THE SILENT QUESTIONS

A SPIRITUAL ODYSSEY

John,
Thanks for
another great
book design.

Doug

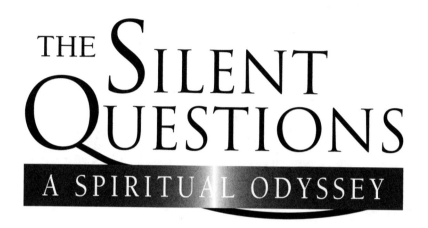

THE SILENT QUESTIONS

A SPIRITUAL ODYSSEY

• • • • •

Doug Marman

SPIRITUAL DIALOGUES PROJECT

The Silent Questions

Published by
Spiritual Dialogues Project
P.O. Box 656, Ridgefield, WA 98642
www.spiritualdialogues.com

LCCN: 2007908804

Publisher's Cataloging-in-Publication

Marman, Doug.
  The silent questions : a spiritual odyssey / by Doug Marman.
    p. cm.
  ISBN-13: 978-0-9793260-2-8
  ISBN-10: 0-9793260-2-8

  1. Marman, Doug. 2. Spiritual biography.
  I. Title.

BL73.M36A3 2007   204'.092
                                                     QBI07-600312

Text design and composition by John Reinhardt Book Design
Cover Design by Phil Wellman, Wellman Advertising & Design
Author photo by Jeremy Boldt
Front cover photo of Sedona by Doug Marman, with thanks to Tor Paulsen

Printed in the United States of America

1 2 3 4 5 6 7 8 9 10

Have patience with everything unresolved in your heart
And try to love the questions themselves…
Don't search for the answers, which could not be given to you now,
Because you would not be able to live them.
And the point is, to live everything.
Live the questions now.
Perhaps then, someday far in the future,
You will gradually, without even noticing it,
Live your way into the answer.

—RAINER MARIA RILKE,
Austro-German poet
(1875-–1926)

To Karen:

Wife, patient editor, and life companion.
You have lived with me through nearly all
of the events of this book.
Your spirit is woven behind every word these pages describe.

● ● ● ● ●

Our conversations will echo through the halls of this world,
Long after we have flown away.

CONTENTS

CONTENTS

THREE

FOUR

CONTENTS

FIVE

SIX

EPILOGUE

ACKNOWLEDGMENTS

I would like to thank everyone who has helped with this book. I've received assistance and inspiration in my life experiences from too many to name, all of which have gone into the heart of this story.

I want to extend my special gratitude to:

PHIL AND MELODIE WELLMAN, who encouraged my writing and read patiently through my early versions. Especially for Phil's great cover design for this book and Melodie's advice on Chapter Six.

DAVID RIVINUS AND PATTI SIMPSON, who offered wise counsel, good editing advice, and showed me the importance of making this a more personal story.

PHIL SHEPHERD, who offered the insights and mirror I needed to see my own words more clearly.

KARLA JOY MCMECHAN, who helped me produce a smoother text, after her careful editorial review and her many useful suggestions.

HAROLD KLEMP, the first person I spoke to about my vision of writing this book, over 20 years ago, who offered guidance, and encouraged me to continue.

MY FAMILY, who have been a part of my life and have shared my journey.

INTRODUCTION

YEARS AGO I SET OUT ON A VOYAGE that changed the direction of my life. It was not a journey I began idly or out of curiosity. I felt pressed into it by a force I could not understand.

Most people are not so haunted by the mystery of life. They don't leave their family and friends to set out on a search for truth. However, after a profoundly moving dream, followed by a number of unexplainable events, I needed to find answers. I could no longer ignore the questions that were springing up within me.

The world teaches us to smother such sparks or drown them in a thousand different ways—through work, family, entertainment, science or religion—but there was nothing I could do to put out this fire. I found only suffering when I tried to run away from the silent questions. My troubles grew until I stopped resisting. Then, my whole life became a part of this quest.

However, this book is not about answers.

Originally, I thought I needed answers. I was lost without them. I felt compelled to search for some kind of map that could explain everything. Then, changes entered my life like new ocean currents that took me far from where I expected to go.

No sooner would I declare victory and stake my flag upon some new mountain top, than life would come along and pull apart everything I

1

thought I knew. Confronted by new doubts, I was once again lured on by the desire to know. I soon learned I was not chasing something fixed and easy to nail down. I was hunting something alive: A reality that unfolded its depth the further I pursued it.

Today, no answers satisfy me. It is only a sense of awe that leads me on.

That's why I'm not much interested in the raging debate over religion these days. Long ago I would have told you that I had left religion behind. I even used to claim such a thing; until the day I realized that my beliefs were so deeply embedded that they were invisible. That's when it dawned on me that the fashionable idea these days about transcending religion was itself nothing more than a religious belief of the times.

So, I must confess right up front that I have been converted. I have fallen in love with a reality so subtle I can't put it into words. It has coaxed me on in stages. It is the force behind the silent questions that compelled me to peel away the veils one by one to see where it was leading. It slowly persuaded me to drop my illusions, showing me something greater than anything I could have believed. This book describes some of the spiritual experiences, discoveries and personal realizations I've encountered along the way.

We live in an age where everything seems to be up for sale. Every new idea gathers an audience and turns into another cult or ism. Wherever I look, I see hawkers promoting "The Answer." They claim to have cracked open the mysteries of the universe. That is the last thing I want this book to be about.

The Answers may promise to solve life's great problems, but I think our appetite for Answers only draws us away from our wondering and our asking. It only pulls us away from the desire of Soul to know firsthand through its own discovery.

Therefore, the knowledge we receive from others no longer seems like a good substitute for personal experience to me. The strength of our life story depends on finding an individual path no matter how many teachers and guides we might have. Otherwise, the way never really becomes our own.

That is why I no longer see the spiritual path as a single system of faith or as one viewpoint about life, but rather as a process of adopting beliefs, experiencing them and then moving on to deeper realities.

The popular adage that all religions worship the same God and lead to the same place sounds incomplete to me. Rather, it seems to me that each teaching brings to the student different experiences and lessons, because they originate from different sources of wisdom. Every level of understanding is a state of consciousness with a reality all its own. However, it is the silent questions that are woven through them all. It is the questions that come back to us again and again that lead us on to something more. And there is always something more.

This brings me to a letter I recently found while going through my old notebooks and journals. Bill was a classmate of mine 30 years ago when we were both freshmen at college. We spent many long nights asking each other questions about life, religion and philosophy. One night, as the dark sky began to lighten with the approach of dawn, Bill and I made a promise: No matter how far our lives would take us, if one of us ever found the answer to our questions, the real answer, he would do his best to let the other know.

A year later I would write Bill a letter. Here was his letter back to me:

Doug,

I have wondered about you since September a year ago. That year has been trying; a year of search, questioning, bewilderment, awe, depression and periods of stagnation. It has carried me into Rand, Hesse, Castenada, Laing, Szasz, Plato, Sartre and many others. I wonder where will it end, or has it even begun?

But now, to your letter. My reaction was one of intense dismay, for at the time I was involved in the philosophies of Rand and B. F. Skinner, utopians with atheistic beliefs. Thus, although your letter has never once escaped my thoughts in the passing weeks, I have waited for the right moment to return to it.

A few weeks ago I bought Paul Twitchell's *The Tiger's Fang*, but I must admit that as yet I haven't read more than the first few pages. I immediately put it aside for later reading, perhaps because I had begun to look at anything spiritual with a skeptical attitude. Honestly, I put it aside feeling that it was only another addition to the world's collection of mythology.

So why am I writing? Since I shelved *The Tiger's Fang*, thoughts of you, the book, and my life and its confusion have been haunting me. Tonight these thoughts and fears have somehow come together in what I hope will be a positive way. They were spurred on tonight with a lecture given by

Dr. Paul Schoolcraft. Unlike my previous experience with the book, my reaction to Dr. Schoolcraft was that he was transmitting something to me that is real.

Yet, I am still somewhat wary. You must understand this; it is somewhat inherent when one has been confronted with the mire of purported truths that have come down over the centuries, moreover, when one attempts to meet them head on. Tonight, I shall begin again to read *The Tiger's Fang*. Where it will lead me, perhaps you know.

Doug, maybe one reason why I am beginning this new branch of my search of truth is that I still have faith in you as I have known you and your convictions. The other primary reason is that I know that there is meaning in this existence of ours. It is for me to find it or to let it envelop me, whatever the true path is. However, you have offered me books. Books, I can buy and read, but what I ask of you, you may not be able to offer. I would like for you to relate to me some of the personal experiences that you have had in your new life.

Thank you for writing. You have set me on a new path of renewed hope. I am glad that you have found LIFE.

Bill

When Bill asked me to relate my personal experiences, I suddenly realized how little I knew. A new life was emerging for me, but it was all too fragile. I thought I had found the answer, yet Bill's letter showed me that I didn't even understand what I had stumbled into.

I tried to share what I could with my friends and family, but how could I communicate my personal inner experiences or the meaning of the spiritual call I heard? It was like finding a fortune of gold and jewels in the middle of the road that I couldn't offer to anyone else. It would just turn to dust in their hands.

It took time for me to realize that this adventure is an inner journey and spiritual realizations are individual gifts; the path is different for each of us. The treasure we find along the way is often only for us.

I lost track of Bill through the years. Life took us in different directions. Yet, finally after three decades I am answering his request. Therefore, I offer this book composed of letters saved, stories written and journals kept.

They don't speak for any teaching, teacher or religion. They represent only my own personal lessons, encounters and realizations.

I hope this book will find Bill somehow, or others like him who might be haunted by the desire to know. I hope it will also inspire others to share their voyages, since I think our stories are the only true answer to life's questions.

—Doug Marman

THE SILENT
QUESTIONS

THERE ARE QUESTIONS that haunt my life, and when these questions arise they come quickly like a cliff's edge suddenly before me; and I must stop to say: Whoa! Where am I going?

Yet sometimes they surface during trying times of great futility when life spreads out like a vast barren desert. I look through the stifling heat waves to the endless horizons and ask: Why am I here?

They are somehow there in my moments of success when all other things have been forgotten and they make me wonder. They come like a vigilant shadow to weep with me when my world looks forlorn and empty. They slip through the meanings of my dreams and shape them.

What lies beyond death? What is the meaning of life?

These are questions I do not look for nor ask out of a curious whim. In fact, I am uneasy in their presence.

But...Who am I?...They make me stop and look and listen, like that great humming sound we call silence. Why must these questions do this? Why must they make me stop and wonder?

I do not know. Yet I do know that somehow I must ask them. Perhaps it is my quest to ask.

What is the purpose of my life? Somehow these have become the most important questions of my life, and only my life can be their answer.

· · • · ·

THESE WERE SOME notes I wrote in a journal some 25 years ago after my search had begun in earnest. I sensed that I was involved in something significant, but I could not explain what it was. It somehow defied being reduced down into words.

It was almost as if I had discovered that it was not I who was asking these questions at all, but that life itself was the asker and my life was somehow the answer.

It was at this point I began to see a great truth: Trying to solve the silent questions, trying to figure them out was the wrong approach.

I had searched through volumes of books in science, philosophy and religion. I had read hundreds of theories and beliefs, but I finally saw that I had been looking in all the wrong places. These teachings were not giving me real answers. They were more like trumpets blaring great sounding concepts, but such noise only drowned out the silent questions.

It now seems to me as if most people try to bury these questions in a thousand different ways because the inner call is too unsettling.

Like many others, I started looking for a new world view, a new belief system, because I thought that would be my answer. But in fact the silent questions came not to offer an answer, but to shake my world and my beliefs.

I remember standing outside one clear night looking up at millions of stars, each a sun with a solar system of its own, spread throughout the endlessness of space. I could see the insignificance of everything I knew. However, something within me had changed. After following the call of the silent questions, I came to realize that something within me was in touch with those stars. I was not something separate, but was connected. My awareness was not limited to a mere body. Therefore some part of me could understand this infinitude.

No theories or beliefs could give me that. Rather, it was something I was remembering. It was something I somehow already knew, like finding a map within myself that had been there all along.

In 13th Century Persia, a Sufi mystic and poet by the name of Jalal al-Din Rumi said this in chapter four of his *Discourses*:

> There is one thing in this world that must never be forgotten. If you were to forget all else but did not forget that, then you would have no reason to worry. But if you performed and remembered everything else yet forgot that one thing, then you would have done nothing whatsoever.

10

It is just as if a king sent you to the country to carry out a specific task. If you go and accomplish a hundred other tasks but do not perform that particular task, then it is as though you performed nothing at all. So, everyone comes into this world for a particular task and that is their purpose. If they do not perform it, then they will have done nothing.

This is the message of the silent questions.

But what is this one thing? Rumi never tries to answer that. How could you ever answer such a thing in words? The silent questions don't come to be answered by some simple formula. Yet how many times do we search for tablets from God where the plan is all etched out?

So, I finally began to see that the questions came to ask me why I was here. They came from some hidden memory, reminding me that there was more to life and I was more than just a creature roaming the earth. It was the opportunity to *know* that drew me on.

Only after my life began pivoting upon a new fulcrum and shifting direction to follow a new course did the underlying significance of the silent questions begin to reveal itself. However, the adventure began long before this. First came the years of searching and doubts.

The Question of a Dream

The silent questions first took root in my life when I was 11 years old. I had a dream that would follow me for years to come. It seemed vividly real and not like any dream I'd ever had. I wrote about it later in my notebook:

I felt the presence of some being standing beside me as the dream began. He pointed and said, "Look at this."

Then it was as if I was suddenly in another world, another dimension, far beyond this earth plane, where beings of great wisdom and awareness lived. I remembered that world. I belonged there; it was my home, but I was lacking something to remain there.

Like an old memory coming back, I realized again that I needed some training, some experience, if I was to stay within the circle of these great beings. I knew something was needed.

I seemed to be a silent observer of the dream, and yet I was a part of the dream at the same time. I was both watching and a participant in the dream.

After a time, the being who seemed both compassionate and firm came back to me, as if some verdict had been reached.

"You must learn about people," he said.

A shudder ran up my back. I looked down into the lower dimensions. Way down into the darkness, I could see the physical worlds with all of their millions of inhabitants scurrying around.

"Why do they act so foolishly?" I asked. "Why do they run around as if they've forgotten who they are, lost in such silly games and battles?"

I said this, thinking it was all below me, but with a sinking feeling that it was not.

"You must become one of them again so that you will understand."

I knew what he said was true. I felt like the American Indian youth facing the test of the wilderness to enter manhood. I too faced a wilderness: the wilderness of Soul. The land of forgetfulness and crude body forms that drives Soul to act and feel like an animal, not aware of its true self.

This I saw clearly from that world above.

He then added, "You will not be alone. We will not forget you."

I felt a presence surround me. It was a bond to this world and its people that would follow me.

I then flew down far below to the blue globe where my life would begin. I looked across the planet, its people and their strange customs. It seemed like only a few moments whisked by. Then, I set a time to take place later in life when I would remember again who I was and where I came from.

Still, I hesitated. The thought of plunging into this world of amnesia held me back. I looked again into my future life and found comfort in knowing I would not be alone. Someone was there to greet me. I would remember my true home again, and the great sciences, arts and freedom of that world. This awareness—that I would one day remember—gave me the confidence to go on.

Then, I made the step and went hurtling down into the Earth world. Down, down, down into darkness and forgetfulness. Down through the veil of illusion, with one thought imprinted upon my awareness: Learn about people. I must learn about people!

My eyes blinked open. I looked around at a strange room. Where was I? Whose bed was this? Gradually I began to remember. This was my room, my bed. I was once again in a human body on planet Earth. My dream had taken me far from this reality.

I lay there, still half in the dream state. I replayed my dream over and over. I tried to bring it back. What was it that made it seem so real? And then I felt the presence of that vast dimension filling my awareness again. Like opening a window, I could see into that realm of wisdom and vivid reality. I was suddenly back in that state of consciousness again.

Without even thinking, a question jumped into my mind. What was this world called? Its name? A word formed in my mind—ECKLON.

"ECKLON," I said, and it seemed to resonate with my home.

Then, another question came: When will I find it again? When will I remember? The answer: When I am fourteen years old!

Then the window into my dream snapped shut, and I was left to wonder what it all meant.

It was only a dream, that's true, and being the son of an engineer I could never forget that it was not real. If I had grown up in another time or another culture I might have accepted this inner experience at face value. But I was old enough to know that it didn't fit in the world where I lived.

For a long time I didn't know what to do with this dream. On the one hand, it seemed more real than anything I had ever experienced. It was nothing like my typical nighttime excursions. And it suggested there was a meaning and purpose to my life. The thought of this filled me with a feeling of confidence, as if it was making me whole in some way. Or was this just wishful thinking?

I couldn't quite accept it, yet I couldn't forget it either. So I did what probably any boy of 11 would do: I turned it into a game.

Why not pretend I was a visitor from a world called ECKLON? Why not imagine my discovery of the sciences and knowledge of another world that would free me from an ordinary life? So, I daydreamed of the day I would remember my true home again, meet others who knew it, and learn I was a part of something greater.

These fantasies brought a great release and sparked a subtle feeling of inner knowingness. However, in the background of my reveries was still the nagging thought: It was just a dream.

What if it was false? The question lodged in my throat. It meant I was just fooling myself. I would then look out upon an empty world, wondering... then why am I here? What is the purpose of this life? The silent questions were never far away when I thought about ECKLON. I dreaded, yet longed for the day I turned fourteen.

. . ● . .

I find it curious this experience would come to me when I was eleven. This is about the age many American Indian tribes used to send their boys out to find their Life Dream. Among many tribes, such a vision was of utmost significance. Often the boy would wander alone for days in the wilderness without food until his inner gift from the spirit world came. This would become his own personal revelation that would set the direction of his life.

Growing up, I felt a strong connection with the American Indian. When I walked through the woods behind our house, I sensed the presence of the people who had once lived on the land. When I followed old trails, listened to the birds, studied the clouds, in my imagination I did so as an Indian. Some of these images came from books, but more often they seemed to come from the land itself. Perhaps it was sympathy with the Indian tradition that brought my own Life Dream.

Yet, I was not an Indian boy, but an ordinary kid living in the twentieth century. An age when dreams were just dreams. Much as I might want it to be real and hoped it might be real, it was still a product of my imagination. Then, why could I not forget the vivid reality of it? Why did it seem to reach into the depths of my feelings?

Looking back, I can now see that something very important was taking place at that time: I was experiencing the emergence of my inner self. Unfortunately, our modern culture doesn't seem to recognize such a thing. We encourage the building of families and countries, our physical bodies and mind, but there is almost a fear of our inner life, as if we might become lost in it and separated from the "real" world.

In primitive societies, children are often instructed to find a secret name, an animal spirit or sacred symbol that belongs to them. These inner images or sounds were not made up, but had to be discovered or received as a gift from a spirit guide. They were kept secret, because to reveal them meant a kind of internal death. Their "word of power" or spirit symbol was a great source of courage and inner strength when needed, whether facing a dangerous enemy or the wilds of nature.

Today we see this all as imagination and magical thinking. In fact, many psychologists encourage people to reveal all of their secrets. Priests and ministers help people confess their sins to relieve people of the burden of their private thoughts and desires. No wonder we live in a world where most people feel helplessly affected by forces around them. They have given up their inmost self.

Sharing our feelings and thoughts with others can help us become more conscious of our own unconscious beliefs. But there is also a part of life that belongs to us alone. We are not just a part of the world. There is something else within us that exists beyond humanity. It is directly in touch with life itself.

Primitive cultures knew the importance of courage and confidence for survival. These qualities radiate from the core of who we are. Much of life especially in primitive times was lived alone while hunting or fishing. But if you give away the secrets of your inner being, how can you find the strength of your individuality? If you have revealed everything about yourself to the world, then you "belong" to the world and have sold your most valuable possession.

Somehow I fell into this wisdom by accident. A series of personal experiences like this dream left me feeling different. I tried to share what happened, but it didn't matter if I told my parents, my brother and sisters, or my friends, none could understand what I was talking about. So, by the time I was eleven, I learned not to share the happenings of my interior life.

While this helped to build within me an inner strength, it also created problems. It made me feel different in ways I didn't like. I felt strange to the world. Looking back, I can see that these subjective events were creating questions and these questions bothered me. As a result, I tried to forget about my experiences. I tried to ignore and bury them.

I was running from something that scared me because it made me feel strange. Here is a passage from a journal I wrote where I described my memories of that time:

> I opened the front door and ran out. The fresh air was filled with the energy of springtime. The grass and trees were sprouting green everywhere I looked. I was free, after a week of being cooped up in the house with the flu. For seven days my life had been on hold, while the world had gone on without me. I had some catching up to do and everything felt good.
>
> But something nagged me, something I didn't want to think about. It wouldn't go away. Like a dark cloud, it crept into my thoughts and I found myself fighting with it again. I had been fighting with it for the past week. Now that I was free I thought it would go away. Why wouldn't it go away?

That was what I recorded in my journal. And not wanting to face what I was feeling, I rushed out the front door to find my friends. Across the street I saw something that could take my mind off whatever it was that was bothering me. Dick had just gotten a new toy: A skateboard. It was the first one in our neighborhood. I asked for a chance to try it.

I took the skateboard to the top of his driveway. Dick suggested I start off slower, but I wanted the danger. I gave a push and was quickly flying down the hill. I felt at ease and in control. It was easy keeping balance. The world flashed by, as I focused on the moment and what might happen next.

At the bottom of Dick's driveway, at just the right moment, I tilted the board to the left to swerve into Dick's garage, but the skateboard didn't turn. I tilted it further. Nothing. I pushed the left side of the skateboard all the way down until it was scraping along the driveway, but it still wasn't turning. Something was wrong!

I felt a strange sense of detachment, as I watched myself heading for the curb at the end of the driveway. Beyond the curb was a short bit of grass followed by a ten foot drop off. I had only a few moments, but I knew what to do. I would let the skateboard hit the curb and step off onto the grass. I would have to stop quickly. It looked a bit tricky, but my instincts felt at ease and in control.

I saw it all clearly, as if I were outside my body watching what was going on in slow motion. I was flying toward the curb, waiting for the skateboard to hit, knowing I must not move before then. And then, suddenly, as if someone pulled the board out from under me, my feet went flying backwards and I crashed down, jaw first. My chin hit smack on top of the curb.

Oddly, I didn't feel hurt. It was Dick who pointed to my face and said something didn't look right. I was soon on my way to the hospital.

American Indian shamans call this kind of accident: being wounded. Our injuries isolate us from the world. They can be physical mishaps like I had or any kind of illness, as well as harm or rejection, that separate us from society. There are a thousand different ways to be wounded.

The shamans say that to be injured helps us learn the lesson of isolation and the grief it brings. To gather strength from suffering is the way of growth. For this reason they have called themselves the wounded ones. Through the power of their own pain they gain the ability to heal others. They know the meaning of illness and isolation better than anyone else. It is this path that makes them spiritual leaders for their people.

I had no knowledge of this back then. I was just an eleven year old boy tempting danger and breaking his jaw.

I had been running away from an inner force telling me to stop and reflect on the meaning of my inner experiences, which was the last thing I wanted to do. So, where did I end up? My teeth were wired shut and my head wrapped in a wire frame. I couldn't go to school for weeks or play sports for months. I could barely talk and had to eat everything through a straw.

For the first time in my life I felt completely isolated. What else could I do but stop and reflect?

What led me to this? I ran it over in my mind to see what was happening. I could then see the fear I had about changes that were taking place within me.

Gradually, it became clear that up to this point life had just been happening to me, like a series of events with no direction. I had been running away from some kind of inner force that was trying to get me to think about the way my life was blindly rushing forward.

Now, stuck at home, what else could I do but stop and think?

From that moment, the silent questions had me firmly in their grasp. I couldn't run from them. I needed to know what they meant. Being wounded taught me that.

The Question of God

The Catholic Church that our family attended from time to time had a very kind and generous priest. One day, out of the blue, I decided I wanted to be an altar boy. It shocked my parents. I remember getting up at 4:30 in the morning, riding my bicycle the 10 miles or so to our little Church, performing a 6:00 am Mass, and then riding my bike back home, where I would catch the bus for school.

The thought of doing this as an eleven year old, on my own, amazes me. What attracted me to do such a thing? I remember the fun I had with the other altar boys. I remember the Father taking us to football games. I remember Sundays, sitting with a row of altar boys in the midst of a solemn Mass, secretly mocking the sacred moment by making hand gestures and funny faces, trying to get the other boys to laugh. I know I would much rather be actively involved, rather than sitting passively amongst the congregation. But I also remember the religious images and the feeling of a spiritual reality that intrigued me.

This all changed after I broke my jaw. I began reading. I found myself with a deep craving to learn. I wondered about everything. I began going through the books in our house, which covered everything from fiction and philosophy to my father's engineering books. I flipped through our encyclopedias. My mother worked as a volunteer librarian for a small local library. I went along with her, reading whatever captured my fancy.

My mother says that I changed so radically after my accident, she could hardly recognize me. I went from being an outgoing, outwardly driven kid who couldn't stop doing things, to a quiet, thoughtful daydreamer and thinker. I remember suddenly feeling that I had so much to learn and I wanted to know it all.

When I wasn't playing with my friends or involved in sports, I found myself turning more and more to science and mathematics. They seemed to offer answers about the world and reality around us. However, the more I studied science, the more I began to have doubts about religion and the idea of God. I remember in 8th grade bringing a copy of Scientific American into school with me. The whole September issue was dedicated to the physics of Light, and for some reason it absolutely fascinated me.

Only two years earlier when I was eleven, I had been an altar boy. Now I was totally absorbed in Isaac Newton's *Principia*, and his book on *Optiks*, the experiments with magnetics by Maxwell and the science of anti-matter. I began studying Einstein's Special and General Theories of Relativity and I read through my father's Organic Chemistry books. I wanted to know about everything.

One day as I lay in bed, I realized that I had lost my faith in religion. I began to wonder why I had believed in God in the first place. True, people have been telling each other for ages that there is a God, but where was the proof? Was it merely a myth?

I started trying to sort through my own feelings and memories. When did I first begin believing in God and why? It seemed as if I had simply accepted it on faith, but the more I thought about it the more I realized this wasn't good enough for me anymore. Was I the only one my age who was thinking about such things?

Between games of basketball or kickball and the day to day grind of schoolwork, I stopped to ask my friends a point blank question: Did they believe in God? If they weren't too uncomfortable with that question, then I would ask them why. The answers fascinated me.

The most common response I heard was: "I don't know. I never thought about it." It quickly became obvious that kids my age were not asking these questions. Some told me in a moment of honesty, "Well, I guess I believe in God because that's what my mom and dad taught me." One boy, out of the dozens I asked, said forthrightly, "It's all bunk. I don't believe there is any such thing as God." I was impressed at his independent thought, since he had obviously considered it, but his belief that God didn't exist seemed no more logical to me than believing that God did exist. Without a good reason, why should I believe either?

I often heard another answer as well. It was an answer that bothered me: "I don't know. There may not be a God," they would say, "but I'm going to believe in God anyway. That way, if there is a God, then I'm safe. But, if there isn't, then how can it hurt?" They would usually smile or laugh when they said it, but they were serious. There was a tone of fear in such a response that disturbed me. It was as if they were saying that they didn't really believe in God, but they would pretend as if they did to avoid putting their souls at risk.

My notebook, written about 7–8 years after the experience, shows some of my memories of what I was thinking back then:

> I remember that dark night when I walked out behind our house and stood there. I felt uneasy, like I was facing an invisible enemy, and yet the rebellious spirit rose in me. I paused, to be sure I knew what I was doing, and then I said out loud, "I won't believe in God without a reason."
>
> I waited for the lightning to strike, but nothing happened. Only silence. But it was not an empty silence. Suddenly I knew I had passed a test. I had faced a fear and been true to myself. Perhaps the greatest fear man has ever created is the fear of God. Immediately, I felt a sense of peace and freedom, as if I had unlocked something that had been holding me back.
>
> But there was also a feeling of loneliness. I now felt like a stranger to both Heaven and Earth.

The silent questions returned and as I stood there feeling the moment and the change within me, I suddenly remembered my Life Dream. The whole memory of it came back. Then I realized I was fourteen years

19

old. The day I had both feared and longed for had arrived. What did it mean?

I had not found the truth of my life's purpose. I had found no one who knew of ECKLON, even though I had dropped the name from time to time to see if anyone recognized it. But something had changed. I was no longer the same. I had awakened in some way.

However, this was far from what my dream had promised. Had the whole vision been false? Had I believed it out of wishful thinking? As I thought back to the vivid images and feelings of my inner experience, a strange thing happened. It was as if a window into that world of my Life Dream opened again. I was once more in that state of consciousness. This was not just a memory; I was actually in that same reality with the same awareness I had before. I could hardly believe it.

Then, just like before, I found questions forming in my mind: Is this it? I am fourteen years old. Is the answer here? Am I just missing it?

I could see my situation, like looking down from above. No, I was not yet ready. I had only passed the first stage. I needed to study more. I needed to prepare.

I didn't like the answer. I had seen before that I would discover ECK-LON when I turned fourteen, but now it was being pushed off. Would I keep pushing it off? Was I fooling myself? When would I admit that it was only imagination? I needed a final date. When would I really know?

The answer came: When I turned nineteen years old. That was the answer I saw. I asked again, and the response came back once more: When I turned nineteen. Then the window faded away, and I stood there under a dark sky with the silent trees around me and I wondered why I was hanging onto this dream?

The Borderland

There are hundreds of biographical stories, but it is rare to find books that focus on the inner experiences and interior growth of children. We hear about the outer events in their lives; the divorcing of their parents, the struggles with illness, the affects of war, poverty, or wealth. But these things only describe outer influences. Looking back, I find that subjective experiences had far more affect on my life.

I can remember such occurrences even back to when I was a few years old. Almost always they were tied to close relationships and bonds of love. Perhaps my strongest connection was with my older sister who was born with a number of birth defects, including a hole in her heart. Since Janet also had faulty knees, we both learned to walk at the same time, even though she was older than me by a year and a half.

I cannot describe even today the ties that connected the two of us. It was like growing up as twins. My mother tells me that one day when Janet and I were talking "baby talk" with each other, she wondered if we actually understood our babbling back and forth. So she asked Janet, "Do you understand what Doug is saying?" She knew exactly what I was saying and went on to translate.

I have since learned that such a private language can develop between twins. However, my memories are not of a private language, but more a knowingness about what Janet was feeling. In fact, I often could not distinguish her feelings from my own and even her body seemed to call out to me, asking me to protect her and heal her. This was obviously an instinctive feeling that sprang out of our bonds of love.

Janet died when I was five years old and it left a void in my life. For many years I would see her in my dreams. At first it seemed like she had not died, but was just away from home. I remember one day hearing Mom and Dad crying in their room. I knew it was over their loss of Janet. I went in to comfort them, to reassure them that Janet wasn't gone. I knew she was okay, but no matter what I said they just didn't understand. I couldn't find a way to explain that my inner connection with Janet was still there.

I can see now that my bond with Janet contributed to a strong unconscious feeling I had that something was missing in my life. It left me with an image that there was someone I needed to meet to fill this void. Someone who would explain what it all meant. This was one of the inner patterns that set me up in this lifetime to feel the urgency of the silent questions, and a need for close relationships to understand people. These are of course the same exact issues I was told about in my Life Dream. It left me with a sense that there was something important I must remember.

I can also recall numerous experiences with animals and nature in my youth that made me wonder.

I felt great pain when my father would chop down trees on the property around our home. It was often my task to cut up the wood later for the woodpile and there were many times when I literally could not do it. I had to drop the cutting saw and walk away from it. I would literally beg my father to let a tree live, to spare its life, and occasionally I succeeded. I used to ask myself, how could Dad take the lives of these trees? Now I see that I was simply connected to these trees in a way that he was not.

There is something about this subject that I find hard to describe. I think it is common for children to have feelings for animals and the world of nature. It is somehow closer to them than to adults. Some children feel this more strongly than others. However, I'm not talking about just sympathy or feelings for trees. It was as if the trees themselves were connected to me somehow.

I ran across a story recently that I think describes what I'm trying to get at here. It comes from an article called, "On The Borderland," by Jerome Bernstein. It was published in the September-November 2000 issue of the *Ions Noetic Sciences Review*.

Jerome was working as a Jungian psychoanalyst in New Mexico when he was contacted by a woman he calls Hannah. Following are some quotes from his article describing their sessions:

One day, a year or so into the work, she arrived at my office very distressed. Driving home from our previous session, she had found herself behind a truck carrying two cows. Her feeling was that the cows were being taken to slaughter. I pursued the standard approach of suggesting that she was projecting onto the cows, that she saw her life circumstance in the plight of these cows. She went along with me for a time. But then she protested in frustration: "But it's the **cows**!" I interpreted her response as identification with animals she experienced as abused. She acknowledged the truth of my interpretations. She began to talk about all animals in the world that exist only as domesticated beings, and their sadness. And again she burst out: "But it's the **cows**!" After the last protest—by now at the end of the session—I became aware in **myself** of Hannah's distress and her identification with the plight of these cows. And I also was aware of a different feeling in the room. The feeling was attached to Hannah, yet it was separate from her. It seemed of a different dimension. It was a new experience for me.

Some weeks later, Hannah recounted how she had gone for a long walk in the country and was followed by some stray dogs. As she described the

22

experience, the room filled with pain and remorse. I asked her what she was feeling. Again we had a go-round like the one with the cows. And again Hannah acknowledged her projection onto the dogs. But this time, out of character for her, she became angry—so angry, she took her shoe in her hand and hit the floor with it. "You just don't get it!" she shouted, slamming the floor again with her shoe. "It's the **dogs**." It was as if she was saying the dogs were projecting something onto her. The urgency of her tone and her uncharacteristic anger jolted me into the realization that my standard interpretations were not enough and somehow off the mark. Something other was happening in the room.

The next week Hannah came in with a dream suggesting the threat of sexual violation by me. The dream jarred me, and I knew I had better **hear** her. I began to listen to her more closely and tried diligently to shut off my mind and training...

Over the next months Hannah struggled to wrench out of her unconscious the words to talk to me. Clearly she was extremely intelligent. Yet at times it seemed she was groping for a vocabulary that was beyond her reach—a vocabulary that perhaps didn't yet exist. Gradually, however, she did begin to communicate her feelings to me. And as she did, I was startled to realize that the things she was telling me I had heard once before.

During my analytical training I had also been learning from native elders and healers, particularly from my friend Carl Gorman...whom I called Grandpa, and a Hopi medicine man, Homer. These men were teaching me a new way of looking at life. I realized that here were people whose involvement with Nature was completely different from the utilitarian, often adversarial if sometimes sentimental, attitude toward Nature that had characterized the Western mind for thousands of years. For the Navajo, religion and healing are the same. The psychic connection with Nature is the source of—and is inseparable from—spiritual and physical health. Illness is a "disconnection" with one's psychic roots. As I listened to Hannah struggle to articulate her emotions, I did "get it." It was indeed the cows. I realized that what Hannah was telling me was precisely the same message the native elders and healers were teaching me—and what my own unconscious was telling me through my dreams: Everything animate and inanimate has within it a spirit dimension and communicates **in that dimension** to those who can listen.

Jerome calls this state, where people find themselves connecting with life at a deep psychic level, The Borderland. He continues:

Hannah is what I have come to call a "Borderland Personality." She lives in the Borderland. Hannah—as do many others—embodies and reflects an evolving psyche that is not only new unto itself, but one that in profound ways is strange and alien to her. Such people are the front line recipients of **new psychic forms** that are entering and impacting the Western psyche. . .

These people **personally** experience, and must live out, the split from Nature on which the Western ego, as we know it, has been built. They feel (not feel about) the plight of animals that are no longer permitted to live by their own instincts, and which survive only in domesticated states to be used as pets or food. Such people are highly intuitive. Many, if not most, are psychic to some degree, whether they know it or not. They are deeply feeling something to such a degree that they find themselves in profound feeling states that seem irrational to them. . . .

Prior to our work together, Hannah could not distinguish between her own feelings and those of the Earth and the animals. When I first encouraged her to talk about the animals she was reticent. She feared, understandably, that I would label her "crazy." And for a while, until I "got it," my insistence on relating her feelings exclusively to her personal history confused and exacerbated the situation.

However, Hannah and I **were** able to sort the psychopathology arising out of her upbringing from the Borderland phenomena. I was able to witness and authenticate her Borderland experiences as **objective nonpersonal nonrational phenomena** occurring in the natural universe for which she was not responsible. And as she came to understand this, she felt more sane and whole, and became dramatically healthier and more functional.

Experiences like these, when you are young, can be very confusing, especially when there is no one around to explain what is happening or to confirm the reality of it. But, of course, to children much of this world is strange and odd, so this was just another mystery. By the time I reached my teens, however, these experiences became a little scary; because by then I could see that others really couldn't relate to what I was experiencing.

Facing Fear

By sixteen years of age, I was following a classic Westernized scientific way of seeing the world. I was immersed in the study of physics, chemistry and mathematics, yet I was having experiences that fit nothing the scientific world recognized. Like Hannah, I began to wonder if something was wrong with me. I began looking through the public library for books on psychology. I must have read dozens of books on the subjects of insanity and psychosis.

Talk about scary! Reading clinical accounts about schizophrenia and insanity as a teenager, while wondering if these problems were describing my own condition created some frightening thoughts! But I had to know. Hiding from my fears only made it worse. I had learned that lesson already.

The books I studied, however, didn't seem to describe what I was experiencing. So, I then began picking up books about geniuses, who also are considered out of the norm. This didn't seem to fit my problem either. There was nothing I could find in the field of psychology or science to describe what was happening to me. I knew nowhere else to turn but to study the matter on my own. I would have to figure this out for myself, whatever it might be.

One day, this inner tension of The Borderland seemed to reach a breaking point. It was as if something beyond me was trying to emerge out of my own subconscious. I realized I could not ignore the issue any longer. I had to face this force that was making me question my own self. I had to know what it was.

I sat down in a chair and tried to look at what was happening. Images filled my mind about what it must be like to go crazy. It frightened me. The impressions from those books scared me, but as I watched my thoughts and feelings I noticed something curious. I could see that my own fears were turning the very thing I was afraid of into something real. The more I imagined the possibility that I might be losing my mind, the more the thought scared me and the more it seemed like it could come true.

This realization seemed even more horrifying. My own dread could create the very thing I was afraid of. Of course I could ignore my fears and pretend they didn't exist. I could search for more books until I understood it better or find someone who could explain what was going on. But, I had already tried all these, and I knew I could no longer put off confronting whatever was taking place within me.

It was as if an earthquake was breaking up the whole basis of my beliefs. Indeed, I had been shutting away my own inner experiences for too long because they didn't fit with society. I had been burying the part of myself that knew, because it didn't make sense according to the scientific theories I had learned. My own consciousness was pushing me to face the understanding that there was something more.

I had no idea what was happening. I only knew there was a force within me that I must confront, and it was either something greater than I knew or something more terrible. I would either find an answer that explained everything, or it would defeat me.

I decided there was only one thing to do. I had to let my fear have its way. I had to follow this sense of terror to its source and see what really was behind it. I had to go where it was taking me and find out what it meant.

I closed my eyes and felt myself falling into a deep, dark hole. I felt myself losing control. I was going beyond my conscious mind and an ominous feeling was racing me toward some end. I accepted it and let it go where it wanted. The more this thought scared me, the further I fell into the darkness. I watched as my own imagination created what I was experiencing, and the more I saw this, the more I realized what was really taking place: I was confronting my fear of fear, itself.

I had been running from something within myself that frightened me and this had only made it seem more menacing. I had to stop running away. It was time to give in and accept whatever was at the core of this. The thought occurred to me that I could lose my mind. That was the scariest thought I could imagine, so I knew I had to face even that. I plunged into it. It was no use fighting it any longer. I had to know if this fear would destroy me or if it had something to teach me. I could see no other choice.

My training in science was lost and of no value whatsoever. This was an experience my mind could only watch. Only my senses and a kind of direct perception witnessed it all unfold. I saw myself drop through what seemed like a black well infinitely deep. I was completely and totally lost.

Then suddenly, without any expectation or warning, I hit bottom. The feeling of falling stopped, and it shocked me. It was as if my imagination could go no further.

There is a bottom to this? Yes, and this new reality felt as solid as rock. My own dread could not touch it. It withstood fear. There was something within me that withstood fear!

I suddenly felt a sense of power and strength I had never known before. I had connected to something that was my own Self, but it was a deeper self than I had ever known. And with this knowingness, this coming to rest on the bedrock of Self, I began to rise up and up through the darkness and back into light. But I was now changed. I felt more whole and complete.

Over the next couple of years, I began to accept and recognize my own differences. I seemed to know things that I shouldn't be able to know. I came to understand, for example, why I could find lost things so easily. I was actually seeing them in my imagination and letting the image guide me. I did it all instinctively without realizing what I was doing. But my friends all knew that when someone slammed our base-ball into the woods, I would probably be the first one to find it. I had thought it was a matter of luck.

It now occurred to me why no one else seemed to see the black rings under the eyes of people who smoked cigarettes, like I did. These rings seemed obvious to me, like night and day, but no matter how I described it to my friends, none could see what I was talking about. Perhaps I was seeing something that wasn't physical?

One day it all hit home. I was riding in a car with a friend from high school and I said to him, as if it was the first time I realized it, "I think I might be somewhat psychic."

"Obviously," Dave said. "I've always thought that."

"You have?" I said, startled by his answer.

"Don't you remember all the things that have happened to you?" he asked.

But I didn't remember. I had buried those things so thoroughly, since they didn't fit my scientific beliefs, that I couldn't even imagine what Dave was talking about.

"Like what?" I asked.

"Lots of things," he said. "Don't you remember the dream you had where you found Sue's house? You had no way of knowing that."

Then it came back to me. One day, shortly after Dave had gotten his driver's license, I told him about a vivid dream I had the night before. I had flown out of my body and up over my house. I then flew over the tops of the trees across town. In my dream, I suddenly realized that I was going somewhere. I began following Main Street, across to the other side of town. I came down lower and was flying perhaps 10–15 feet off the ground. I swerved unexpectedly down a road I'd never been on before. I then turned suddenly to the left down another road that was also new to me. I flew perhaps halfway down this road and then stopped. I turned to the left. It was Sue's house, a girl friend I had known from school since first grade. I'd never been to her house before, but in my dream I knew it was her home.

After I told Dave about my dream, he said, "Hey, let's check it out."

The idea that Dave now had a driver's license and we could just jump into a car and go there seemed amazing in itself. So, with me giving directions from my dream, we made our way right to the road and the house I had seen in my dream. It looked just as I remembered it, except in my dream it had been late at night, as if lit by a full moon.

When I pointed to the house, Dave said, "That's it."

He had known where Sue lived since he had been there before, but he wanted to see if my dream was for real. However, I was more surprised than he was. In fact, until I got out of the car and walked over to the mailbox to prove to myself that this was indeed her house, I didn't believe it.

A couple years later I had completely forgotten about this, until Dave reminded me. Dave also reminded me of another experience I had forgotten. One day I told him that it seemed as if I could sometimes sense what was in a book before I read it.

I often went with my mom to the library where I would just run my fingers across the books. I didn't even know why I liked doing this, until one day I realized it was because I was getting something from the books. Being scientific, I wondered how real my feelings were. Was I really receiving something from the book? I began testing it, by picking out books I knew nothing about, noting my sensations, and then reading the books to see if I had been close.

I found that, with some accuracy, I seemed to tune into the author's state of mind and viewpoint and a general sense of what the book was about before reading a word. But was this a fair test?

So, I told Dave my thoughts one day while visiting his home. "I'm not sure, but it seems to be true." I said.

Dave said, "Let's run a test."

"What kind of test?" I asked.

"I'll pick out a book you haven't read," he said. He went to his bookstand and found a bright yellow paperback book with the picture of the sun on the horizon, which I had never seen before. There was nothing else on the cover but its poetic title, which gave no indication of what it was about, and the name of the author, who was Japanese.

I held the book for a few minutes and soon began to feel something from it creeping into my body, like a stream flowing into my senses and nerves. I felt feelings that were obviously not my own. All at once it hit me and I threw the book down on his bed.

"Ughh!" I said. "This man is sick. There's something wrong with him. I think he is mentally ill. I hate this kind of book. I can't stand to read them. They bother me too much." And for the first time I began to see why certain books had caused me problems when I had to read them for school. It was the consciousness of the writer creeping into my thoughts that bothered me.

Dave looked at me with a blank stare. "I can't believe it," he said. "I picked out that book for a reason, because when I first saw it I thought it was going to be a cheerful story, with the rising sun on the cover. But it turned out to be the diary of a man who commits suicide. You described it pretty well."

I had never tested my impressions before with anyone else. I still wasn't convinced by the experiment, but it seemed to confirm what I had been feeling. Later, as Dave was recounting it, I began to realize how difficult it was for me to accept my own experiences. It was just as if I had been burying my own self and the things I knew because they didn't fit the world I had been taught. But how did I know these things? I had far more to learn.

So, the silent questions came to me again. I was somehow connected to life in ways I had not suspected. The questions were drawing me on to discover more.

True Desire

The wind is blowing snow in flurries outside our dorm. Winter comes cold in these northern parts of New York and never wants to leave, but it doesn't stifle activities any. It has only cultivated a unique form of "indoor sports" among my college classmates.

I have learned the wisdom of peeking cautiously outside my door before entering the hallway. Who knows what might be flying by at the moment. A soccer ball? Frisbee? Someone's sneakers? This evening, however, silence managed to make a temporary assault, and with my roommate gone there was nothing left to do but homework. So, I began my assignment for philosophy class. The task: to discuss the difference between comfort and happiness.

I began putting my thoughts down, but suddenly found new ideas entering my awareness, and realizations began flowing into my thinking one after the other. I'd never experienced anything like this before. It was like writing down a Socratic debate, leading to a conclusion I never would have expected. It went something like this:

How can one find true happiness?
By following one's desire and seeing it come true.

But surely not all desires bring what they promise. What of the desire for power or money? People who achieve them don't always find happiness.
Then those must be false desires. Follow only your true desire.

But how can one know a true desire from a false one?
The true desire brings what it promises; happiness and satisfaction. Achieving one's true desire leaves one wanting nothing else. And thus, there can be but one true desire.

One?
Yes. For one has no desire after achieving it. It leads not to wanting more and more, but less and less.

And what might this desire be? Can it be stated?
It is not hidden. We simply miss it beneath the cravings of our senses. But surely, to give and give only is our true desire. To give to our family, country and world. To give to life, and our own self. This brings true happiness. To give totally and completely—this is at the heart of every true desire and the beginning of true satisfaction.

I was stunned. How could I have written these thoughts? One thing was clear: a moment before I had not known these ideas. Where did they come from? Reading the words over, retracing the thread, gradually I could see an inner light had guided my thoughts and my pen. I wondered; is this same inspiration the source of all great thought?

My own question amazed me. It overshadowed anything I'd ever thought about. Was there another way of knowing and understanding besides sitting in a classroom or reading a book? Yet, what even shocked me more was realizing I could tap into this pool of wisdom and learn from it myself.

I wrote this down some years afterward in my journal. In fact, having discovered that I could learn through my own writing from this experience at college, I began writing regularly. This is when my notebooks began.

The paper I handed in for philosophy class came back graded with a B+. The professor wrote: "Don't know if what you say would withstand a critical examination, but it's terribly interesting!"

I couldn't believe it. How could he not give the paper an A? I went to see him. After a few minutes talking, however, I could see that we were on different wavelengths. He was concerned about critical examination and I was captivated by a light of inspiration that could open up my awareness where I could suddenly see life clearly.

For the next year I poured over every kind of book on religion, philosophy and life after death, looking for mention of this inner knowingness, but found nothing. I read some interesting ideas and beliefs, but there was no mention of how to enter into this state of consciousness and explore its knowledge.

Flipping through my notebooks from those days, I can see moments of inspiration, followed by long periods of doubt and questioning. I felt the need to solve this problem, yet realized that my sense of urgency was itself getting in the way. I was starting to worry about what I didn't know. Where had all my beliefs come from? Did everything I accept come from others? How had I adopted those convictions as my own?

I uncovered a piece to this puzzle one day when I ran across a book on hypnotism in the college library. In those days, hypnotism was not widely accepted by Western science. It was considered quackery by most and mere parlor games by almost everyone else. Yet the book I found claimed to show how to hypnotize others. Why not try it out?

I asked a friend if he would help me run an experiment. I would try to hypnotize him, with another friend as a witness. He thought it was a great idea. Both of us doubted much would come of it, but since we were engineering students, what better way to get to the bottom of it than through experiment?

Jerry lay down on his bed. I sat in a chair with Curtis acting as our witness. I began the process of putting Jerry into a hypnotic state. I tried to get him to relax and settle deeper and deeper into a state of relaxation. It didn't seem to be working, so I made suggestions that he was feeling relaxed. I went through all the steps I'd read about, but I had the feeling that Jerry was just lying there listening to everything I was saying and nothing had changed. Jerry was one of the brightest thinkers I'd ever met, so I wasn't too surprised at the lack of my success.

I finally gave up trying to take Jerry into a deeper state and decided I would just have to give him a hypnotic suggestion and see what happened. I knew it couldn't be anything too dramatic, because it didn't even look as if he was even in a hypnotic state at all. He was just lying there, with a sort of smile on his face, like he was amused with the whole thing.

So, I said to Jerry, "When I say 'Go' you will lie in bed for exactly five minutes. Then you will wake up."

I turned to Curtis and showed him my watch. When the second hand swept past the 12, I said, "Go!"

Curtis and I watched Jerry. Both of us were sure he was going to immediately jump up off his bed, but he didn't. He just lay there. After 10–15 seconds Curtis and I began to look at each other in disbelief. What was Jerry doing? Had I actually hypnotized him?

We stepped out of the room so that we could talk. As soon as we closed the door behind us, I blurted out, "Is this for real? Is Jerry just kidding with us?"

Curtis said, "It doesn't look like it. He's just lying there!"

We were both in a state of disbelief. We had never seen anything like it before, and it was even more incredible because of Jerry's obvious intelligence. It seemed impossible that I had hypnotized him.

As the fifth minute approached, Curtis and I went back into the room to see what was going to happen. We stared at the second hand on my watch. Exactly as it swept past the 12, exactly when five minutes were up, Jerry jumped up from his bed and said:

"It didn't work."

Curtis and I both howled. Then we looked at Jerry again. We couldn't believe it. Jerry was serious.

"It didn't work," he said. "I was just resting. I heard everything you said. Nothing happened."

"But Jerry," I said. "Why did you wait exactly five minutes to say that?"

For the first time, Jerry's amused smile left his face. "I don't know," he said. "I just felt like resting for a while."

It then dawned on him that he had no other good reason for why he had waited exactly five minutes except that I had suggested it. Indeed it had worked. But what amazed us even more, was Jerry's description of what being hypnotized felt like: He didn't feel anything at all. He felt relaxed and at ease. That was it.

In other words, he didn't even know he was hypnotized!

This triggered all sorts of questions for me. I began to wonder how many of our beliefs are really things that we have accepted through the suggestions of others? Does our subconscious take the trust in our friends and family and accept their suggestions as true?

I could see how often we fall under the spell of outer authorities, accepting them as experts and therefore accepting what they tell us. We are also bombarded with advertising messages and people selling causes they want us to join.

These thoughts deepened considerably when I went home for Christmas break. I decided to try another experiment with hypnosis. My youngest sister, Carol, agreed to be my test subject. My brother, Tom, and sister, Joanne, agreed to observe. As soon as Carol lay down on my bed, I began the process of putting her into a hypnotic trance. I could immediately see that she was going under deeply. I took her to a very deep state to see what was possible. Here is what I recorded in my notebook:

I told Carol to open her eyes. Joanne and Tom watched as I took out a deck of cards and performed miracles of magic that any magician would have died for. Except I was using no magic tricks at all. I was using only suggestion.

I showed three cards to Carol. I laid them face down on the bed. I flipped them over one by one and asked her what they said. Then I turned them face down and did my magic.

"Now watch this," I said to Carol. "When I turn up this card it is going to be blank." I then turned up the card.

"How did you do that?" she asked. Joanne, Tom and I watched in amazement since I hadn't done anything at all. The card wasn't blank to anyone but Carol.

I then mixed the cards up and Carol still picked out the right card and still saw it as blank. I then turned the card back to its original form and then made the whole deck blank. Carol couldn't believe her eyes since I never covered or moved the cards. I simply said "presto" and they changed right before her eyes.

I then decided to try something I'd never tried before: a classic post-hypnotic suggestion. We've all seen movies or read books about such things. Could they be true? I asked Carol to lie back down and close her eyes. I took her into a deeper trance. I then told her that in exactly 10 minutes after she woke up, she was going to feel thirsty and she would go downstairs to pour herself a glass of milk. I also told her that when she woke up she would remember nothing since being hypnotized. I then counted backwards from 10 and woke her up.

Her eyes blinked open and she looked at us watching her. "Well?" she said.

"Well what?" I asked.

"Well, when are you going to start?" she said.

Joanne, Tom and I roared with laughter. Carol looked at us and said, "What? What's going on?"

I then explained to Carol that she had been hypnotized, but that I'd told her that she would forget it all, which is why she couldn't remember anything. Needless to say, she didn't believe a word of it. She thought I was joking.

I had to show her the cards and go through all of the tricks and tell her what I had done. She was finding it hard to believe, but Joanne and Tom made it clear to her that it was for real. I could see that the whole thought bothered her a little bit, just as it was bothering me. How could her perceptions and memories be so completely altered by my mere suggestions?

Then she suddenly got up and began going downstairs. The three of us followed her. "Where are you going?" I asked.

"I'm thirsty," she said.

We watched as she opened the fridge, took out a carton of milk and poured herself a glass. It is hard to describe the feeling of bafflement, wonder, humor and disbelief that struck us as we watched. It had been exactly 10 minutes since she woke up. Apparently, not only do hypnotic subjects take suggestions very well, but they seem to have a more accurate sense of time than any conscious person I have ever seen. In both of my experiments, they had matched my suggested time right to the second.

Once I realized the power of hypnosis, after this second experiment I never hypnotized anyone else ever again. I was deeply disturbed by the thought that others would accept suggestions so readily. Was this something I wanted to encourage? Would they become even more open to suggestions from others? It shook me up.

I began to wonder if indeed the world view of the whole human race was the result of hypnosis. How much do we really know for ourselves? How much have we just accepted the suggestions of others? It was not just religious beliefs that I was wondering about, but even basic concepts of what we thought was real such as: Why do we think clocks really keep an accurate account of time? When someone is winning a game, why do the losers always feel bad and the winners feel good? How much of society's concepts of success and failure are simply the results of mass hypnosis? Is the world really as it seems to us, or is it just a subconscious construct?

Rather than having made progress, I now felt like I knew nothing. Should I reject everything that I believed? How could I? How can you throw away everything you believe?

Higher Education

After my freshman year, I decided to quit college. I realized that what I was looking for could not be found there. I had studied physics, chemistry, and mathematics. I thought these were the path to understanding what life was about, but I began to realize that they represented only an outward study of life. In fact, the sciences never arrive at the original cause or meaning of anything. Science answers how things work, as if life were a long chain of causes and effects, but never the source of all causes, or their real purpose.

I was looking for something more—a higher education you might say—and it was not a mild curiosity pressing me on.

However, I was entering waters uncharted by science. Even something as simple as hypnosis, which almost anyone can prove for themselves, was a field that most scientists rejected in those days.

Now that I could see the far reaching affects of hypnosis and how we accept so many of our beliefs simply out of trust—and how real this can seem to our subconscious, especially when "everyone else" believes it—I also realized that experiment and personal experience were the only real paths to knowing and understanding.

As a result of my exploration, I became convinced that I needed to start looking within myself for the ultimate answers. This was a major shift for me, because up until this time I had accepted the common belief that we cannot trust our own subjective senses. We fool ourselves too easily. However, it now occurred to me that the moment we accept this suggestion, which is just like a hypnotic suggestion, we force ourselves to depend on outer authorities for our answers. This is what happens when we start believing that we can't trust ourselves. In fact, the opposite now seemed true: The only thing I could really trust was my own experiences. I might not know what they meant, but I certainly could know what I was experiencing.

Then a new question came to me: If hypnotism could fool the subconscious, could it also help one learn to discover new areas of consciousness and reality? What if I asked the subconscious for guidance, rather than telling the subconscious what was true? Could it be used to make contact with the pools of wisdom that I had experienced before? Could the subconscious find the way to these states of knowingness?

It started merely as a strange thought, but I soon realized the question I was really asking: Is there a higher wisdom that I possess that my inner self is a part of, and could my subconscious open the door to this understanding?

My notebooks from this time are filled with experiments and realizations. I tried a form of self-hypnosis. But instead of giving myself commands to feel more self-confident, think clearer, or other forms of self-programming, I used suggestions to see truth as it was and to find the states of knowingness that my own beliefs were preventing me from experiencing. In other words, instead of telling my subconscious what to do, I was telling it that I trusted it to lead the way.

My notes show the results of my experiments:

When the conscious mind becomes confused, the subconscious mind takes over to solve the problem...

Confusion creates gullibility because the conscious mind looks elsewhere for suggestions...

Confusion is loss of faith in the conscious mind...

There is a struggle in every person between day and night, the fight between our conscious mind and the subconscious...

Fear is an extreme case of worry, which is the battle between the conscious and subconscious. The conscious mind worries that something might happen. The subconscious takes this as a hypnotic suggestion and experiences it as true. The conscious mind then rejects it as wrong and dangerous thinking. Relaxation and patience are the answer. Relaxation is allowing the subconscious to roam free...

Worry is negative thinking...the mind worries too much. This is the strain of the conscious mind. Trust brings out the wisdom of the subconscious mind...

It is impossible to live a life without worry unless one has faith in some guiding force, whether it be God or the subconscious. Did Jesus understand this?

To direct one's faith is fruitless. Use the built-in homing device. It shall guide you to truth...

Whenever a parent says to a child, "Don't get into trouble," it is like worrying. It creates a suggestion to the subconscious of the child to get into trouble. This is why children get into so much trouble when they have parents who don't trust them. The conscious mind of the child is not strong enough to stop from acting out the suggestions created by the parent's own worrying...

The opposite of worry is faith...

Trust reduces worry between people ...therefore total hypnosis would involve total trust...

God represents total freedom. People will constantly strive for freedom until they realize it is the freedom from worry they are looking for...

Jesus said faith can move mountains, but this is not faith in knowing you can move the mountain. It is the faith in something greater than our conscious abilities.

It is fascinating to look back at these notebooks and see how my exploration of hypnosis and the subconscious was leading me into a spiritual search. Suddenly I had a new perspective on Jesus' teachings about love and faith. Was he really showing how to trust in a higher force because this trust opened the subconscious up to that guiding power?

In fact, was the battle between good and evil that the Bible talks about simply this struggle between the conscious mind and the subconscious? The conscious mind wants to have control, but the subconscious is far more powerful. As soon as the conscious mind imagines doing something "wrong" the subconscious seizes this image as a suggestion and treats it as if it was real. Was the answer for the conscious mind to develop trust in something greater than itself, so that the subconscious could act upon higher impulses rather than lower?

I decided to read the Bible and search for its deeper meaning. I had long felt the Bible held some kind of second dimension of meaning hidden between the lines. That is what it felt like to me when I held the book. So I tried a hypnosis experiment to see if I could discover what the added dimension was: I would take the whole message of the Bible and trust it.

I put aside all my worries. I accepted only trust in truth itself to lead me.

I then saw something clearly for the first time: When we fully trust that there is a greater reality and purpose and that this Truth is guiding us toward awareness of the whole, then our conscious mind and subconscious mind become aligned. It feels like an inner healing. I didn't yet realize that I was really just contacting Soul, a higher part of myself than my mind. But I could sense that I was onto something real.

We have taught ourselves to distrust the impulses of the subconscious mind, since the subconscious is so easily fooled by almost any suggestion and accepts almost any suggestion as if it is true. However, it is our fears and distrust that create exactly the wrong kinds of suggestions, which the subconscious then seizes with a force so powerful that it seems out of our control. This is why, when the conscious mind loses faith in the subconscious, we begin to experience our subconscious as a source of wild and dangerous impulses. This break in trust between the conscious mind and subconscious mind leads to a suggestion of distrust, which then sets the subconscious mind in motion to become exactly what the conscious mind fears.

It is like a ready made trap. When the conscious mind cannot trust, it has nowhere else to turn but to its own rational thinking or to depend upon outward authority to tell it what to believe. However, this leaves us divided from our own inner selves and puts us in a battle against our own subconscious. We fight against our thoughts and desires because we don't see that our fears originate from our own suggestions of distrust. That's where it all begins.

This is the message I found hidden in the Bible. There were two ways of living: in trust of Truth and a greater reality, or in distrust. In the Garden of Eden, or outside. Eating the apple was turning toward the knowledge of the conscious mind for guidance, rather than God. Trusting only in our conscious mind leads to a world of worry, wars and fear, because it is based upon distrust in our own inner self. My notebooks show some of the thoughts that concluded this experiment:

One must die in his conscious mind before he shall find this truth. To die means to lose all faith in the conscious mind and find only faith in truth itself.

This is what you realize at the moment of death.

Perhaps a part of me did die.

Indeed, I felt the deep underlying feeling of worry I had been struggling with begin to subside. My thoughts became friendlier, more trusting and more inspired.

When soul longs to know, follow it, for it is led by the wisdom of all life, while you can only lead yourself with the experience of one man...

I used to believe that you should not believe in God unless you know it is right. However, no one ever pointed out that I was putting my faith in this very belief without knowing it was right...

To learn, you must learn with your heart. You must have faith in truth. If it is wrong, your heart will show you.

For the first time, I saw that it was my responsibility to believe, not because it was the result of some kind of logical conclusion, but because this was how the subconscious worked. By believing in the guiding force of a greater reality, my inner self would find the way. In other words, belief was a creative act.

It was a double-edged sword. If I believed something out of fear, then it would become true to my subconscious. If I only allowed myself to believe in the results of rational thought or the truth established by outer authorities, it was like giving up my creative ability to believe, and this created a world view of limitation and solid external reality because it was based on a suggestion of distrust.

Science had taught me to see this outer world as real and that subjectivity could not be trusted. However, to the subconscious, every thought, emotion and suggestion is experienced as real. According to science, this only shows how easy it is to fool the subconscious. But suddenly I realized that in fact this was all backwards and the subconscious was witnessing another truth, a greater truth.

Every experience we have is indeed a real experience. It is not the subjective experience that fools us, but the interpretations concocted by our conscious mind that get us off track. The feeling of God's presence, for example, is not necessarily a proof that God exists, but it is still an experience that is real in itself. The feeling of God's presence is as real to the subconscious as any other experience.

We ask ourselves if we believe in God, but this is the wrong question. Would we ask ourselves if we believed in the moon? The real question is: What is our experience of God? It is a subjective experience, but it is no less a real experience than anything else. The experience itself is what the subconscious knows. It knows that direct experience, free of connotations, is the only thing that is real.

To accept these inner experiences as real experiences is to trust our inner selves. Once I trusted my subjective experiences and perceptions, I realized that I was in fact believing in Soul to guide me. This led to another interesting idea.

If it was my choice to believe whatever I decided and I wanted to believe something that could lead me to the pools of wisdom that I was looking for, then why not believe that my subconscious could lead me to Someone or Something that could teach me these secrets? Even the idea itself seemed to thrill my imagination. And if it was my responsibility to choose what could turn my own subconscious toward the greatest positive force, then why not choose to believe this?

What I tried next seemed natural. Making use of self-hypnosis again, I relaxed and began believing I would meet Jesus inwardly and ask him for his guidance. My imagination, with its new found powers of creativity, seemed to leap at the suggestion and I soon found myself shifting in my state of consciousness. I was rising upward, it seemed, going through layers until I felt myself stop in a beautiful world that stretched out in every direction around me. I saw someone approaching and soon realized it was Jesus.

I didn't say a word, but he knew immediately what I wanted as if he was answering my call. He looked at me with his kind and gentle eyes and said, "I can't help you."

What? He couldn't help me? How could that be?

I looked at him, feeling confused. Had I done something wrong? Surely, there was something he could do? But his eyes seemed to say that my case, for some reason, was beyond his control.

After a moment, his expression changed a bit. It was as if he had an idea. He then looked at me and said, "I'll pass your name on. Perhaps they can help you," and he walked away.

What a strange experience! Jesus was telling me that my case was out of his hands and he would have to pass my name on to someone else. Was my subconscious also passing me on to something else?

One week later I found out.

Soul Travel

Walt and Pat, my uncle and aunt, had watched me growing up and recognized the spiritual search I was going through. I think they understood it better than anyone else in my family because of their own experiences. They were two of the earliest chiropractors licensed to practice in New York State, fighting against a medical profession that was continually trying to portray chiropractic as quackery in order to shut them down.

A lot of their friends were also searching spiritually; trying yoga, studying with teachers from India, exploring new thoughts and ideas. It was, after all, the late sixties and early seventies, and there was a strong surge of spiritual renewal transforming society.

When we got together that summer weekend after my freshman year at college, we began talking and we talked most of the night. It was a great feeling to find others who felt the same interest for a deeper and truer way of life. They found my realizations interesting, and it soon became clear to them that I was a serious seeker looking for more.

Before my family left to return home, Walt handed me six books from his bookshelf. He said to me, "Pat and I have a strong feeling we should give these to you. We're not exactly sure why—we haven't read most of them—but we think they might mean something to you. I guess we're just unknowing channels. We're interested to hear what you think of them, especially *Jonathan Livingston Seagull*."

Besides the book by Richard Bach, they gave me three books by Paul Twitchell and two booklets by the Self-Realization Fellowship. The energy I felt from the books told me there was something special in them.

I've often thought back to what Walt said to me that day. How could someone know they were an unknowing channel? Yet, that was exactly what he and Pat were for me, just as Walt said.

When I got home, I began flipping through the books, just feeling their energy without reading them too closely. *Jonathan Livingston Seagull* seemed like a fascinating story. The Self-Realization Fellowship booklets felt heavy and solid and did not attract me. But the books by Paul Twitchell had such a strong presence to them that they vibrated

41

in my hands. I'd never felt such energy from books before. While the Bible seemed to radiate two dimensions when I held it, these new books seemed filled with too many dimensions to count.

I just sat there with my eyes closed, letting the energies from the books flow into me. I was afraid to open and start reading. I was afraid that the energy I was feeling would disappear if I started reading. I had seen this before—the energy from a book was somehow lost in the words, as if the author himself did not know what he had created.

In My Soul I Am Free was a biography of Paul Twitchell and his own spiritual search, which led him to discover Soul Travel and an ancient teaching he called Eckankar. *The Tiger's Fang* was a story of Paul's inner journey through spiritual worlds and his personal discovery that there were many heavens, each greater than the next. *The Far Country* was a book that laid down the philosophy of Eckankar, written as a dialogue between Paul and his Tibetan spiritual teacher, Rebazar Tarzs.

Needless to say, there are many spiritual paths and teachers, each right for some, and each offering something different. If I was describing adventures with well-known traditions such as Buddhism or Taoism it would probably be easier for many to understand. However, I was on a different kind of journey. I wasn't looking for an ancient teaching or a group to join. If spiritual truth was real, I should be able to find it through personal study. Paul Twitchell's books fit perfectly.

He was not writing about religious dogma that should be accepted on faith, but described an inner directed, individual path. He didn't plod through deep intellectual ideas, but wrote about spiritual experience and self-discovery. He explained that our consciousness does not have to remain trapped in our body, but can travel freely into subtle realms where life can be seen from the viewpoint of the whole.

Such principles, it turns out, are as old as any religious creed on this planet, but they rarely gain the recognition of popular faiths. The reason for this is that no single tradition ties them together. They have re-emerged in every age under new names and different forms. This is a result of the individuality one finds amongst those who follow this line of personal spiritual experience. Each person shapes and forms the path to fit them in their own unique way. This was why I had not heard of these teachings before.

However, the thing that amazed me more than discovering someone who knew about direct inner experience and the many states of knowingness, was the realization that this man, Paul Twitchell, some-how knew how to connect a kind of spiritual power to his words. His books held an energy that I could see he knowingly put there. It was this sensation that caught my attention more than anything because this was an immediate and direct experience for me.

The books sparked my imagination and seemed to blow open the doors on my subconscious with new suggestions. I was peering into a new world that my intuition sensed was true.

However, I was at heart still a scientist, so I watched my own reactions cautiously. It was time to test his ideas. Paul wrote that one could Soul Travel at will and he gave techniques. It was time to try it out.

My notebook tells the story of my first attempt:

I concentrated on seeing with my imaginative eye. I started forgetting all my senses, because the picture I saw was the clearest I have ever seen. I then decided to stop trying and just let my intuition take over.

I suddenly became a viewpoint. I wanted to see something that I could verify later, so I began to think about my friend Dave. I felt myself flying through space and then began hearing voices. It was Dave with our friend Doug. I was in Doug's car, listening to them trying to remember the name of the author of the book, Kim. Both made some wrong guesses. I then said, "It's Rudyard Kipling," but they didn't hear a thing.

I wasn't surprised, but it was amazing to see and hear everything that was going on, yet they couldn't see or hear me. I was right behind the passenger's seat and Doug was driving. I listened for a while longer, trying to remember whatever I could.

I then saw a white light coming down into my eyes. I sensed that this was purposely being projected so that my eyes would stop bothering me, almost as if the light was healing my eyes. Then I found myself coming back inside my body, but I was looking at my eyes from the inside out.

In my left eye I saw a symbol of some kind. I worried about it and instantly I was outside my body again. I then told myself not to worry and once again was inside my body. I then saw that the symbol was blue and shaped like a steering wheel. I followed it and found myself in a whole new world. [I had not yet heard about the blue star, which Paul wrote about in other books.]

I forgot most of what happened next, except for what happened at the very end. I was in what appeared to be a space ship with a middle aged blond man talking to me. At this point the experience was more dreamlike, al-though I was still consciously awake and aware of everything and completely in control. I felt detached, watching, yet when I imagined something it would either happen or it seemed like it was something that would happen later.

I then lost interest and withdrew back into my body, which I had forgotten about. It seemed like I woke up for a while, but then I woke up again. I immediately looked at my watch. Almost two hours had gone by. Obviously, I'd forgotten most of it.

My experience progressed in an interesting way. I started just as a point on the inside of a car, but eventually became like an all-seeing eye. I learned not to worry and I saw the immediate effect of worrying. Everything came to me through my intuition.

In the beginning I had a hard time looking directly at people, but in the end I could examine even a pin on someone's clothing quite clearly. I had three full senses; hearing, seeing and knowing. My whole energy seemed focused on seeing. The hearing and knowing came naturally.

After the experience, I tried calling Dave, but couldn't reach him until the next day. He confirmed that at the exact time I had my Soul Travel experience, he was indeed in Doug's car, with Doug driving down the road I had described. He couldn't remember if they had talked about the book, *Kim*, or not, but he did confirm some other things I had seen.

Such an experience might sound like proof enough to convince anyone, but I've found the mind to be a strange thing. With experiences that completely shake the foundation of what we believe, the conscious mind can find ways of doubting anything. While it seemed to prove that Soul Travel was real, my experience had turned dreamlike in the end. That bothered me, and I began to wonder how different the dream state was from Soul Travel.

My experience was real, that much I could accept, but was it a real experience of the same outer world, or an experience that in some way paralleled the outer world? I had seen something actually happening miles away from my house, but what I had seen seemed different in some ways.

The next Soul Travel experience didn't come so easily. My mind wouldn't relax, and no sooner did I feel myself slipping out of my body than I would begin thinking about it and pop right back in. For the first time I could see how little control I had over my own thoughts and imagination.

Through Soul Travel experiences I was beginning to see that spiritual knowledge was something far different than book knowledge. Paul's writings seemed to be speaking in a language my subconscious immediately recognized, but I didn't want to accept something just because I read it. I wanted to experience it for myself.

I found myself filled with inspiration one moment, as if a great light had turned on and was illuminating the world, but then would end up back in the dark, feeling limited by my own thoughts soon after. It was a strange up and down cycle, which I've heard many others describe as well.

From my notebook of those days:

Upon realizing all things are equally comfortable,
  We gain Wisdom.
Upon discovering all things are equally authoritative,
  We gain Freedom.
Upon seeing all things are equally important,
  We gain Power.

Inwardly I was making progress, but I'm sure it all looked very different from the outside. My father was getting a little tired of seeing his teenage son lying around the house daydreaming, or whatever it was that I was doing. He was deeply disappointed I had decided to quit college and was sure I was throwing away a great opportunity. My father had fought hard to have a chance at college, having grown up in a family with six kids. His father had died when he was young and he was raised only by his mother on a small income.

College had changed his life experience and he could not help but feel that I was wasting my life away on daydreams. So, one day he told me that he could not house and feed me any longer. It was time for me to earn my own way and find a new place to live. If I needed to figure out what I was going to do next, I would have to do it somewhere else.

The Hermit

Late summer in the Connecticut State Forest was a beautiful place to contemplate. Dave's brother had set up a tent there earlier in the year. Since no one else was using it, Dave drove me out there to stay.

The forest was thick with oak and birch trees. Pines were peppered about here and there. Squirrels, raccoons and possum were my most frequent neighbors, although I soon discovered I had a live-in tent-mate as well: a silver-gray field mouse. Occasionally, deer would pass through the woods and the owls came out at night.

It was not a far walk to a small stream for water. A long hike brought me to a nearby apple orchard, where I picked up freshly fallen apples for lunch. All the pressures of civilization were gone. The nights were long and quiet, and the stars shown bright in the late summer sky.

I thought a month or two would help me sort through what I should do next. I also thought that life with nature would help my spiritual exercises. However, my mind wandered. It seemed harder to concentrate, and for some reason I didn't feel at home amongst the trees, but more like an intruder. It took a while to settle in.

I wanted a direction, but strangely my hermitage in the woods seemed to show none. Life just went by, day to day, amongst the plants, insects and creatures. I was able to free my mind from the craziness of mankind, but it didn't seem to be bringing me any closer to the states of consciousness where all of life was clear. It was not going as I expected.

It felt like I was in some kind of limbo and I realized that I needed to make a choice. It was time to start a whole new life. I could go anywhere and do just about anything I wanted. But what did I want?

I thought about Eckankar, Paul's teaching. I could fly out to Las Vegas and track down the address on the back of the books. That seemed a long way off, and who knew what I might find.

I had the feeling that there should be something that made it clear for me, as if I would suddenly know exactly what I should do. But as the weeks went by, I didn't feel as if I was getting any closer and I didn't know how else to make my choice. So, I waited. And while I waited, I studied my books and practiced exploring the new spiritual teachings I had found.

The weeks passed by. Then, one beautiful clear day I heard someone trudging through the woods. It was Dave and he was carrying a sack of civilized food. Real food.

He laughed at my beard and long hair. I didn't even know how it looked since I had no mirror. It was great having a visitor, and as we talked I began to realize that it was time to rejoin the civilized world.

We sat in the clearing by the tent, soaking up the sun that filtered through the trees, when I suddenly realized I had no idea how long I had been living in the forest.

"What's today?" I asked.

Dave told me the date and my jaw fell open. It was my birthday! I had no idea.

I was nineteen years old! It caught me totally by surprise.

But there seemed to be something more. What was it about turning nineteen? It seemed like it meant something more.

Suddenly my Life Dream came back to me with a shock. I would know the answer when I turned nineteen. I would find the teachings of my true spiritual home. What was the name of that world again?

ECKLON came back to me again, and like a flash of light I realized that it was ECKANKAR!

In those days we called experiences like that "mind blowing." I can't think of a better way to describe it. I was speechless. I couldn't explain what I was feeling. I couldn't even think what to say about it.

"What is it?" Dave asked.

"It's my birthday," I said, which were the only words that came to mind. The rest was too unbelievable to describe.

"Could you pick me up in a week?" I asked Dave. "After I pack things up here, I've decided where I'm going next."

Death Comes Knocking

My parents agreed to let me stay home for a few months while I earned enough money for my trip. My mom even found me a job painting the Little Red Schoolhouse Library, as we always called it. The community volunteers running the library decided the building needed a new coat of red paint and were looking for a painter.

The outer shingles were long overdue. They needed to be completely scraped free of what little paint was there. The edging needed to be done in white, and there was the bell tower at the top that would need painting from the roof.

No sooner did I begin the job than I felt a real sense that what I was doing was exactly right. I think Paul Twitchell was dead on when he said that most Westerners do not do so well spiritually when escaping into the wilderness, unlike stories about hermits from the East. There is something about our work and involvement with others that plays an important part in our spiritual unfoldment. The conflicts and struggles we face are keys to our growth.

I thought, like most people, that we can think most clearly when our surroundings are peaceful and serene, but what I began to see for the first time was that life has a flow to it, and our life becomes most full when we are in synch with that energy. In other words, rather than thinking clearly to decide what I needed to do, I was better off catching the flow wherever it might be and going with it. We then become more like surfers catching waves and following the currents where they might lead.

Life, therefore, is active and not passive. The spiritual path is not only being receptive to the subtle lessons and currents, but actively participating and co-creating.

As the mystery of this was beginning to dawn on me, I wrote this poem. My writings at this time were all fairly simple. I wasn't trying to author works of art worthy of publishing. I simply found that describing in words something as subtle as the ebb and flow of life helped me see more clearly:

LIFE

O lovely life,
   Singing your melodies of silence,
So often I wish to grasp you firmly
   In fear of you leaving my presence.

Yet escaping my fingers of desire
   And chains of reason,
You leave me gripping my own hand
   And chained to the past.

What essence are you of
   That when I let you be,
You tug my chains to pieces
   And loosen my fingers with ecstasy?

Are you any more than an enchanting dream?

Though many times I fear
   Your powerful crushing breakers,
I'll sink and splash, until at last
   I see I must pass your borders.

Yet, the cliff remains before me, save
　　While I ride your foamy waves
And am lowered to my shore
　　Where your ebb beckons for more.

Are you any more
　　Than an enchanting dream?
Are you anything
　　But that of which you seem?
Are you truly being,
　　Or but a mirror of my Soul?
Answer me, life!
　　Or am I just a fool?
Then life echoed back these words,
　　With a ring of laughter in her voice:

"Are YOU any more than an enchanting dream?
"Are YOU anything but what you seem?
"Are you truly being, or but a mirror of MY Soul?
"Answer me! Answer me! Answer me! Ha!
"Or are you just a fool?!!"

One morning before heading out to my painting job, I found myself with a strange feeling that someone was nearby, watching. I couldn't figure out where the idea came from, or why I might be feeling such a thing, so I forgot about it. When I got home in the late afternoon, I sensed the feeling once again.

It was a very strange experience for me since I couldn't see any reason for it. So, once again I simply ignored it and gave a call to my friends to set up some fun for the evening.

I got back home late and decided to read one of Paul Twitchell's books before heading up to bed. The feeling began to creep over me once more. However, this time it seemed stronger and darkly foreboding.

I tried to concentrate on my book, but the sense of a dangerous presence began to grow and I finally realized it was just too much to ignore. I was clearly sensing something.

In fact, as the whole perception began to hit home, I realized that as impossible as it all seemed, there was someone nearby and they were waiting for me. My mind simply didn't know how to accept the idea since there wasn't a shred of physical evidence to support it, but the inner awareness grew stronger and stronger. I couldn't ignore it any longer.

Was it a warning? Was an intruder nearby? Was my family in danger? As it grew stronger, I felt a tingling on my scalp and finally realized, with a kind of strange horror, that someone was indeed already in the house, but they were not someone physical. It was some kind of spirit entity.

I began to walk around the house to see where the feeling was coming from. It was well after midnight and everyone else was asleep, which only added to the darkness and bizarre feelings. I finally decided I should just go to bed and ignore whatever it was. However, as I went up the stairs to my bedroom the sensation got stronger. I got to my bedroom door and knew without a shadow of a doubt that someone was waiting for me in my room.

I immediately turned around and went back downstairs. What should I do? I thought seriously of waking my father, but I couldn't for the life of me figure out what I would say to him. "I'm scared, Daddy. There's a bogey man in my room." The thought made me laugh, but the feeling of sheer fear was something so real and palpable that I literally didn't know what to do.

I tried to relax and calm down, but my pulse was racing. I paced downstairs, but as I did I finally realized that it was not my imagination. I was not creating this. It was real and this being was waiting for me. Finally, with almost a sense of desperation, I realized I could not stay up all night. I couldn't run away from it. I would have to face whatever it was.

I slowly began marching up the stairs, turning out the last lights on my way up. The presence grew stronger as I approached. As I entered my room, I saw my brother asleep on the lower bunk. How could Tom just lie there sleeping? There was no longer any doubt at all that someone else was there. It was some kind of being and it was waiting for me. While my brother slept, it felt like I was facing death itself and I began to wonder if perhaps it wasn't time for me to die.

Well, if it was, then I guess it would have to be. I wasn't going to walk away. I would face it. But, I was going to fight whatever it was. I wasn't going quietly!

As I drew the covers of my bed, I could feel the being there just above me. It was waiting. It was time. I closed my eyes as I lay down and...

BANG!

I was out of my body with a bang and found myself face to face with a being of incredible power and strength. It was trying to take me away. I fought it with every bit of energy I had.

But strangely, as I flung my fists, I found only empty air and light all around me. I spun around and struck out again, but couldn't grab hold of anything. I then began to realize that I was involved in a battle with my own self. I was fighting myself! The being was standing just out of reach watching me foolishly flail my arms.

For the first time it dawned on me that perhaps this being of death was not my foe, but a friend. I then immediately thought of Rebazar Tarzs, Paul Twitchell's Tibetan teacher. Suddenly the embarrassment of it all struck me and I remembered the story of Jacob in the Bible, who found himself fighting an angel on the ladder to heaven. I realized I was doing the same thing. My own imagination had turned it into something fearful.

It was the thought of death that had frightened me, but I had spent so much energy trying to fight my spiritual guide that I had passed through the portals of death without even a blink. So there I was standing on the other side, having crossed over, and finally I saw it all clearly. My own imagination had created these fearful images of death. Once dissolved, I could see I was in the hands of some great being, although I didn't know for sure who it was.

He reached out his hand and I grabbed it, and he took me all the way through the experience of death. I found myself crossing over and coming into a great light. I could feel a great heaviness and darkness falling away. I was dying, but it was beautiful. How could I have ever feared such a thing?

My inner guide was just a ball of white light, but he took me up higher and higher and I began to notice another change. It felt like I was dying again. A whole new sense of heaviness was falling away as I left everything behind as I crossed into a yet higher level. I began to wonder if I was being taken up through the inner planes as Paul had described in his book *The Tiger's Fang*. I wished I could see more, but the light was so bright that I could only make out the feeling of the worlds I was passing through.

Even though I could not see much, the sensations were incredible. The new world seemed limitless compared to the place I had just left behind. The light seemed infinitely more brilliant and the feeling of Love and Truth hummed around me.

Once again I found my guide leading me upwards, or at least it seemed as if I was going higher, and I found myself dying again. The energies were becoming even finer and more subtle. I had read the stories that Paul had written, but this was nothing like what I had expected. It was all of life itself that I was seeing. This world was even greater than the last world; the light even brighter. It was becoming difficult to sustain my consciousness because the feeling of bliss was so great.

For the first time I could see, as we traveled up through the inner planes, that these worlds were all connected like a great cone that was coming down out of the completeness of Reality above. The lowest plane, where I had left my physical body, was the lowest point of the cone. It was also the narrowest and smallest part.

As we traveled up toward the open end of the cone, the inner reality became larger and greater, with more freedom and awareness and love.

My guide pulled me on higher and it seemed that everything I understood was being pulled away from me. I had no thoughts anymore. I was only a sense of awareness. The beauty of it all was too much to take, and I could feel myself slipping off into a sleep state. I tried, but could not sustain awareness at that level. By then, my guide had taken me through five planes up into the pure spiritual state of consciousness. I could see from this state that the cone we had traveled up was but one of millions of cones, and that each cone represented completely different universes and realities, yet they all came together at the fifth plane.

Each cone was different from the others. The laws within each, the creations within each were different, like completely independent yet parallel universes. In other words, the inner planes that have been described by many spiritual travelers down through the ages were unique to our cone only, and were not the same for any other.

From this standpoint, these cones seemed more like drops. Separate droplets of creation, dangling like stalagmites from one great Ocean of Reality.

The subtleness and bliss was so great that I could stay awake no longer, and drifted off to sleep.

· · • · ·

My instinctive response after such an experience was to try dissecting it all to pieces. What did it mean? What really happened? Was that Rebazar Tarzs? Did I really travel up through the five planes?

I decided that the experience itself was too precious to analyze like that. I didn't want to mangle it and alter it beyond recognition. So, I just let it be what it was—an experience.

However, there was one thing I knew without a shadow of a doubt: This experience was REAL and had taken me closer to a direct experience with LIFE than anything I had ever experienced before.

What I didn't realize is that I had just scratched the surface. This experience, I later learned, was just my First Initiation.

I don't like using the term Initiation. Like so many of the words used in the field of spirituality, it is loaded with unintended connotations. Every religion and spiritual teaching seems to develop its own expressions and vocabulary to describe the subjective life, and I know I have done the same in my book. The problem is that these terms can be filled with different meanings for different people. When we first read a word like initiation, for example, we might picture images of primitive rituals or we might remember joining a fraternity at college. These are obviously far from how I'm using the word, so I know I run a risk in using such terminology. This is one of the challenges of writing a book like this. I hope the reader will bear with my particular use of vocabulary to describe what in many cases is beyond what any language can describe.

However, as I've been trying to say, I don't know a better word for describing the many experiences and inner stages I have passed through over the years. But, I think I should take a moment to explain what I mean by Initiation.

To initiate something is to start something. Therefore, it denotes a beginning and entering into something new. When we read about a spiritual teaching, we can learn a variety of things, just like gaining knowledge from school and books. However, this is nothing like what we learn once we make a commitment to a living spiritual path.

Idries Shah, the Sufi teacher, once told some academic researchers who were asking him questions about Sufism that they could never understand it without becoming Sufis. The whole of the teaching came from working with it and participating in it. It is nothing like knowledge we find in books. Unfortunately, as Idries Shah pointed out, these researchers could not believe him or understand what he was saying. They just thought he was hiding something or trying to make it sound more mysterious.

This whole reaction comes from our educational training, which gives us a sort of mentalized learning about things. It doesn't show us the difference between book knowledge and real wisdom. It doesn't show us how much more we learn from what we do and the commitments we make.

When moving to a new country, many people will notice a significant change in their dreams, as their inner consciousness tries to work out the new environment and adapt to the new culture. This is a form of initiation. When we make a change in careers, we find the same thing. Our inner life changes when beginning a new relationship. Our consciousness evolves whenever we start something new.

We can read about places to visit or about the companies we plan to join, but there is a big difference between what a tourist sees and what a citizen experiences. We find the same thing with relationships. It is one thing to date or go out with a friend, and it is another thing altogether to make a commitment to live together.

Unfortunately, the term "initiation" is often used to refer to the outer ritual or symbolic gesture that reflects these stages in life we pass through, rather than the inner experience and the inner shift in consciousness as I am using the word. Everyone recognizes the marriage ceremony, the promotion at work, joining a fraternity or sorority, or graduation from high school and college, but we often forget about all the invisible ways a person adapts to these new states of consciousness. In other words, we see the outer rites of passage, but not the inner transformations.

Sometimes we picture our lives as if they were made up of mileposts, like a train chugging along through new cities and states on our way through life. We can easily overlook that the most significant events of our lives come from the choices we make, and that these choices determine when our own lives become mixed with others or with forces and ideals greater than ourselves. These involvements change us.

These are what I call the initiations. They are the changes in our states of consciousness and the experiences that come when we become involved with something new.

In this case I call the experience I had my First Initiation because it came from my first real commitment to the spiritual path. I had decided to see where this path was leading. My experiences changed dramatically after this point. I began to recognize a spiritual current entering my life and changing the course I was on. Yet, it all took place without a word spoken or written by anyone.

A Journey Alone

I was ready to take the next step on my journey. I decided to visit Las Vegas to find Eckankar or whatever else might be there. Through Pat and Walt, I met a chiropractor friend of theirs who knew about Eckankar. He told me that Paul Twitchell had recently passed away. This was disappointing to hear. He told me that Eckankar had a new leader, Darwin Gross, but didn't know much more about Darwin than that.

I wondered for a moment if I was going to be wasting my time going all the way to Las Vegas, but everything within me was telling me it was time to leave. It was time to start a new life—one of my own making. And, as Walt put it, I was also going to the source to find out what Eckankar was really about.

Walt and Pat dropped me off at the airport. I wrote the following in my journal about my voyage, which took me thousands of miles from anyone I knew:

I stood in JFK International Airport with hundreds of strangers passing me by, and thought about all the reasons I had for going. With almost my last dollar spent on a flight ticket, I wondered if I was jumping in too fast. But I put my worries aside; I knew I had to go.

I was a teenager, leaving a world of school books and classes; a world of cooked food on the table and a warm house at night; leaving the security of my family and friends. I had this desire to start out life on my own two feet. It would be a new life, full of possibilities.

It began as a dream, yet suddenly I found it happening when my aunt and uncle handed me some books to read. These were books describing a knowledge I knew was true, deep within me. They described worlds and states of consciousness beyond the physical, and these books offered something else to me: A destination and a goal, something my new life could be built upon. Like a boat with its sails trimmed and ready, I took the wind when it blew.

Standing in the airport with hundreds of strangers passing me by, I was nervous. I knew no one where I was going. What would I find in Las Vegas? Was anything there besides the post office box listed on the back of the books? I had no idea, and I could feel myself shaking at the idea of what I was doing. But, as my plane rolled up to the gate for boarding, I suddenly found comfort in an unexpected way.

A man dressed in suit and tie, with chestnut brown skin, walked up and sat next to me. There was something about this man I had never experienced before. Emanating from him was a sphere of love—a globe of energy so distinct that I could measure its boundary with a yardstick. As soon as he was closer than five feet away, I felt it surround me, and all my fears and anxieties began melting away. I was overwhelmed by this soothing relaxation washing through me.

I could only think: Does this man know the effect he has on people? Doesn't everyone feel this flow of . . . but I didn't know what to call it.

"Is that our plane over there?" he asked me.

Looking out the big window, I saw it approaching for the first time. I nodded.

"Did you check in yet?" he asked.

I nodded again.

"Well, then I'd better check in too," he said, and with his springy step he got up and left.

The instant he was five feet away, the whole sphere of warmth went with him and I felt all my worries and tensions returning. It was incredible. And as soon as he came back, I felt the globe of energy around him engulf me once more.

What was going on? Who was he? By the color of his skin, it seemed as if he had just stepped off a plane from India, but his English was flawless, without a trace of any accent. And here he was in a business suit and tie sitting next to me in worn jeans, a beard and long hair, acting like we were making the trip together.

I could not fathom it. I could only accept it and let this warmth flow through me.

Our flight arrived in Las Vegas during the night, with city lights stretching everywhere from horizon to horizon. What I saw from above shocked me into realizing how naive I was. This was no small, young city as I expected.

Seeing Las Vegas by day, I knew another thing: My plan to live off the vegetation, berries and plants as I'd done in Connecticut was hopeless. This was desert world. There weren't any berries. There was only sand—lots of sand, and perhaps some of what they called chaparral, which looked more like clumps of barbed wire. It certainly didn't look digestible.

As for camping outside with my sleeping bag for warmth and a sheet of clear plastic for my tent—it had just snowed the day before. I never knew it snowed in the desert. The temperature was dropping below freezing at nights. But I heard we were lucky to be having such a warm spell!

Now it struck me how far I was from the world I knew. I'd never seen how small my life was until I tried changing tracks. Still, I had to go through with it. My whole life lay ahead of me. It was pulling me like a magnet and leading me on. I had to start it off on my own feet, and I had to make the journey alone.

It didn't occur to me until long after I wrote in my notebook, that I had not really made the journey alone at all. The signs were everywhere, but I didn't yet see what I had set into motion through my new commitment. What took place in the next few days was truly extraordinary. I didn't know what to make of it all.

When we arrived in Las Vegas, I found myself walking behind this strange man who seemed to be from India. I will never forget his springy step that contained incredible vitality. I walked behind him on our way to pick up our luggage and I tried to mimic his step. The strangest thing happened when I did this. I could feel his energy flowing through me. Although he was 15–20 feet ahead of me, I began feeling his whole spirit and confidence filling me as soon as I began mimicking his stride.

When we arrived at the baggage carousel, he stood next to me again while we waited. The first bag to come out was my knapsack, sleeping bag and sheet of plastic all bundled together. The second bag was this man's briefcase. No other bags came out for quite a while. Just our two bags. He picked his up and headed out the door of the airport. I wanted more than anything in the world to follow, but like suddenly hitting a glass wall, I stopped and realized I had nowhere to go. I could follow him no further.

It was late and I couldn't afford a taxi cab or a hotel room, so I was forced to sleep on some empty seats at one of the airport gates. No one bothered me, but it wasn't my most comfortable night of sleep either.

I did have a plan and a map showing campgrounds near Lake Mead, where I thought I could make a temporary home until I found work in the city. As morning came, I slung on my backpack and headed out the door. I walked into the parking lot and tried to orient myself. Which way would it be to the road that ran out of town toward Lake Mead?

I was turning around looking at the signs, when a pilot came out of the terminal building on the way to his car.

"Need some directions?" he asked.

"Yes," I said. "I'm heading out toward Lake Mead. Do you know which road is the best way there?"

"I'm heading that way, myself," he answered, "care for a ride?"

I couldn't believe my ears. What a stroke of luck. What a coincidence, I thought.

"Sure, that would be great." I said. "Thank you."

During our long ride to my destination, I began to realize how far away it really was from the city. It would have taken me probably an hour of walking just to reach the freeway that headed out of Las Vegas, and who knows how much longer to catch a ride or how many rides I might have needed to get to the Lake Mead Visitors Center, where the pilot dropped me off. It did indeed seem like a stroke of luck.

The fact that Lake Mead was so far away from the city was not good news, however. I had planned to live at the campgrounds, catching rides into the city and back again until I could earn enough to find an apartment. The distance was going to make it difficult to spend much time in the city and still hitchhike back and forth. Yet, that wasn't the worst of the news.

I soon learned from a helpful lady at the Visitors Center that the only free camping spots were on the opposite side of the lake. It would take literally hours to hike just one way. The campgrounds near the main road cost $3.00 per day. With only $35 in my pocket, that was more than I could afford. Had my string of luck run out?

I didn't know what to do. I felt the strong instinct to just do something…anything. But I didn't know what. I walked around the Center to see if any ideas came to me. I looked through the brochures. Hours ticked by. I felt stuck. I also felt strangely helpless. I had no experience with this sort of thing and had no idea where to turn.

I went back to question the lady at the information counter a number of times, but realized that she had helped all she could. Where should I turn? I finally realized that I had nothing else I could do but to turn the whole thing over to Life. If I was here for a reason and there was a purpose in my journey, then something would have to work out. None of the alternatives I had would work. There had to be something else.

With that I just sat down on one of the seats in the Center and just gave up all my worries. There was nothing more I could do.

No sooner had I finally given everything up, than the lady from the counter came over to me.

"You know," she said to me. "I've been watching you for the last few hours and I've been thinking there must be something else I can do to help. And something just occurred to me.

"There's a squatter's village off one of the main roads about half-way back towards Las Vegas. It's just some folks who've pulled their trailers off the side of the road. It doesn't have any facilities. I think they are mostly retired folks who stay for a while, until they decide to move on. It wouldn't cost anything.

"I've never actually stopped there, although I've driven by it a number of times, but maybe that could work for you."

It was the perfect answer. A free camping site, half the distance to the city. What a stroke of luck! I thanked her profusely, picked up my bag and headed out the door. It felt good to be moving again.

I arrived at Nixonville, as the squatter's village was called, before dusk, thanks to another helpful ride. There were perhaps a dozen or so trailers parked across the barren sand. I spread out my bag and plastic cover just in time to see the lights of Las Vegas coming on in the valley. It looked like a bowl of brilliant jewels in the distance.

The night was cold, the air was clear, and life seemed somehow more alive than ever. I will never forget those nights out under the stars.

After a day of getting settled in, I got up early to try catching a ride into Las Vegas. There wasn't much traffic in those days going by to the city. It took me almost four hours before someone stopped to offer a lift.

The driver was a young man, a few years older than I, who was willing to drop me off at the Eckankar Center address. I had picked up the address from a phone book at the airport before heading to Lake Mead. It was nice knowing there actually was an address and not just a PO Box, but life played another little joke on me before we arrived.

Following my map and trying to find the right address, we found ourselves staring at an empty lot with nothing but sand where the address should have been. I had worried this might happen. In fact, it was almost as if my own fear had come true just as I imagined it. We checked the buildings up and down the street, but the number we were looking for was definitely right where the empty lot was.

The only thing I knew to do was go to the nearest phone booth and call. However, while we were turning off the street, I noticed another road with the same name. In fact, we had taken the wrong turn. Sure enough, half-way down the block I found "ECKANKAR, The Ancient Science of Soul Travel," painted across the windows of a small office. What a relief!

After looking through all the books and reading about the study program, I spoke with the receptionist. Cheri wore bright, colorful clothes, and struck me immediately as quite a different sort of person. She explained that to receive the discourses would cost $42 per year. Fortunately, I could start with $15 and pay on a quarterly basis. That was almost half of all the money I had, but seemed worth it, since my whole voyage had brought me to this point. However, remembering my financial situation, I also asked if I could fill out a job application at the same time.

It turned out that a new class was starting that very night. It was free and they still had room for a few new students. What a coincidence, I thought.

The class was held at the local ECK Center down near the airport. After pawing through the books, which I couldn't afford to buy quite yet, I decided I'd walk down to the ECK Center and look for jobs along the way. When I reached The Strip, which is the main road through Las Vegas, I took a wrong turn and began walking north instead of south. It took me a couple blocks to realize I'd made a mistake. Just as I was turning around, I heard someone off in the distance yelling, "Eckankar!"

I looked across a sidewalk full of people and saw a young lady looking at me.

"Eckankar?" she asked.

"Yes," I said. "How'd you know?"

She pointed at my discourse envelope. Nancy filled me in on the city and the ECK classes. She gave me some suggestions where to start looking for work, which led to my first job. She would also later help me find my first place to stay in the city.

If I hadn't made the wrong turn I never would have bumped into her. The odds of running into an ECKist, as they call themselves, when less than 100 lived in this city of nearly 300,000 surely seemed like another bit of luck.

After meeting Nancy, I headed down toward the ECK Center and arrived shortly before the ECK class was ready to begin. Along the way I stopped off at a gas station, where I asked the attendant if I could use the electricity in their bathroom for my shaver. I decided I was better off without a beard since it seemed to be giving people the wrong impression.

For some reason people assumed that if I had a beard I must be into drugs. In fact, one of my hitchhiking rides on the way toward Nixonville was a car full of teenagers who were sure I would welcome their offer of "some good grass." They could not believe that I wasn't interested and insisted I had to be joking. When they finally realized I was serious, they started thinking I must be some kind of undercover narcotics officer and suddenly became very quiet.

The message was clear. If I wanted to find a job, my beard had to go.

On my way out of the gas station I thanked the attendant, and he looked at me strangely.

"For what?" he asked.

"Thanks for the use of your bathroom," I said.

He looked at me strangely again and I realized he didn't recognize me as the guy with the beard. I had a good chuckle over this.

When I arrived at the ECK class, Shirley, the class leader, was expecting a young man with a beard. Apparently Cheri had called her to let her know I would be coming and she had described me as a young man with a beard and long hair. They had discussed how it might be a good idea to mention that drugs and Eckankar didn't mix, so Shirley laughed when she heard why I'd shaved my beard off.

That night after class was over and Shirley stayed late to answer some of my questions, somehow she got the idea that I was far away from home. I hadn't said anything, but she asked:

"Do you have a place to stay tonight?"

Her question surprised me, because I hadn't said a word about it during class or to Cheri. I said, "Well, I thought I'd probably just sleep in the airport again, like the other night."

The thought of this seemed to pain her. I assured her it wasn't that bad, but she insisted that there had to be something better than that.

"Well, I'm camping out in the desert in a little squatter's village about 20 miles outside of the city," I said. "It's a little place called Nixonville."

"Nixonville?" she said, startled. "That's where Fritz and Eva are staying."

"Who?" I asked.

"Fritz and Eva and their three boys are ECKists. They live out there and work in the city," she said.

Well, with that, the coincidences had gotten out of hand. It had gone a little too far and I couldn't consider it luck any longer. Out of a dozen families living in Nixonville, one of them would turn out to be ECKists? And in fact, Fritz turned out to be a specialist in desert flora and made a little side living by gathering wild desert ginseng, desert herb tea, ephedra and other valuable herbs. So, I learned how to forage in the desert after all.

How wrong I had been about taking the Journey Alone.

61

I believe we are interwoven with all of life, whether we realize it or not. The moment we make a commitment to Life, Spirit, the spiritual path, or whatever you want to call it, then Life responds back. When we begin to listen to Life's subtle whispers and follow the flow of its currents, then it is just as if Life begins to listen to and follow us as well. When we make a commitment to Life, it also commits to us.

I was hardly alone on my journey.

Old Friends

As I thought about the new direction my life was taking, I looked back through my childhood. I could see this same force had been there all along. I wrote the following story shortly after arriving in Las Vegas to try capturing the subtle inner guidance I had experienced long before, as a child:

> I enjoyed the challenge of trying to get home fast. Pulling hard on the handlebars, standing up and pedaling fast, I raced over the small hill by our house. I loosened my grip to a light touch and guided my bike down the dark road. I could take the path around the back side of the house.
>
> Slowing down, I swerved left and flew onto the dirt path. The trees robbed me of even the moonlight, and so guiding my bike from memory, I waited for my eyes to adjust.
>
> I noticed how quiet it was, and scanning the well-known woods, I caught my breath. The stranger may not have heard me riding by. I slowed down and watched him over my shoulder. Carefully, I leaned my bike against a tall birch and crept up slowly.
>
> Was he asleep? I felt nothing strange in the air, only that silence which made me wonder. Yet, I could see he was just sitting with his eyes closed. It looked like he might be waiting for someone.
>
> While I was inching up closer, my foot slid from a rock and a stick snapped. His eyes blinked open and looked in my direction. He smiled. Then after a few moments, he said, just loud enough to hear, "Hello. Would you like to come over and talk?"
>
> I hesitated. I wanted to be friendly, but was nervous. I could already feel my shyness taking over, so to break through I blurted out awkwardly, "Are you waiting for someone?"
>
> "Yes," he paused, like the calm that comes in the middle of a storm. "I have been waiting for you."

My thoughts flew furiously. Questions filled the shadowy night. He knew me; I could see he knew me. But what did he want?

I was thinking of the best ways for escape, when he spoke again. His words were like waves upon a beach, soothing and relaxing. I didn't move.

"You need not fear me; we are old friends. We are as close as the wind is to the air." This was all he said, as he moved his hand through the breeze.

He began to smile and his eyes sparkled in the moonlight. Then, before I knew it, we were both laughing. Not loudly, but inside ourselves. It was as if something tickled us inside. I had the thought that I remembered who he was, but as I chased after this image it vanished.

I sat as close as I could to him then, so I could see his eyes and feel the warmth that surrounded him. He started to talk.

"Laughter is a true sign of learning. You are right to think that when your schools have little laughter, they have little learning. Your teachers can only teach you tools for the average child to help live in this world. But you are different, for your heart is open to a life beyond this world. You must listen to the forest and its teachings. Also the sky and its message. You must listen to all things and to your enemies and friends, for I am in all of them.

"You see the leaf?"

My eyes searched the dark night, following the direction of his finger. Then, at that very moment, barely visible, a leaf loosened from its branch and began gliding down.

"It knows when it is called and falls willingly, guided by the currents."

He talked with great love toward this leaf, so it seemed proper when it glided into his lap. But he was not looking at it anymore. His eyes were burning deep into mine. He continued softly, "I shall be with you always. Never worry of love again. Now, you must go, for your parents look for you."

With that he rose, with a walking stick in one hand. I started for my bike and turned to wave good-bye, but he was gone.

I wasn't sure quite what I was trying to describe here, but it was about the recognition that indeed I had been watched over by something or Someone who was helping guide my life. It was as if some kind of seed had been planted in my heart and through the years it had grown into the silent questions that set me upon my quest. Was I simply trying to return something that had once been given to me?

I could not yet see that the Inner Master was a part of myself. I was not ready for that understanding. In fact it wouldn't have helped me even if I had been told that. I still needed to see these qualities reflected in Another. I was still operating from the physical level of understanding that comes with the First Initiation. Each lesson comes at its appropriate time.

The Symphony

A golden field swayed to and fro by the changing breeze, as if a mighty hand was making patterns upon velvet. The trees played their subtle music with the wind and I was raised up as I followed the song of Life into the heavens. The symphony was grand and I stood in its middle. A small rabbit parted the velvet hay and vanished. I then realized I was a part of this performance of life just by my being.

No more was I the spectator. The birds seemed to sing in approval of my new awareness. I conversed with a rock who talked of the years. He seemed to mock my young age. Time had disappeared long ago and the moment opened up before me.

Then, suddenly the theme changed. A small boy with stick in hand came running through the woods, banging on the trees, throwing rocks at the birds fleeing his attack and chasing a squirrel up a tree. He saw very little and I was fortunate to stay unnoticed. I adjusted to this violent interruption much the way the music did.

After the boy left and a soft melody crept back, I realized the coarseness of his instrument did not set him outside of the symphony. Some day, perhaps, he would play a keen silver flute. Some day he would see what I have just seen. No part of life is set apart from the music, for it is life itself. I wish all could see it this way.

I was trying to capture the changed consciousness I was experiencing. Through writing about the subtle feelings that had crept into my life and describing this new awareness, it was as if I was waking something up within myself.

What was it?

The silent questions drew me on with all the enchantment of a beautiful melody.

How Do You Begin Soul Travel?

Doug,

I had a dream that I came to Las Vegas and met you and you were showing me around, which by the way may come true...

Since reading *Letters to Gail* [a book by Paul Twitchell I had sent] I have been able to more clearly see the importance of non-attachment... The book was a support to many ideas which I feel are fitting.

How did you begin Soul Travel? Actually, how did you change so many socialized thoughts so quickly? Did you have much confusion before you found ECK?

I've got many questions at this point in my life...It is so vast and un-answered.

Love, Sue

This is the same Sue whose house I had found through my out-of-the-body dream experience many years earlier. We had stayed in touch, and she saw me changing since I began my spiritual search. She was trying to understand how I could have adopted such a new life so quickly, while at the same time it is clear that she too was called by the silent questions. But in fact, for the first time I began to feel as if things were finally falling into place and making sense to me.

About a year later, Sue found some answers of her own.

Doug,

I'm writing to you because of something which baffles me. Twice I have had an experience which I cannot explain, or shall I say I don't know if they are the beginnings of Soul Travel or what.

Both experiences have been when I was very tired, not asleep but waiting for sleep. I all of a sudden feel this loud blackness accompanied by a feeling of fast motion. The first time I tried to stop it and became frightened. When I opened my eyes I had no feeling in my body.

The second time I tried to relax and the intense noise and movement almost came to a stop. I started to float but it all just stopped and I went back to my knitting. Oh, and the first time, I was dreaming before it happened and you were in the dream!? Last time I was awake.

Well, I haven't been reading or thinking about Soul Travel for a long time so I wonder if that's what's going on. I thought maybe you could give some insight on the beginnings of Soul Travel and what it's like?

Love, Sue

In another letter, shortly after, Sue wrote:

I've had some more Soul Travel experiences and they have helped me to believe in my other bodies, and to be introduced to others who have these awarenesses.

Just as Sue did, I learned it was my own experiences that mattered and little else. All the books I read, the popular theories, the scientific facts and philosophical concepts, all these fall away like a house of cards in a breeze before our own experience. Yet we each have to decide for ourselves what they mean.

The experience of my Life Dream when I was eleven years old took me to a world I called ECKLON. Now I had found a teaching called ECKANKAR. Was this the teaching my dream had foretold? Would it show me the science and art from the world I had seen in my dream? What about my mission here? What did I need to learn about people?

At this point I had barely begun to learn the meaning of these questions. However, there was one thing I had discovered so far:

People have a great desire to know. This is why the silent questions come. We want to be aware of who we really are and the greater meaning of life. We need to be conscious. Living in the dark brings suffering.

However, the senses of our physical body overwhelm us. We become so caught up in our sensations that we can't even imagine moving our attention beyond the body. We don't believe it is possible. So, we forget who we really are and why we are here.

I was just beginning to remember how to see Life from outside the human consciousness. I made it a practice to move my attention wherever I decided to put it. It became a daily exercise for me, so that I could move my awareness at will, even outside my body.

However, this was just dipping my toe in the water. The real adventure commenced when I discovered an inner current that was so alive it captured my attention. Pouring my attention into this spiritual flow of life created a new conscious center. I then made my second commitment to link myself inwardly to this stream and it gave birth to a new state of consciousness.

It really was that simple. I can see that now, but how could I make contact with such an inner wave when I didn't even know what it was or how to find it?

It helps to have someone who can show the way; a teacher who points out where we can place our focus. But even more important than finding a guide, I believe, is the need to ask. I needed to start by following the silent questions. I had to ask. Asking was the first step in expanding my awareness and learning the path that lay ahead.

THE PATH

THERE WAS THE PATH. Stretching forever, hot and aching from the blistering sun and pounded by so many feet. Yet the path was still there. It was the path of humanity, and it was cracked and bruised with age.

The sun hung like a hot iron in the sky and the people passed by, looking down. Slowly and painfully they walked by, looking up only in glances from the path.

I didn't follow the path any more. I took to the forest and to the mountains where the way was hard, yet the air was clear. Still, I often turned to look back at the masses upon the path. The path that leads to their jobs, to their villages, and to what they call home. It was years since my feet had felt the hot rock or my lungs had coughed from the congestion. I was happy to sit alone beneath the tree.

I was raised on the path, like all of the rest. I was taught to become hardened to the heat and the congestion. I tried learning to believe in the path and to depend on it.

But the way was too harsh and my feet too tender. I could not bear the pain.

Onward the path goes, ever onward toward some unknown end, if there is one. It reaches and connects with all other paths because it is the path of humanity. All is one, they say, and the slogan weeps from misuse. For they use it as a rope to hang with or as chains to bind. Yes, the path aches with ages of restrictions.

Most never see me beneath the tree in its shade. Hundreds just drag by, only looking up to check that there are no changes in the path. Only hoping the path may be a little easier today.

How different is the experience of he who is consumed by Life, drawn by IT, and filled with IT. To him there is no path, only compassion.

· · • · ·

I WOKE ONE morning, having just read these very words in a dream. It was the first page of a book called *The Path*. I quickly grabbed my notebook to record on paper exactly what I had just seen, but could only jot down the above passages before it faded from memory.

The book seemed real in my dream. It did not seem like my own words, but felt like some secret text that spoke directly to my condition. It was describing feelings I was just beginning to recognize. Somehow I was stepping off the path of humanity. The weight from ages of traditions and expectations was slipping away.

Where did these words come from? Had some unconscious part of me made them up? If so, why did it feel as if they had been written by someone much wiser than I? How could written words come from within me in a dream, and yet seem completely beyond me?

I had taken another step on the path. I was now starting to work directly with the inner teachings, but it was not what I expected.

The Inner Teachings

I had read about the Second Initiation. It signifies a conscious connection to the Astral Plane, the first spiritual world beyond the physical. This is the world where Soul goes after death. It is a world of imagination and emotion. I had read these things in books by Paul Twitchell and other authors, so I imagined I knew what they meant. But when the inner teachings began entering my consciousness, I realized the experience of it was far different from what I had read.

I knew theoretically that the second stage of Soul's journey comes after we are linked to spiritual currents beyond the physical. But what did this really mean? How does this link take place? What is the Astral Plane?

Thousands of books have been written about spiritual teachings down through history. Most are based on theories, tradition and myth.

Few are written from direct experience. However, even discovering first-hand accounts could not prepare me for the reality of it. I had formed all sorts of ideas about what it would be like, but I was completely wrong.

If the experiences I described from the first leg of my journey seem remarkable, they were nothing compared to what happened next. The whole of my life suddenly shifted, as if an unexpected wind filled my sails, pushing me into uncharted waters. I had drifted off the map of humanity, but where was I going?

A number of changes took place in my life at this time. For example, after I discovered a box of taped talks by Paul Twitchell, which had been abandoned in a loft at the Eckankar Headquarters, I found myself with a new job working for Darwin Gross the spiritual leader of Eckankar. It was quite a step up from busboy at the Silver Slipper Casino, and it was my first job starting up and managing my own department.

I also met a beautiful girl who, it seemed, loved the same things I did: Hiking in the mountains, swimming in the many lakes and rivers nearby, sleeping under the stars, writing about spiritual subjects and working with creative arts. We loved spending time together. Karen and I were soon married. For our next 5 jobs we worked at the same companies so that we could be close. We are still together over 30 years later.

Karen and I also brought our first family member into our home around that time—an extraordinary black and white cat, who lived with us for 20 years.

However, while these might mark significant physical events in my life, they miss entirely the real meaning behind them. It is not the physical mileposts that jump out from my notebooks, but the inner experiences. A shift had taken place. It was not the outer story of marriage, career or family that filled my many journals from that period of time, but a whole new life—a new dimension of reality that began revealing itself to me.

In fact, behind each of the events I just described above was a story that no camera or a microphone could capture. For example, the moment I walked into the General Administrator's office at the Eckankar Headquarters to introduce myself and ask for a job, I immediately realized something was happening.

It was the first time I'd met Bob. I had been to the office a number of times before, visiting to flip through the many books. I would talk to Cheri, asking her what she thought my chances of getting a job there might be. She said that Bob had never hired anyone under 21, which didn't look promising for a 19 year old, and I had only been studying the ECK discourses for one month, which meant I was a complete newcomer. But she suggested I talk to him directly.

One day, about a month after arriving in Las Vegas, I woke up and suddenly had the feeling it was time to introduce myself. I rode my bike down to the office, walked in the front door that led into Bob's office. He happened to be standing there behind his desk, so I reached out my hand and said, "Hi. My name is Doug Marman..."

Before I could say another word, Bob looked at me with this shocked look on his face. He then looked out his office door into the next office where Cheri sat. He said only one word: "Cheri?"

I took a step forward to see Cheri sitting there grinning from ear to ear, with her hands thrown up. She said only, "I didn't do a thing."

Like I said, no microphone or camera could have pieced together what was happening, but somehow I knew immediately that I had just been given a job. I didn't know how I knew it, but I did. I turned back to Bob and said, "You're kidding," which would have sounded even stranger to anyone observing, but Bob and Cheri knew exactly what I meant. The whole exchange had taken place without words.

Bob then explained, "I just got off the phone with Darwin, and he told me to offer you a job. We need some help back in the shipping department."

Or take the time when I first began seeing Karen. I met her at the Eckankar Office shortly after starting work there. It turns out she had just moved to Las Vegas one month before I did. We hit it right off and soon began spending time together. I could see it was getting serious pretty quickly. I wondered: Was I rushing into the relationship too soon?

I decided to let Soul, my higher self, make the choice.

On our next weekend afternoon together, Karen drove me back to my apartment in her blue Volkswagen beetle. We sat together silently for a moment in the car, when suddenly I felt this wave of spiritual current lifting me up. The current was so strong it pulled me out of my body and I found myself with Karen in our "light bodies". We were like two globes of white light in a sea of energy. From this point I could see how close we were together in spirit. It was easy to see the love that swirled around us. I was in this state of consciousness for what seemed like five to ten minutes, then found myself returning to my body.

As soon as I was back, Karen turned to me and said, "See?!!"

I intended to ask her if she had experienced what I had, but with her one word I knew. We both knew.

Or take the story about when Karen and I found Cyper, our black and white feline. We decided one day to adopt a kitten. We'd heard about a "no-kill" animal shelter on the outskirts of Las Vegas run by a lady named Betty Hahn, who promised to take in any animal free of charge. We visited her shelter and found ourselves walking amongst acres of peacocks, pigs, goats, cats, birds, snakes, dogs and almost any kind of pet you could imagine, mostly roaming free within her fenced property. One row of cages held just families of kittens, newly born.

As we approached one of these cages, I noticed one little kitten, barely able to walk, meowing loudly and crawling out over the top of its mother, brothers and sisters to the front, as if to greet us. When we stopped to look, it began climbing up the side of the cage. Karen and I were both struck by its boldness and by the strange feeling that this little kitten was trying to reach out to us.

She was mostly black with a white belly and a splash of white across her forehead. She had the deepest blue eyes I'd ever seen. The incredible effort she made to climb up the cage with her shaky little legs, barely able to hold on, touched us. It was as if her whole life energy was being spent in trying to grab us as we strolled by. However, Karen and I had decided not to adopt just any kitten. We were looking for a special one. So, we continued on down the row of cages.

As we walked, I looked back to see the black and white kitten shakily backing down off the cage and returning to its original place, beside its mother. The eagerness of this kitten to greet visitors touched me, but what surprised me more was what I saw happen next.

Another couple came walking down the same row behind us. As they stopped in front of the same cage, I nudged Karen to see what was happening. In fact, nothing was happening. The kitten didn't move or make its plaintive cries. Karen and I looked at each other.

After we had looked at the whole row of kittens, we decided to visit the black and white kitten's cage again. And just like before, even as we approached, this same kitten began its loud meows and stepping over its brothers and sisters to make its way to the front of the cage, where it climbed up to greet us. The feeling was unmistakable. We were being chosen.

We had come to pick out a special kitten, but the kitten had picked us instead. I wonder if the spiritual path isn't exactly the same as this. We think we are searching to pick out the best path, when in fact the path actually finds us.

Of course, we told Betty Hahn we would like to take this black and white kitten home with us. However, she said that the kitten was just a new born and had not been weaned yet. Betty would give us a call when the kitten was ready. She thought it would be about ten days.

One week later, I woke up from a vivid dream where this kitten came to me and made it clear that she was ready. She was quite adamant. There was no question in what she was saying to me. It was time to come get her and bring her home.

I told Karen about my dream and she was amazed, because she had just had a dream where this kitten had climbed up to sleep on our bed with us. Even though it was three days early, we called. Betty told us that yes; in fact, our kitten had just been weaned the day before. We could come by whenever we wanted.

We brought her home in a shoebox. For the first day she stayed close to the box, as if this big new world outside of her cage took some getting used to. I laid the box down on its side, so she could walk in and out. As I did this, she began walking toward me on her little shaky legs. I got down on my hands and knees, and she came right over. When I turned my right hand palm upwards, she climbed up and lay her little head down on my palm, placing one paw on my thumb. She had achieved her goal and claimed me as her own. Exhausted, she fell asleep.

I named her Cyper. It was a name that came to me inwardly the day she arrived. I felt the strongest attraction to her, and she became attached to me immediately. As the days and months went by, she would learn to jump onto my lap, where she would curl up as I read or did my spiritual exercises. There was something in her presence and love that tugged at my heart. It was as if I was remembering something about her. It was as if she and I knew each other from long ago.

In other words, what I'm trying to say is that behind the events of my physical life a whole new dimension came alive. Had it always been there? It seemed more as if I was awakening to another parallel state of being that fit hand-in-glove with the physical. These were not two separate worlds, but were somehow interwoven.

Up to this point, I had thought the path was something outside of myself. I had been trying to follow a path, or what I thought was The Path, but I discovered in a strange way that there really was no path. There was no path of outward rules or expectations to follow. Yet, I was still following something. Some inner trace, some inner current or stream of Truth seemed to be guiding my steps.

I asked myself: What was this Eckankar? Paul Twitchell wrote that it was not a religion, a philosophy, or set of beliefs. This suggested something far different than anything I had seen before. What was it? I read through his many books and I still came back to this same question.

I couldn't find a satisfactory answer. I became even more aware of the dilemma any time someone asked me what Eckankar was. This shouldn't be such a difficult question, I thought, yet I found myself giving a different answer every time. It seemed as if the only proper response was a spontaneous one to explain what seemed right for that person and that moment in time.

After a year of struggling with this question, the realization finally dawned on me that the spiritual path is nothing more than seeking out and discovering what The Path is! It is not a set of theories or teachings in books. It is not rituals or tradition. It is a reality that can only be found and known by continually seeking out what it is. It is nothing more than this.

Mystics down through history have given out this same truth. The *Tao Te Ching*, written 2500 years ago in Ancient China, says,

The path that can be spoken of
Is not the eternal path;
The name that can be named
Is not the eternal name.

In other words, reading books and listening to talks can only point to The Way. The physical teachings are no more than hints or clues. The path of itself must be contacted directly via the inner channels. Through dreams, spiritual exercises, or moments of inspiration, the heart opens up and catches a vision of the next step on our own individual path. The real path begins when we commit to these inner teachings and begin to follow them.

I started studying the ideas and feelings taking place within me more closely. Little by little I saw how my life was shaped by a continuously changing panorama of subtle, almost imperceptible experiences occurring within my inner worlds. These were the inner teachings.

To become more conscious of these subjective events that were coursing through my life, I tried capturing them through writing. I wrote to give form to these subtle, formless events.

Some of the things I recorded were my dreams.

For example, I had a dream where Paul Twitchell's teacher, Rebazar Tarzs, came to me and took me to a graveyard. He brought me to a small mausoleum. The feeling was creepy. The last thing I wanted to do was go inside, but Rebazar Tarzs beckoned me to follow him. He said there was something important for me to see.

I entered the dark structure and found a metal plate for each member of my family. Each plate contained strange text that I couldn't read. However, I had the sense that this place had been designated as our burial places, and our life's fate was sealed by this plate. I had the strong feeling that what was written in the text was my life story.

Rebazar Tarzs waved his hand over the text and suddenly I could read it. Immediately I saw a life that seemed trapped and controlled by the events of the world, as if my life had been sold and paid for, like some kind of business transaction. Rebazar Tarzs then removed my metal plate and handed it to me and told me to leave quickly.

I woke from that dream, and although I didn't understand it all, I had the incredible feeling that my fate was now in my own hands. Somehow the course of my life had been taken out of the control of the physical world and was now free to be re-written.

Besides dreams, I also tried writing stories that might capture the subtle inner events I was sensing. I tried exploring the essence of these experiences to understand them better. One day I sat down to describe the deep inner connection I felt with Cyper. It took the form of a simple children's story about a man called Bird Friend, who was a healer of birds in the mythical land of MU in a time, long ago. But this piece of fiction would end up having a very real impact on my life. Here are a few excerpts from the story:

Bird Friend

Suddenly, from the rocks above, jumped a mountain lion twice my size. His head searched back and forth with fear and confusion. His eyes met mine with a pleading for me to help, but his pause almost cost him his sight. For, out of the sky streaked a white falcon who's claws barely missed the lion's face. The cat's jaws dropped open and out fell a ball of white feathers. Then he raced to the woods with the falcon still chasing.

The falcon's threatening screams faded over the hills and the river's playful gurgling returned. Yet I wondered:

"Could those feathers be a baby falcon stolen from its mother?"

Sure enough, that is exactly what it was, and it was pure white like its mother. I lightly touched my hand to its warm body. The heart was still beating. It was still alive!

Carefully I lifted it, holding its weak neck in the palm of my hands. I stood silently wondering what to do, when its two small eyes popped open. A thrill of joy swept through me and with it, like an echo, a feeling came of an old memory awakening. What was this memory that I couldn't quite grasp? What were these little eyes reminding me of?

Slowly I understood. Bit by bit, it was coming back. Somehow I knew this baby falcon from long ago . . .

Yet here was my very same friend, now a baby falcon. I knew I must help.

· · • · ·

By the eucalyptus tree, in its shade, I rested listening to the baby bird's beating heart, hoping help would come soon. My thoughts were filled with warmth, stirred by the water rushing by and memories with my friend bubbled up. Yet the thought came over and over: How strange that she would return. How strange that we would meet again!

A rustle of leaves nearby brought me out of my dreams. A tall man walking with a long stride approached.

"My name is Bird Friend," he said in a deep yet soft voice. "Bluening told me that there is a boy by the river who has a baby falcon needing help. So I came right away."

"I came looking for you," I said. "My name is Lone Star."

"Come," Bird Friend said, "this little falcon needs quick help!"

As I followed Bird Friend with his fast pace, I looked up and saw all kinds of birds following from tree to tree. Many kinds I had never seen before. They were all beautifully colored, some with orange, blue, and even green, and they were all singing wonderful music. Bird Friend himself was whistling bird songs as we walked.

Finally we arrived at the small clearing where he lived. He showed me a small nest in a bush where I could lay the baby falcon.

Then Bird Friend said, "You must go now, because I will need time to heal her. Then she will soon be flying to find her mother."

"But can't I stay?" I said with all sorts of disappointment. "She is a friend of mine from long ago, and I don't want to say goodbye to her when I have hardly said hello."

Bird Friend smiled. "Every man should have a bird friend," he said. "And it is good you have found one, but she is very young and she was taken from the nest without the word of her mother. So you must go for now. But when I speak to her mother I will tell her what you said. Then I will send Bluening to bring you back when it is time to return."

As sad as I was, I said goodbye to my baby falcon friend and left. Her small eyes opened again for a moment and I heard a faint chirp. Then, exhausted, she fell asleep.

· · ● · ·

Bird Friend raised a hand over his head and all the woods became silent. Then in a mighty thundering voice he said, "I proclaim Lone Star faithful friend of Bird Friend. Let any bird who finds Lone Star in need of help, help him and fill any request he may ask. So states Bird Friend, keeper of birds!"

The trees exploded with colors and music as all the birds flew over my head. Then for the first time did I realize who Bird Friend really was. He was not just a friend of birds. He was Lord of all birds, their guardian and keeper!

"I could never be more honored," I said.

Even while the birds were circling and dancing through the air, Bird Friend disappeared behind a tall bush. Then out he stepped, a white falcon on one shoulder.

"Can this be the same baby falcon?" I thought to myself. "It has grown so much bigger. It looks so strong!"

"Here is your friend," said Bird Friend, "and with her goes her mother's blessings."

With those words, in the background, a big white bird took wing to the sky and vanished in the heights.

Bird Friend added with a chuckle, "and this falcon is the fastest I have ever seen, and getting faster every day."

I held out my hand and she jumped from Bird Friend's shoulder to my arm. As I drew her closer I noticed a diamond shaped patch of black on her white forehead. The black spot would grow larger even as she grew and it would always seem to me to be the crown of a princess on her head.

80

It was not the last time we saw Bird Friend, lord of all birds, but that day I even forgot to say goodbye. I felt nervous like when you meet a new friend. Yet inside I was running faster and jumping higher than ever before. She stayed on my shoulder the whole trip back.

I named her Cyper, which means flash in the wind, and any who ever saw her fly said she was well named. We traveled together and slept together and always a young princess she stayed in my heart, though the years went by.

From the moment Karen and I first brought Cyper home, it was clear she was not an ordinary cat. It is hard to explain the connection between us. In her younger days, she often went off exploring on her own and could be gone for days at a time. Karen worried that she had been hurt or trapped somewhere, but Cyper always let me know inwardly she was fine. However, one day I had an intuitive feeling that she might need help. Karen and I went out searching around our house and found her down the block behind some bushes. She had been in a fight and was seriously injured.

She used to go on hikes with us up in the mountains. She would race up ahead on the path, then circle around and come up from behind. She climbed up the rocks to look down on us from above, and would sometimes sneak attack us from the bushes. As we passed others on the path, they would stop to stare. They had never seen a cat on a hike in the mountains before.

She also had the strangest habit of wanting to perch up on my shoulder. She liked to sit there like a falcon as I walked around the house or around our yard. She would jump up from a chair as I walked by, or from the floor if I leaned over.

I discovered another odd thing early on: Whenever I whistled, she came immediately. I used to enjoy whistling while working around the house and often didn't even realize what I was doing, until I found her at my feet looking up at me with her questioning eyes—like, "You called?" It took me a while to realize that I simply couldn't whistle without her coming.

It's interesting that Cyper developed these strange traits after I had written my story about her. It made me wonder how true my fictional story was.

This inner connection we had, and her love for me stirred deep feelings.

I tried to capture it somehow with the story I wrote. I then realized that this in fact is the essence of art—this reaching out of the spiritual senses to express the realities of the heart.

The Reality Revealed by Art

Someone once asked the great artist, Michelangelo, how he came up with the images for his great sculptures. He responded that he saw these shapes as if they were frozen in the stone and all he did was free them with his chisel and hammer. Beethoven continued writing his music even after becoming deaf, claiming that he heard it within himself. His only regret, he said, was that the music he heard was so much more beautiful than anything he could write. Debussy, the composer, said that his music seems to have no beginning and no ending because he felt as if he were listening in on some eternal melody and could only capture a part of it.

We've been raised in a technological world, so we like to think that imagination has nothing to do with reality, but I was beginning to learn otherwise. Our imagination, in fact, is like a fine sense that can, if trained, see invisible realities all around us. I felt as if I had crossed over into another world, as I began to see the difference between mere creations of the mind and truths that our imagination can see.

This explains why some works of fiction, such as *Star Wars*, or *Lord of the Rings*, can touch millions of people and leave a mark on society as clear as any real historical saga. And yet, other books seem empty and shallow, even if creatively written. All works of imagination are not equal, because some capture an actual reality that exists in the inner worlds.

However, this was just the beginning of my lesson with the Second Initiation. I was soon to learn that imagination has a far greater power than just its ability to move feelings. Here is an entry from my journal. The notes describe a physical experience I had shortly after writing my story, *Bird Friend*:

Spiritual Laws

While walking down the street, just a week after I'd written a story about a friend and healer of birds, I suddenly found a flurry of feathers circling my head. Three feet away and cawing, the friendly bird surprised me. It was as if he was trying to communicate something. Could this be?

He landed in the tree next to me. I looked closely into his eyes. What was it? I took a step closer and he flew off.

I walked on, but as I neared the next tree he came again, suddenly out of the sky, black feathers and cawing. He circled around my head. He was trying to tell me something, but what was it? He landed in the tree I was approaching; then flew off as I came closer.

Although other people were not far away, again and again, as I neared the next tree along my walk, out of the sky he came and circled my head, flying a few feet away and then landing next to me. I'd found a winged friend, but I had no idea why.

Every day after that for a week, when I went on my walk, I'd call out in a whistle and from as far as a mile away I saw him coming to greet me! He flew from tree to tree as I walked. "Caw, caw," he would joke, almost laughingly, and yet his eyes held a curious wondering look, as if he were asking: "Why am I doing this? Why do you call me and why do I feel I must come when you do?"

I was asking exactly the same thing.

I was so awestruck and amazed with this special bird companion that I made a mistake. I invited my wife to see him. Although my bird friend came when I called, and Karen saw the same amazing sight of this wild bird flying right to me from a mile away, yet his eyes told me I had hurt him in some way. I had broken our secret friendship by showing off what belonged between us.

Just like that, I could feel our bond was broken. It was over. I could never find the heart to call him again.

This was a real experience recorded in my notebook, not a work of fiction. Yet it was clear the story about Cyper and Bird Friend that I had just written a few days before had somehow crossed over from imagination to reality. I could hear Bird Friend's words from my story:

"I proclaim Lone Star faithful friend of Bird Friend. Let any bird who finds Lone Star in need of help, help him and fill any request he may ask."

Indeed, outer and inner realities are not separate like we sometimes think, but are echoes of each other. The images and ideas that we hold in our attention influence life around us, sometimes in surprising ways.

However, the bigger lesson that hit me from this experience was that there were Spiritual Laws that must be followed if I wanted to make that path on the Astral Plane a reality. Certain things must be kept silent. I felt a great loss from what I'd done, and could sense that I had let Life down in some way. Suddenly it became painfully clear that the grace of Spirit, like gifts from a lover, should never be shown off. The intimacies of the path become profane when displayed before the world for reasons of vanity or social recognition. That's also when I realized that there was something more important than the physical world, and for the first time I could feel it within my grasp.

Spiritual travelers call this the Way of Love, because blessings and subtle miracles follow the steps of those who have established a bond of love with Life. They become drenched in the color of this love. What greater loss can there be than to lose such a treasure? The wealth of the whole world seems meaningless in comparison.

These graces are meant for us alone as Soul. The inner teachings slip into our life bringing gifts that we cannot show anyone else because they mean nothing to the world. Like whispers between lovers, the world has no business knowing what transpires. It is for this very reason that although I would love to share everything through the pages of this book, holding nothing back, yet it is as if a finger is placed on my lips, silencing me. Out of love I can give out only what Life blesses.

"Do not share all," Life says to me just now. "Do not lay out the whole of the path as if it could all be explained or followed from a book. These are things meant for the heart to discover and understand."

Therefore, Life does not give out the path in black and white because we must discover these mysteries within ourselves, and we cannot make such discoveries until we learn the Laws of Love. It is this process of discovery from the depths of our awareness and being that makes for spiritual growth. That is how the path was unfolding and revealing itself to me.

Rumi makes an interesting point about this in chapter two of his book of discourses, called, *It Is What It Is*:

> If you bring a lamp before the sun, do you say, "I see the sun by means of this lamp?" God forbid! If you did not bring the lamp, the sun would still shine. What need is there for a lamp?
>
> This is the danger in associating with kings. It is not that you may lose your life—we must lose our life in the end anyway, whether today or tomorrow does not matter. The danger arises from the fact that when kings enter upon the scene and the spell of their influence gains strength,

becoming like a great lamp, the person who keeps company with them, claims their friendship, and accepts money from them will invariably speak in accordance with their desires. That person will listen to the kings' mundane views with the utmost attention, and will not be able to deny them.

That is where the danger lies; it leads to a fading respect for the true source, the true sun. When you cultivate the interest of kings, that other interest that is fundamental to the spiritual life becomes a stranger to you. The more you proceed down the path of kings, the more that direction where the Beloved dwells becomes lost ... Going in the direction of kings renders you subject to their rule. Once you have turned down their path, in the end God gives them power over you.

It is a pity to reach the ocean and to be satisfied with a little pitcher-full from the sea. After all, there are pearls in the sea, and from the sea come a myriad of precious things. What is the value in just taking water? What pride can intelligent people have in that? This world is a mere foam fleck of the True Sea. That Ocean is the science of the saints, and within that Water is the Pearl Itself.

The Spiritual Path is not the same as the path of humanity. This is what I came to learn. Looking for recognition from the world and worldly rewards was following the path of kings. This was a new principle for me—a new law that I must learn to obey if I wanted to enjoy the secret blessings of the path. This experience with my bird friend brought this home for me.

So, I began to turn my attention to the subtle interaction between my inner perceptions and the creative process. There was something important for me to learn here, about how it worked. I could see that. My notebooks contain some of my observations:

Through studying the inner creative forces, I have found that each day a certain number of ideas develop for writing. They seem to begin as seeds of inner forms, fleeting images or an interesting thought. They begin to take on shape and I can feel them pressing in on me, as if they want me to give them birth into the physical.

That is when I need to release these forms by finding words to express them. If I try to write before or after this inner pressure from only my own ideas, I usually find it goes nowhere. It never has the same sense of life.

It seems these creative forces are always at work during the day developing into inner forms. It takes a certain amount of attention, daily, as they rise up in my thoughts to grab a few moments of my awareness. It is just like growing a garden, we need to water it once in a while, and it needs a few minutes of sunlight to grow. Without this cycle of inner attention and discipline, the inner forms never completely come alive.

Also, if I don't release and give expression to these creative forms, they stop growing. This happens sometimes when these forms seem too alien or are at odds with my own perspectives. They hardly ever develop the way I expect. Even though some part of me is giving life to them, they still seem to have a life of their own.

When I try directing them too strongly, I end up struggling with an inner pressure, as if it is bottled up. It makes me irritable and I find myself creating all kinds of problems around myself, until I realize what is going on and sit down to write. I wouldn't be surprised to find, some day, that someone discovers that improper use of the creative force is an underlying cause for many diseases of the body and mind.

We don't want these forces controlling us, but it is true that the muses work for us if we work for them.

When I began learning how to weave and work with these invisible realities, I found my life changed and I could no longer live like I had before. The inner teachings were gentle, but they made the whole world look new. "The trees are no longer just trees; the mountains, no longer just mountains," as an ancient Buddhist text once put it. I knew exactly what this meant. I could see an inner fiber shining through and shaping these outer forms. It was revealed like a tapestry of Spirit, and I was now connected to this fiber.

In other words, I was beginning to see the laws and operating principles of the Astral Plane. It was not what I expected them to be. Sometimes called Turiya Pad, Sahasra-dal-kanwal, Anda Lok or dozens of other names in other religions, the experience of this level of being was far different from anything I had read in books.

The Indirect Path

The spiritual path at this second stage was an indirect one. The things I strived for never quite turned out the way I expected. Everything seemed to have a life of its own, yet would surprise me by the way things worked out. I struggled with this for a long time until it finally began to sink in.

It seems as if no answers are held back from me inwardly, but I cannot demand them or get them when I want them. However, if I carry the questions around, rolling them around in the back of my thoughts and let them go as if I was sending them out into life, I find the answers coming to me from the strangest directions.

I wrote this in my notebooks as I began to ponder how it worked. I started calling it the "Magnetic Forces of Indirectness," as I tried to describe the way that answers could be drawn to me by just holding them in my thoughts.

Suddenly I realized that in the past, in fact, throughout my whole life, I had been trying to push answers—to force them. I had been trying to solve them through my mind, when all along there was a much easier way. I wrote:

We hardly gain anything by forcing things, yet when we find something new the whole world changes in the blink of an eye. We then find a new feel for life and our old desires fall away. So many times we may start toward a goal with specific objectives in mind. Then, after we have reached a new point, we look back and say, "Well, that goal wasn't the reason I took this path at all. I took it only to get here."

In fact, the true Way when practiced properly seemed almost effortless. It was as if magnetic forces attract to us experiences based on what is within our consciousness. So, we only need to hold our attention on what we want to attract. The moment we make a place for the path within us, the path comes to us and leads us on.

I wove my newfound discovery into a story, along with some other lessons I had learned:

Concerning Pushitis

Late one night, I was reading the notebooks of Leonardo da Vinci when I ran across a rather strange discovery: Every muscle in the human body works by the force of pull, through contraction. No muscle has the power of push.

"I never knew that!" I thought to myself.

With images of this genius still floating through my thoughts, I found myself suddenly feeling tired. In a few seconds I had drifted off into a deep sleep, while still sitting in my chair, with the book flopped open on my lap.

I was standing by an operating table looking at a pale body lying on it all clothed in white. I jumped back, shocked, when I realized it was my body. A feeling of panic rushed through me. It looked dead!

The room I was in was like a large, white room with only one light shining down over the table from above. I didn't see any walls, but I sensed they were there. I was in the room alone, except for another man bent over examining the body. When he stood up and turned to me, I recognized him as Leonardo da Vinci. He looked exactly like the self-portrait from his notebooks.

He shook his head back and forth. "It's a shame," he said, "but death had to come sooner or later. All the organs were failing, his muscles were losing strength. He must have been in a great struggle to the end."

"How did he die?" I asked, really meaning how did I die, but I couldn't quite admit it was my body yet, lying there on the table.

"An acute case of Pushitis," he said, as he pulled a white sheet over the body. I was relieved when he covered the body, because it was uncomfortable staring at myself on the cold metal table. But pushitis?

"What's that?"

"What? Don't you know?" Leonardo asked, piercing me with his eyes. Then he turned very soft and frowned. "I guess that's the worst part: They never know they have it.

"Pushitis begins when people think they can push their muscles. Those poor muscles. They do the best they can, but they can't push. They can only pull!"

I laughed. "You mean I died of that? That's ridiculous." I thought he had to be kidding. It must be some kind of joke.

Leonardo nodded, stroking his gray beard. Then he started grinning. "I'm glad you're taking it so well," he said. "Usually it takes time to adjust to the news."

His answer startled me. He wasn't joking. I felt a sudden fear seize me. My life was over? I wanted to make everything stop. I wanted to go back to my old world. I felt a deep urge to force it all to change, when Leonardo pointed to a picture on the wall. The picture was of a man with his name inscribed underneath: Descartes. There was also a short quotation: "I think, therefore I am." I had heard that saying before.

"His was a sure case of Pushitis," Leonardo said. "He felt he had to think or else he would cease being. But he got over it too. Maybe you'll see him around. He usually works near the library."

"Wait a minute," I said, still trying to fight everything off. "What's going on here?"

"What?" Leonardo looked at me, surprised. "Don't you see yet?" He paused and turned to look at the sheet covered body, thinking quietly for a moment. Finally, he sighed.

"I'll tell you what. Let me give you an explanation," he said, "and I'll start from the beginning. But first let's get out of this stuffy place."

Suddenly we were in the middle of a velvety grass field under a large oak tree. A small stream of clear water was bubbling on its way to a shimmering blue lake, only fifty feet from us. The sky was spotted with four or five clouds that were moving and changing before my eyes in a strange kind of pattern. The shapes these clouds were forming caught my attention, because for some reason it seemed as if they were expressing thoughts I was feeling inside. The sight fascinated me, as I tried to figure out what it was that was really happening. I don't know how long I stood there watching. I was startled when a large black raven flew by and landed on Leonardo's shoulder. I then realized he had already taken a seat.

"It's not such a bad place after all, is it?" Leonardo asked as I sat down in a wood rocking chair. Then I remembered seeing my dead body and about Earth, my old home. I couldn't believe I had forgotten it all so soon. The physical life now seemed like a dim and insignificant memory.

"I've never seen a place so beautiful. The colors are so alive, but will you please start from the beginning like you promised?" I asked.

He smiled wisely and said, "There is no beginning, really, but I suppose I can make one. Did you notice the body you have now doesn't have muscles?"

Isn't that something! I hadn't even noticed, but he was right. Every movement I made followed directly from my thoughts. Realizing this evoked a tremendous feeling of freedom, like being released from a cage. I don't know how to describe such a wonderful sensation, but it comes closest to that feeling of flying in dreams.

"That's why the Pushitis wears off," he continued. "Not that this body is perfect. The fabric of this world is emotions and imagination, and everyone's supply is what you might call—limited. This body can get hurt. In fact it will even die sooner or later, but few realize this because its lifespan can be thousands of years long."

Leonardo paused for a while, probably to give me a chance to absorb what he had said. It was all too much even to begin understanding.

"Anyway, everyone has the ability to imagine, and that's how I created this." He said, while waving his hand in a wide arc, as if he had just painted the whole scene with his paintbrush. "You'll be making your own scenery before you know it. In fact, I think you already began when you were playing with those cloud shapes."

"Playing?" I said. "But I wasn't doing anything. Those clouds were doing that by themselves."

"You mean you weren't pushing them. It was more of a mutual connection, wasn't it?"

I think what Leonardo was talking about started to sink in because I began to see that something was happening all around me. It was barely noticeable at first, but the whole landscape was changing bit by bit. The stream slightly shifted course. Small bushes in the distance began growing flowers while I watched, and the clouds continued making patterns in the sky. It may have been going on the whole time I was there, or maybe it didn't happen until I realized it was happening. I wasn't quite sure, but there was no doubt that the world was moving in harmony with the emotions I was feeling inside. Not that I felt like the creator of it all, but rather as if the whole world was somehow a part of me and connected to my own imagination.

"This world IS a part of you," Leonardo said, as if I had been thinking out loud. "Why don't you try imagining a cloud or something? You know, image it forth."

"But I don't even know where to begin," I protested, feeling foolish.

"Good for you," he chuckled. "That's what people call beginner's luck, because beginners don't know enough to even try pushing. That's why it comes to them naturally. Actually, you can't push an image any more than you can push a muscle, so don't waste your time trying. Yet there are people who believe both are possible. Quite frankly, the worlds of God simply do not recognize the push, and I would say man has had nothing but trouble since he invented the idea!"

"But you are wrong," I said. "I have been pushed before, both physically and with threats, and you don't forget such things!"

"Aha! You are quite correct. Some people say 'Don't do that!' or 'That is wrong!' They are trying to push and control people through negation. But examine a little more closely. They have no effect unless we accept their authority. We give them power when we go along with their rules. You see, we draw all of these influences to us just like a muscle drawing tight. Unless we pull them in, they float on by. Our life is completely our own doing."

He explained it all so clearly, there was nothing I could do but see the truth in it. However, I didn't care for what he was saying, because just thinking about it left me feeling like a complete fool. I had been creating my own problems and never even realized it.

90

Looking around me I saw the world seething and swaying in rhythm with my thoughts and I wanted to stop it. I wanted it to go back to being a reality of its own, as I had imagined it before. I didn't like the idea of being responsible for everything. But how could I change it back if I couldn't push? A fear began growing as the thought occurred to me of all the evil I might be creating unconsciously, which I had no power to stop! And just as I had this thought, the beautiful world around me suddenly started becoming a nightmare.

Everything began closing in, but what could I do? The stream started circling around as if trying to trap me. The clouds grew into black mammoth claws pressing closer and closer. I was creating it all, I knew, but I could not find new thoughts within myself to change anything. My own fears seemed too powerful. Suddenly the bushes flared up in flames. The tree I was under began grabbing at me with a thousand icy hands, and the island I was on was shrinking moment by moment. Leonardo was nowhere to be seen.

The sky turned pitch black and the flames flared brighter. I tried to run but it was no use. I tried every possible thought I could find to stop it, but it only made things worse because I was pushing. I was destroying myself and I couldn't stop it. I flung myself to the ground, exhausted, and gave up. There was nothing else I could do.

Everything suddenly went quiet. The fire at my back vanished. Nothing seemed to be moving anywhere, but I didn't want to open my eyes. I just lay there listening to the silence. Enjoying it. Or was there something? It sounded far away, like someone running. They were coming closer.

I opened my eyes. I was lying on a mound of dirt, all that was left above water. The tree next to me stood motionless. The fire had died out and the sky began to brighten. Over the hill came Leonardo. He ran up to the edge of the water.

He had a big grin on his face. "I had a rough time keeping up with all this moving landscape," he said.

"Yeah, what a mess," I said and we both laughed. I looked around in amazement. Finally, I dove into the clear warm water and swam to shore. Leonardo helped me out.

"When a person stops pushing everything," said Leonardo, "he unleashes a thousand forces. To control all this energy he must let go, give up. It's like a vacuum, when we empty ourselves of everything, we draw Life to us. But I knew you'd pull through." He laughed again, at his own pun.

It was like a great weight had fallen from my shoulders. I breathed in deeply and felt lighter and freer. I could feel a positive energy flowing through me. Yet, when I turned around I was still taken by surprise. "Did you do that?" I asked, pointing at a round picnic table with an umbrella on top. On the table was a pitcher of lemonade with two glasses. It startled me because I had just been thinking about a tall, cool glass of lemonade, and that was exactly how I pictured it!

"No," said Leonardo. "Isn't it yours?"

"Well, I guess it is," I replied.

"You look surprised," Leonardo responded. "Once you have decided about something in this world, you set it in motion. The fabric of this world takes care of the rest. Just as when you decide to start running on Earth, your muscles take care of the rest."

"It all sounds too simple," I said, reaching for the pitcher. "But since it's here, would you like some?"

"Just a sip. That's all there's time for. Since you wanted me to create a beginning, I must also bring this to an end."

Even as I was draining the glass of lemonade and thinking how I would miss Leonardo, someone started shaking my shoulder. I couldn't figure out who it was or why I was sitting in an arm chair. Then I recognized a friendly face.

"You'll sleep better in bed, dear."

"I suppose so," I said, "but if only you'd wakened me just a little later. That was the best lemonade I've ever had!"

When I first stepped out of the physical world into the Astral Plane, I found myself face to face with all of my imaginative creations. This same thing is true for everyone. If people use threats to try controlling others during their life on Earth, they find those very forces of fear taking shape and coming back at them when they cross into the Astral. This is why some people are truly afraid of dying. On the other hand, our generosities also return to us in the form of helping hands from long lost friends.

This explains why people see their life flash before their eyes as they come face-to-face with the sum of their creations and choices. For many, this can be scary, until the fearful images are dissolved and seen for what they are—merely our own unconscious offspring. This whole experience brings about a universal feeling of standing before the Lords of Death, or the Judges of Death, as they have been called. It is a feeling that nothing in our life is hidden any longer and everything is seen for exactly what it is, as if it were being shown to us by wiser and more knowing beings.

I have to laugh at the kind of scientific thinking that leads some people to say that all of this is nothing more than imagination. They call nightmares simply bad dreams and believe all of religion is no more than an empty myth—which means a lie. Such foolishness.

Art and fiction attempt to discover the archetypes, images and elemental stories that strike a universal inner chord. They become teaching stories, in a sense, because they awaken us to aspects of our own selves that remain hidden in our day-to-day lives. This is why such forms find their way into our dreams and inner lives.

We might call them myths, but they are more than mere stories or lies. The movie *Star Wars*, for example, captured the imaginations of millions, not because it was merely a story, but since it was woven from the elements of a legend about another world that speaks to us through the language of imagination. Hundreds of copycat science fiction movies failed because they did not have that essential spark of Astral truth. The same could be said of *The Wizard of Oz*, when it first came out.

These works of art were not successful by accident. George Lucas consciously took what he had learned from Joseph Campbell's teachings on mythology to create a modern day epic. He wanted to tell the story of an everyday boy who becomes a hero when thrust into an adventure that forces him to find the means within himself to overcome even the most powerful forces of an evil empire. We immediately recognize the empowerment of the individual from this story.

The Wizard of Oz struck the consciousness of its day, not simply because it created a wonderful dream world of imagination, but also by showing how tricks of authority, like the Wizard himself used, are often established to make some people or ideas look godlike. Thus the movie in its day was a conscious statement of our own self-creating reality, and that we always have within us the powers that we need to find our way home. We only need to realize it.

The experiences of these stories are universal because these emotions are indeed something real. We might not be able to measure them with a scientific instrument, but we all feel them. Even if they are constructed from the fabric of imagination, which is the very substance of the Astral Plane, our experiences with them are still just as real as anything physical. In fact, emotions *are* realities on the Astral Plane. They are just as visible there as anything here in the physical.

For example, some jobs have extreme pressures. These stresses affect our health and attitudes, even though they only exist in our imaginations. We also know that music and humor can bring relief and make us feel better. In other words, we experience emotions and imagination as if they were very real things. This is what artists, musicians and entertainers work with every day. For scientists to say that such things are nothing but imagination is incredible. These are powerful forces that shape our world.

Paul Twitchell wrote in the "Introduction" to his book, *The Tiger's Fang*:

> Some will say this book is the wild fantasy of a highly developed imagination, but one must understand that there is nothing in the world of God without some degree of truth. Even fantasy is cast out of the material cloth of God, so how can fantasy be a complete untruth?
>
> This statement should stagger the mind of man and shake the foundation of the teachings of orthodox religions, philosophies, and metaphysical concepts. However, I am prepared to make my statements out of pure experience and one must remember that all experiences are unique only to the experiencer.

Why should this stagger man's mind? Because, fantasy can be just as great a source of truth as any religion or philosophy. In other words, the seriousness and gravity that often surround matters of religion, philosophy and even science are nothing more than an imaginative creation to give weight and a sense of authority to such teachings. But that very weight pulls us away from Truth Itself, which speaks to our hearts directly.

Cannot poetry capture spiritual truth as completely as any religious text? In fact, are not the holy books of this world simply poetic works and artistic expressions mixed with thousands of years of emotion?

I began to realize this truth, and that I could face and deal with these imaginative creations, just like I might work with any other living thing. I didn't need to wait until after death. I could cross those borders through Soul Travel. I could dissolve my fearful, unconscious creations and replace them with expressions of awakened realizations. In other words, merely visiting the Astral Plane was not enough. I must, in a sense, become a citizen there, while still living my physical life. I must become a citizen of two worlds. Life, then, took on an added dimension for me.

Neville Goddard, also a citizen of that world, captured great insights into the laws of the Astral Plane. This is from his book, *The Power of Awareness*:

> Man's chief delusion is his conviction that there are causes other than his own state of consciousness. All that befalls a man—all that is done by him—all that comes from him—happens as a result of his state of consciousness...
>
> To be transformed, the whole basis of your thoughts must change. But your thoughts cannot change unless you have new ideas, for you think from your ideas. All transformation begins with an intense, burning desire to be transformed...
>
> In giving birth to your ideal you must bear in mind that the methods of mental and spiritual knowledge are entirely different. This is a point that is truly understood by probably not more than one person in a million. You know a thing mentally by looking at it from the outside, comparing it with other things, by analyzing it and defining it, by thinking OF it: whereas you can know a thing spiritually only by becoming it, only by thinking FROM it. You must be the thing itself and not merely talk about it or look at it. You must be like the moth in search of his idol, the flame...
>
> Your imagination is the instrument, the means, whereby your redemption from slavery, sickness and poverty is effected. If you refuse to assume the responsibility of the incarnation of a new and higher concept of yourself, then you reject the means, the only means, whereby your redemption—that is, the attainment of your ideal—can be effected...
>
> There is no order in Nature corresponding to this willing submission of the self to the ideal beyond the self. Therefore, it is the height of folly to expect the incarnation of a new and greater concept of self to come about by a natural evolutionary process. That which requires a state of consciousness to produce its effect obviously cannot be effected without such a state of consciousness, and in your ability to assume the feeling of a greater life, to assume a new concept of yourself, you possess what the rest of Nature does not possess—Imagination—the instrument by which you create your world.

In other words, we are either creating unconsciously or consciously, but whether we are aware of the fact or not, our imagination is continually giving birth to our world experience. Once I realized this, I knew that I must take the responsibility and become the author of my life. I needed to start consciously choosing my feelings and attitudes.

An Experiment with Time and Space

One day, around this time, I curled up on our couch to read one of Paul Twitchell's spiritual fiction books, called *The Talons of Time*. It was the tale of a scientist, John Skally, who had discovered the secret of time. He was captured by the Time Makers, beings from the Astral Plane, who didn't want their secret being revealed, because they used the concepts of duration to control the world. It was a fascinating book that explored the beliefs we unquestioningly hold about time and the many ways these ideas can limit our imaginations.

After reading this story, I realized that any time I wanted I could change my state of consciousness and thereby change my life. I didn't need to struggle through stages of grueling effort and time to arrive at a changed life. I didn't need to carry around the baggage of my past actions and mistakes as if I had to overcome my past sins. I didn't need to change the outer form of my life. I could simply assume a new state and live FROM it, attracting to myself new experiences through the Magnetic Forces of Indirectness.

This new thought made me so curious that I decided to try an experiment using the awakened imagination. How far could changing my way of seeing things influence my experiences?

Karen and I arranged a Saturday afternoon with our friends, Roger and Ros. Roger and I made plans to play tennis, while Ros and Karen wanted to walk through a nearby park. I had the sense that Roger was a fairly decent tennis player. It sounded as if he had kept his game up by playing off and on. I, on the other hand, hadn't played since high school. I knew my game would be rusty.

However, I decided to forget these excuses of the past and these imagined disadvantages. In fact, I decided to play this game of tennis from a completely imaginary level and not worry about my physical playing at all. I wouldn't tell Roger, because I wanted to see what would happen.

Our first volleys showed immediately how out of practice I was, but rather than accepting this as a hardened reality, I focused on what was going on in my imagination. I wanted to create a whole different reality on the Astral Plane, you might say, rather than letting the Physical Plane dictate my emotional experience. So, each time I missed a shot, no matter how badly, I replaced the image of my physical mistake with a feeling of winning the point, as if I had made the shot perfectly. In other words,

I refused to accept my physical failures as if they were defining my inner feelings. Rather, I pictured in my imagination the state I wanted to experience the game from.

The effect was amazing. As we began playing, I found that I could lose a volley, yet feel like I had won. Instead of imagining Roger beating me, I pictured myself in a state where I was winning every stroke. This generated a feeling of growing confidence. As a result my play improved dramatically and I found myself having a lot more fun than I expected.

In fact, Roger was beating me pretty badly at first. But after the first set our games became well matched. I thought it would take time to get my game back, but my sudden improvement surprised even me. More importantly, I didn't go through any of the self-recrimination I usually experienced. I just replaced my mistakes with an image of how the right stroke would have felt. I was so busy focusing on thinking FROM the place where I wanted to be that I had no room for feeling dejected. The result was that I bypassed the inner struggles I usually went through.

For the first time I saw that all these struggles were nothing but battles with my imagination. In the past I had tried forcing myself to change, rather than simply changing my state of consciousness.

The second thing I realized was how powerful a sense of self-confidence can be, and how important it is to assume this self-confidence. I didn't need to wait for success to feel self-assured. I could assume that feeling first. Success would then confirm it.

In other words, most people lack self-confidence because they think they should wait until after they attain something worthy before gaining confidence. Yet, those who are the most self-assured simply allow themselves to assume this feeling first. They become far more successful in life, even if they are no more talented. Their own self-confidence gives them strength to overcome difficulties, because they hold the expectation in their imagination that they can solve whatever problem comes their way. That is the state they assume and work from, thus making what they expect come true. This, then, further builds their self-confidence.

Halfway through this game with Roger, I realized that all my life I had always experienced a feeling of defeat whenever losing a game, no matter what kind of game it might be, as if it were a programmed response. I had indeed fallen victim to the Time Makers' trick and had accepted a limited idea of time and space. I had only allowed myself to feel successful if I won. Yet here I was experiencing the full sense of winning, and feeling great about how I was playing, even though Roger was beating me.

I soon realized that this whole pattern of emotion is tied closely to the worship of rank, which we often hold in our imaginations unconsciously. People who hold a higher position of authority can create a feeling of awe and make us feel less powerful, when in fact this is nothing but an image we have accepted into our imagination.

Once I could consciously control my own imagination, I found outer authorities had no more power over me from an emotional standpoint. As a young man of twenty-one, this gave me a tremendous feeling of self-empowerment and freedom.

There was another interesting result from this experimental tennis game that fascinated me. While I felt better and better about my play as the game went on, Roger, on the other hand, seemed to feel worse and worse. While I experienced the full emotions of winning even though I was losing, Roger seemed to be going through the exact opposite reactions. It suddenly struck me that it was just as if I was beating Roger on the Astral Plane, while he was beating me on the Physical.

Our last set was a close one, but Roger managed to pull out a win. I still felt great about the whole game and wonderfully rejuvenated and satisfied. Roger, on the other hand, seemed to feel badly about how he had played and was criticizing himself for his mistakes. I was trying to console him as we walked over to our wives. I told him he played pretty well and I enjoyed the game. It never even occurred to me how all of this looked to Karen and Ros, but after we left to go home, Karen turned to me and said:

"You must have beaten Roger badly."

"Why do you say that?" I asked.

"Well, it was obvious. He was feeling horrible, and you obviously were feeling great about the game."

"No," I said, "Roger actually won."

Karen did a double take. She couldn't believe it. I explained to her my experiment. She admitted that it absolutely seemed as if I had won. Well, in a sense I had, but not on the physical plane. This proved to me that the whole feeling of winning and losing is an emotional one, just like the feelings of success and failure.

This led into an even more important discovery concerning relationships. Seeing this impact on Roger, I began to notice the days when I was feeling great and on top of the world. Strangely, it seemed as if

Karen often felt depressed on those same days. On the other hand, when Karen was on a roll and everything seemed to be going her way, I would start feeling down and out. One day I recognized the similarity between this emotional see-saw and the game I played with Roger. I then saw how our emotional creations were affecting each other.

An amazing mystery suddenly became very clear to me: In striving for that feeling of being on top of the world, I was also creating an image that this was a better state of consciousness than what other people were experiencing. This was affecting Karen and probably others around me. The reverse was true when Karen was feeling on top. I could then see why we attacked each other in little ways when we felt down. We might complain or grumble, but we were unconsciously trying to bring the other person down to our level. The other person's immediate reaction was how unfair these little attacks were, not realizing that they were partly responsible for what was happening.

This struck home for me one day when I happened to be the one having a great day. I suddenly realized that Karen's feelings of depression were partly my own creation. When she started complaining about something I had done, I stopped my normal cycle of reaction. I realized what she was really asking was for me to come down so that she could rise up in her feelings. It was incredibly subtle, but unmistakable. I decided to intentionally come down from my great feeling to see if it helped, and she immediately began feeling better. I then knew that love and sharing was more important than being on top of the world.

This was one of the greatest lessons I learned from those days. Apparently, I still had a lot to learn about people. Yet, it was only after stepping off the path of humanity that I could see the subtle forces influencing the human consciousness. This led me to another realization, showing how limited my previous thinking had been.. Here is what I recorded in my journal:

True or False?

Teachers of logic claim that a statement is either true or false. Most of logic is spent in trying to determine between the two.

The real sticklers of logic state that there are, in fact, two other categories for a statement. For example, a statement can be meaningless, like

"What is the difference between a duck?" Or, it can be self-contradictory, as in "This statement is false," which is neither true, nor false, nor meaningless.

However, I have just realized that the field of logic has failed to recognize perhaps the most important kind of statement of all, which fits none of the above.

Take this example: "This statement means more than it says."

It is not true of itself, or false. It certainly seems to have meaning and it does not contradict itself, therefore it fits none of the above four categories. Yet, in this statement is captured the essence of the greatest aspects of poetry, language and human communication.

Once we realize it is hinting at something greater—that there is meaning and purpose beyond mere words—we realize it is describing an altogether different kind of truth. Yet, it is an understanding that becomes true to us only when we recognize the greater meaning it is referring to.

On the other hand, it is false to anyone who refuses to believe it. If you cannot catch its hidden meaning, then it means nothing more than it says, and is therefore wrong.

The implication of this seemingly simple thought was staggering. The more I thought about it, the more it shook my whole foundation of rational thought. I suddenly realized how little our lives and human existence are tied up with True or False statements. Love and beauty, friendship and happiness, loyalty and wisdom - all of these invisible realities mean far more than words can describe. Yet, how much time had I spent trying to fit everything into the pigeon holes of True or False?

I thought back to when I was fourteen years old and had asked my friends at school, "Do you believe in God?" I could see that I was trying to decide if God was true or false. In fact, that was the wrong question. What really mattered was the meaning of God. What greater truth was this idea of God describing?

Now I could understand why people who believe there is nothing more than the physical world often see the idea of God as false, while those who believe there is more meaning to life see God as true

In other words, God is neither true nor false the way a scientific fact is. Rather, it is a symbol describing more than it says and more than we know. It is a doorway that leads to something more. What is the point of declaring the doorway true or false? Why not step through and discover where it is leading?

This also explained why some scientists claim that out-of-the-body and near death experiences are false, or that spiritual experiences are nothing but delusions. They don't believe anyone can know subjective events are true or are anything more than the neural synapses firing in our brain. In other words, unless someone can prove they are valid scientifically, they are merely products of imagination.

The error in their logic was suddenly clear to me. They were trying to fit spiritual experiences into the category of true or false. They didn't realize that spiritual experiences are in fact describing something more than they are. They are experiences that awaken us to a greater realization about life. The moment we experience what it is like to transcend death, the whole meaning of death changes for us. We no longer see it the way we did before. Such experiences are filled with meaning and self-discovery. They lead us to a greater truth, a greater awareness, just as if Life had been trying to communicate to us and we finally grasped its meaning.

This new kind of truth statement simplifies many things. We don't need to ask if another person is true or false when they say, "I love you." We only need to understand what they mean. What are they trying to communicate? Such a phrase is a symbol that means something different to each person, for each occasion. It is the same as someone saying they have attained self-realization or God-consciousness. It is what they mean that is important, not the impossible goal of deciding whether their statement is true or false.

I could now see how people who become sold on religion often fall into this same trap, arguing that their religion is true and feeling they must defend it. In fact, all that really matters is what their religion means and where does it take them? What do we learn from it and how does it help us connect to a greater life? This is what matters about religion—not whether it is true or false. Therefore, a teaching might become a doorway to truth for a period of time and then suddenly no longer seems to help. It may, in fact, become like a closed door that stands in our way.

I began to realize how deeply this error in logical thinking had affected mankind. Centuries of battles have been waged over the true and false, as if the matter could be determined by force. Religion tried to establish the belief that only it was true, and this brought about the Dark Ages in Europe. Science now claims to have destroyed this dragon by declaring such religious practices as false, but this only raises science up as The True in its place.

This is the whole danger of true and false. We search and struggle to catch a glimpse of truth, and after great research and study we finally arrive at a greater understanding. We then name it The True. Yet, as soon as we declare it The True, it starts becoming false because it no longer means more than it says. It starts to become a religion that defines and limits what we believe. The silent questions no longer draw us on because we have stopped to tell the world about our answers instead. In other words, the path no longer transcends its form, but starts to become something concrete, something fixed. It becomes an icon to worship and we become lost in it.

The moment we declare something true or false we stop looking to see what it means. Therefore, the battle over true versus false closes the door to meaning. We get so caught up in the sense of power that comes from knowing The True that we forget that real truth is something more than words can describe.

Victor Frankl has shown through his "logotherapy," which means therapy through meaning, that people need meaning in their lives to survive. Our sense of purpose is not something imaginary and unreal, but a vital necessity of Soul to grow and thrive. It is bread for our spiritual being.

In his book, *The Unheard Cry For Meaning*, Frankl writes,

At an American university, 60 students who had attempted suicide were screened afterward, and 85 percent said the reason had been that "life seemed meaningless." Most important, however, 93 percent of these students suffering from the apparent meaninglessness of life "were actively engaged socially, were performing well academically, and were on good terms with their family groups." What we have here, I would say, is an unheard cry for meaning, and it certainly is not limited to only one university...

This happens in the midst of affluent societies and in the midst of welfare states! For too long we have been dreaming a dream from which we are now waking up: the dream that if we just improve the socioeconomic situation of people, everything will be okay, people will become happy. The truth is that as the *struggle for survival* has subsided, the question has emerged: *survival for what?* Ever more people today have the means to live, but no meaning to live for.

On the other hand, we see people being happy under adverse, even dire, conditions. Let me quote from a letter I received from Cleve W., who wrote it when he was Number 049246 in an American state prison: "Here in prison...there are more and more blissful opportunities to serve and grow. I'm really happier now than I've ever been." Notice: happier than ever—in prison...

This is not only a matter of success and happiness, but also of survival. In the terminology of modern psychology, the will to meaning has "survival value." This was the lesson I had to learn in three years spent in Auschwitz and Dachau...if there was anything to uphold man in such an extreme situation as Auschwitz and Dachau, it was the awareness that life has a meaning to be fulfilled, albeit in the future.

As Frankl shows, people often turn to suicide when they have lost their sense of meaning in life. Their whole world seems false. They can no longer have faith. In other words, after believing in what they thought was true, their disillusionment from discovering that they were wrong overpowers them and makes everything appear false. The answer, as Frankl points out, is to begin the search for meaning...to begin looking for the hidden purpose of their lives.

In fact, we create meaning the moment we look for it. We bring meaning into being by our recognition of it. And for anyone living on the Astral Plane, this is something that comes into existence right before our eyes! Our purpose suddenly fills us with something real.

Why do we become trapped by the idea that things must be true or false? Where does this come from?

It took me a while to understand this, but I eventually came to realize that this issue is all a cover and a mask for a deep, ancient instinct. It is built into our biological machinery to worry about whether someone is friend or foe. If a foe, our whole perception changes and we begin looking for and finding dangerous intentions, even if there are none. Our unconscious imagination creates exaggerated and fearful images to put us on our guard. Thus, a piece of rope in the dark becomes a snake.

It is our fear and instinct for survival that can change a friendly thing into seeing a dangerous one. And once we've switched, it can become almost impossible to see the thing for what it is.

This is why various religions declare certain beliefs evil and sinful so that religion can be the friend to defend against these foes. Science often tries to do the same, as do logicians and rational thinkers who believe statements must be true or false. Their intentions are all good, but they miss the fact that even more important than survival is meaning. More than we need safety, we need to know why we are here in this world.

Back in the 1970's, some anti-cultists wrote a book called *Snapping* describing how cults converted people to a new worldview. For years anti-cult groups tried to convince the public about the dangers of "brainwashing" and "mind control." Finally, in the 1980's the American Psychology Association made an investigation into these claims and found no evidence whatsoever to support brainwashing or mind control as something real. How could this be?

In fact, terms such as brainwashing, mind control, and even "cult" are simply ways of labeling others as the foe: Cults are dangerous, cults are false. When, in truth, people down through history have often created new cultures out of their search for meaning. Every religion known today started just this way. Even science began this way.

Ironically, the whole problem with declaring others the foe is that we can no longer see them as they are. We cannot see the unique meaning they bring to this world. We cannot see their truth and purpose shining through their eyes, because we can only recognize such things if we first believe they might be our friends. How can we see from their viewpoint if we don't first look for their meaning? This is so ironic, because cults can become dangerous the moment they declare the outside world as their foe. Yet, this is exactly the tactic the anti-cultists have used in declaring cults our enemy.

Victor Frankl calls this reductionism. He describes it as a procedure that pretends to be scientific, but takes human traits and reduces them down to subhuman. Love, for example, is described as a sexual drive, the same as animals experience. Such an approach, says Frankl, only blocks a true understanding. In other words, reductionism rejects that our actions can mean more than their outer appearance.

He writes in his book, *The Unheard Cry For Meaning*:

> Love is really one aspect of a more encompassing human phenomenon which I have come to call self-transcendence. Man is not, as the predominant motivation theories would like us to believe, basically concerned with gratifying his needs and satisfying his drives and instincts... Rather, man is—by virtue of the self-transcendent quality of the human reality—basically concerned with reaching out beyond himself, be it toward

a meaning to fulfill, or toward another human being lovingly to encounter...

Language is more than mere self-expression. Language is always pointing to something beyond itself. In other words, it is always transcendent—as is human existence at large. Being human is always directed to something, or someone, other than itself, to a meaning to fulfill or another human being to encounter. Like the healthy eye, which does not see itself, man, too, functions best when he is overlooking and forgetting himself, by giving himself. Forgetting himself makes for sensitivity, and giving himself, for creativity.

Which brings us back to: This statement means more than it says. It is only true if we are willing to transcend language. Then we discover a whole world of meaning, which is real in a way that affects every experience of our life.

In other words, Life means more than the physical world only if we are first willing to love and search for greater realities. It is through love that we transcend ourselves and discover our own meaning. Then we know that our life, too, means more.

The Group Consciousness

The transcendent search for meaning is the key to the spiritual path. This was what I learned at this point of my search. If I approached spiritual growth only for my own sake alone, the way became slow and difficult. It is the ability of a teaching to expand our feeling of love—which means our willingness to go beyond ourselves—that marks its effectiveness. Therefore, what I learned was how to transcend my physical life by working for something greater.

This led to discovering one of the strangest paradoxes: The role of the group consciousness.

The last thing on my mind when I started studying Paul Twitchell's books was joining a group. Group-think seemed to me to be nothing more than mass hypnosis, and most religious organizations seemed more interested in social causes than spiritual exploration. I had already rejected authorities of every kind. This was exactly why Twitchell's books appealed to me. He was describing an individual path based on personal inner experience.

However, it didn't take me long after arriving in Las Vegas to realize how much more I learned when studying with others. I felt a clear energy and presence enter the room after class began, and hearing from others and their unique insights helped me understand aspects of the path I would never have recognized on my own.

I find it interesting that Paul Twitchell began Eckankar as an individual study. He wrote his first monthly discourses to be read on their own. However, he soon realized that most people wanted to study in groups, and they learned faster in the company of fellow seekers.

This was no small adjustment for Paul, since his own experiences had taken him to the realization of how alone the seeker of Truth is in this world. In other words, the path had taken him far beyond any groups or group experiences, to the individual path that Soul ultimately grows into. However, for most people the path begins by learning through group study.

This is one of the strangest paradoxes: The Way is an individual one, revealing itself differently to every man and woman, yet we are drawn into groups to learn about this individual path.

This opened up insights into how groups influence our thoughts and views of the world. Groups can both expand our horizons and limit them. Each group develops a culture all its own. Once I saw this through the inner vision, I could see that this was all the influence of the Astral Plane on our lives, since group consciousness is an emotional experience.

Now I could see why, whenever a book or song became popular, an audience formed. When fans meet to share their common feelings, they can feel the influence of the group consciousness. They begin to think like a group, rather than as individuals, yet these feelings can connect them to something larger. This whole influence comes through the Astral, which is why it is invisible to our physical senses.

I've heard from friends about their experience at the Woodstock music festival, in 1968. It was powerfully moving for them. They called it a "happening" because no one was in control. It had a life of its own and developed spontaneously. It formed out of a common love for music. This was a group consciousness experience. It rippled out and influenced others across the world. It created a culture.

We have seen how J. K. Rowling's Harry Potter books formed a new audience. It began when children started telling their friends. They found a new world of imagination that they could share with others. It drew them together into an experience of something greater. They could feel the reality of the new group consciousness. Millions of children and adults felt this and joined in.

I wrote in my notebooks:

> Emotions are experiences. Not like our physical experiences, but sensations of a finer, more subtle nature.
>
> Looking across current events, we can see that emotional tides create major influences over people. Like clouds that change with the wind, these Astral tides blow storms of emotion across our culture. At other times they bring peaceful feelings that seem to lift up our hopes with a sense of serenity.

We can sense the emotion of a group consciousness. Some groups are open and creative. Others are restrictive and political. However, it was this new vision of cultures and groups that led me to some of my deepest insights about the true meaning of individuality. I remember thinking how ironic this was.

The contradiction became clearer after talking with a student at Stanford University who was interested in spirituality. He launched into a series of questions about what I believed, what the books said, and how could I know my experiences were true? I explained that nothing was taught like that. We needed to discover the path ourselves through inner recognition. No one could tell us whether an experience was true or not except ourselves. It was an individual path.

He clearly related to the sense of freedom I was describing. He became more and more interested, until he suddenly stopped and put up his hand as if he'd had enough. "I agree with everything you are saying," he said. "It all sounds great. I can't see anything wrong with any of it. But I don't believe in joining groups." And with that, he stood up and walked away.

I remember thinking about his final words for the longest time. After all, he was enrolled at Stanford. What did he think being a university student meant, if it wasn't joining a group? How ironic it seemed, since this was one of the reasons I quit college. I found it way too controlled by group thinking. I needed to get outside of that consciousness to find my own life path. Yet, my discovery of the inner Self was now expanding my awareness through a deeper understanding of groups.

During an Eck business meeting, this whole issue culminated into a breakthrough for me. Local Eckists had come together as volunteers to manage the needs of a local Eck Center. Who would set up and lead new classes, or pay the rent? Who would give public talks for those asking for more information? Who wanted to put up posters or run ads for the free public events? One thing was always amazingly clear amongst those who called themselves Eckists at that time: They were individuals through and through, and loved doing things their own way. However, this didn't always make group activities easy to organize.

At this particular meeting, a pattern began to emerge that I had seen before: A growing feeling that the group as a whole was not accomplishing as much as it should. Everyone loved their freedom so much that acting for the sake of the group was a challenge. As a result, group events would fall apart. The discussion became heated as people tried to move the group into action, like you might fan a flame into a fire. However, the group consciousness did not seem to respond. No one felt inspired to follow what the group as a whole wanted to do, even though they were a part of the group that voted to do it.

The whole inner conflict suddenly became clear for me. I saw it from the Astral Plane and realized that group consciousness, itself, could not act. It was individuals who must lead the group, not the group deciding what individuals should do. The group itself was merely a shadow of the individuals. In other words, the whole challenge we were struggling with and trying to solve was how to move from being a follower of the group into becoming leaders.

The simplicity of the answer hit me: If any of us, as individuals, felt something was missing in the group, this was an indication—not that the group should take up this activity—but that those who were inspired by this thought should be the ones to turn it into a reality. The inspiration came to those people for a reason, and if they could spontaneously put it into action, it would become a reality for the whole group. This was the way individuals could thrive in groups—by leading.

As this realization dawned on me, I stood up and shared it with the group and suddenly the consciousness of the room seemed to open up. The whole spiritual principle we had been struggling with was learning how to become leaders of the group consciousness. It was like a light turned on in the meeting. The answer was through our own individual action—not trying to push or sway the group. Groups are drawn on by the vision and the initiative of individuals. This is leadership. Once again, pushing is not the answer.

This idea developed into a realization that changed my life. By carrying out what I saw was needed, I was helping to lead. The moment I became a "co-worker" as Paul called it, I was no longer following the group consciousness. I was being cause rather than effect. This might seem like a simple lesson in social responsibility, but it was a great spiritual education for me. It was through this insight that I began to see how the spiritual teachings take us far beyond group consciousness.

Being with others who come together in the name of Truth can open us up to the spiritual teachings. But this is only the beginning. To take the next step means stepping beyond the group and continuing on as the individual.

How strange it was to find the greater strength of individuality coming from studying with a group.

Looking back, I can see that all of this was a part of my growing realization of what it meant to be a responsible "citizen" on the Astral Plane. It meant that the group cultures of the world were not something to struggle against. Rather, it was my job to help lead them and show them the way. They needed the eyes and hearts of individuals to grow and breathe, and this was also the way of retaining my own individuality.

I began this path by trying to develop an inner spiritual connection with Spirit that was independent of any group. Yet, I found the connection at first was stronger in classes and discussion groups. Like Jesus said in the Bible, "I am there whenever two or more come together in my name." He was speaking about the amazing way that group consciousness can open the doors for individual spiritual experience. However, leadership was the way of emerging from the shadows of a culture into the light.

Freedom from the Path of Kings

Not everyone involved in the organization of Eckankar felt this liberating freedom of individuality as I did. I could see that some started off this way, but became more and more interested in gaining positions of rank. It was as if their way of finding strength and inspiration within themselves was to seek power through the group.

I came face to face with this phenomenon the first time I attended an Eckankar seminar. Darwin Gross called a special meeting in his hotel room for his leaders from around the world. Since I was working at the Eckankar Office, I was invited, even though I had only started studying just a few months before.

What I experienced was incredible. I felt a powerful spiritual current flowing through Darwin to the group. I never saw anything as strong as this when Darwin visited the Eck office. It was much subtler then. In this meeting, however, it seemed as if Spirit was pouring out of him and lifting the whole room.

The energy was so overwhelming I had a hard time staying in my body. Soul wanted to follow this current to its source and forget everything else. However, I also wanted to hear what Darwin was saying, and felt that it was important to listen. This wasn't easy balancing the two, but after a few minutes I learned how to keep my attention on both the inner current and Darwin's outer words at the same time. This was something completely new to me.

After the meeting, I was floating a few feet off the ground as we left Darwin's room. An Eckist waiting nearby asked us what the meeting had been about. I told him that it was just a meeting of Darwin's "outer circle," as Darwin had described it. The Eckist turned green before my eyes. (Astral green that is.) I could see the emotion of envy pouring out of him. I never thought that anyone would have such a reaction. After all, the "inner circle" seemed like the place to be—which of course meant those Masters who led the inner teachings—rather than the outer circle.

After a while I came to appreciate what Darwin's outer circle had accomplished and why he chose them. They began as volunteers in their local areas, helping with classes and giving talks, gradually taking on more and more responsibility in the organization until after many years they were recognized as leaders. My case, on the other hand, was nothing like this. I had simply taken a job at the Eckankar office one month after enrolling in the classes. I hadn't done anything. I felt outside of what was happening to others. I couldn't relate to those who felt envious of me, as if I had achieved some position of rank, when I hadn't done anything at all.

I resolved not to get caught up in these desires for position and rank. This was far from the individual spiritual path I was interested in. However, I soon realized how much more there was going on beneath the surface.

I still had a lot to learn about people.

Six months after starting work at the Eckankar office, I was called in by the general administrator. Bob had left a few months before and a new man, Bill, had taken his place. Bill and I got along fine. He offered sincere compliments and seemed to respect the work I was doing. However, he called me into his office one day to ask me a strange question. He had heard about another Eckist working in the office who had gone to the hospital for a personal matter. Apparently Darwin knew what it was about, but Bill did not, and he wasn't happy about this. He thought that being the general administrator, he should know.

It struck me as not quite right, but he asked if I knew why this Eckist had gone to the hospital. I said, yes, I knew. He asked me what it was about. I said, "Have you asked them directly?" Yes, he said, but the Eckist wouldn't say.

"Well," I said, "if they don't want to share their reason, then I don't see how I can. They asked me to keep it in confidence."

"Perhaps you don't understand what I'm saying here," Bill said, suddenly pulling his rank on me. "I'm not asking. I'm telling you to tell me. And if you don't, you are fired!"

"I can't do that," I said. "I made a promise."

He looked at me shocked. He hadn't expected me to refuse him. He then said, "Pack up your things. You're fired!"

I walked out of his office stunned. I thought over the whole drama. What else could I have done? I couldn't renege on a promise, especially about someone else's personal affairs.

However, rather than feeling hurt or depressed about what just happened, I unexpectedly found the most incredible inner sensation. A great light came down and surrounded me, lifting me up and smoothing out all of my emotions. I felt almost as if I had passed an incredible test inwardly and was now being rewarded spiritually. But what had I done?

It was one of the strangest experiences. By all accounts I should have felt bad, as if I had been wronged and treated unfairly. Instead, I felt like the "inner circle" had come to surround me and pat me on the back for doing what was right. I realized once again that I was not on the path of humanity, but something else was charting my course.

I thought about it again, but still couldn't see how I could have done anything different. I had to say what I said. My actions seemed insignificant, as if I just happened to be in the eye of a storm. But as I thought about it, I was reminded of something that Paul Twitchell once said: When someone hurts us or wrongs us, it is as if they take their own spiritual wealth out of their own inner bank account and put it into ours. In other words, as strange as it might seem, Bill had just given me a gift! By firing me unfairly, he lifted me up, spiritually.

I went to see my friend in the hospital and shared what had happened. They were upset that I would be fired over them, but I said not to worry about it. I felt great about the whole experience. In fact, it was wonderful. I laughed because, of course, it didn't make any sense from the physical perspective. This glow lasted for days.

The next night I got a personal call from Darwin. He had heard about my firing and wanted to know the rest of the story. It sounded as if he already knew, but wanted to hear it from me. I told him what happened. He then asked me to wait. He would get back to me in a day or so.

A few days later he called to ask if I would like a new job working for him. He wanted me to start a new audio and recording department. A few weeks before, I had shown him the abandoned tapes of Paul Twitchell that I found in the loft at the office, and I had already started trying to sort them out. He wanted me to make it my full time job, organizing the tapes, recording new talks at seminars, editing them for production and then setting up cassette duplication equipment to make tapes for sale. That was how I ended up starting the audio department. It began by just doing something I felt needed to be done.

The whole thing couldn't have worked out better. I spent more time working closely with Darwin, where I learned about his plans and how I could help. Bill, on the other hand, was replaced within a couple months by a new general administrator.

After thirty years of studying different teachings, I've seen experiences like this happen over and over again to many people. Some have often wondered what could have gone wrong that spiritual seekers would become corrupted by positions of power. But I've come to see a whole different perspective on this. Rather than this being a sign of something wrong, it is, in fact, an important experience and is part of the way we learn. If we can get beyond the idealism of how we think things should be, we can see an amazingly subtle, yet valuable, lesson.

Here is what Babuji Maharaj, a spiritual leader in the line of Radhasoami masters said on December 22, 1937, to his students:

Sooner or later, anyone who takes up the spiritual path will find that occasions arise to test one's regard for the world. The sense of fear and shame, timidity and hesitation out of concern for the world and worldly power will have to be discarded, or one's love for the path will fade. It is not necessary to show off one's independence, but if anything concerning the spiritual path is at stake, then no one in the world should be able to stop us. We should not be afraid of anyone, even if everyone becomes displeased.

Devotees have gone through all sorts of humiliating situations. When they first joined Satsang here, pressure was put on them from all quarters to try and stop them. Their social caste-fellows kicked up a row. For a long time, devotees could not find husbands for their daughters to marry. None of their caste-fellows would marry them. When, finally, marriage did take place, then no one would take part in the ceremony. Things even came to such a point that many were threatened with losing their jobs. They were asked to submit letters of resignation if they did not stop with Satsang.

But those who were true and sincere did not give in. They made it clear that even if they lost their jobs and everything else, they would not give up the ways of Satsang and the spiritual path. In the end, no harm came to them. They neither lost their jobs, nor were they forced to submit their resignations. Rather, things took such a turn that their honor and reputation increased.

These moments test our faith, but more importantly they show us where we are putting our faith. If we believe more in the authority of those who threaten us than in our own inner guidance, then we have given them power over us. This means we have chosen the path of kings, as Rumi put it. If we take the path we know is right, then we gain unexpected spiritual rewards. Things even end up better for us physically as well, if we can just let the injustices work out on their own.

From this experience, I learned not to be afraid of doing what I knew was right, no matter what authority I might be facing. As Rumi said, the danger of kings is not in losing one's life, since we must all die one day anyway. It is forgetting the Greater Way. I discovered the most incredible spiritual treasure from seeing the true power of the Path. It was a pattern that would enter my life many times in the coming years.

I didn't go looking for these kinds of confrontations, but eighteen months later I found myself being fired from the Eckankar office again. This time by a new general administrator who felt threatened by me.

Apparently, he didn't like seeing someone who felt freedom and was not afraid of his authority. However, I knew I was working for a higher purpose. For some reason this raised his hackles, so he decided to teach me a lesson and fire me. One week later, he broke his arm, while inwardly I felt myself being lifted up into what seemed like spiritual light, and was once again floating on cloud nine.

The second time I was fired, Darwin didn't hire me back right away, but I didn't need his help this time. I realized it was time to move on. I wasn't quite sure of what changes lay ahead, but looking back I can see that this was when I moved beyond the group consciousness. It was exactly the jolt I needed to make the shift.

We should never be afraid to follow our inner guidance. We should never be afraid to do what we know is right, nor is there any reason to bow down to others who want to be worshipped for their position or power. And we should not be afraid of being shunned by any group. The path is far more powerful than any of these little things, as it shows us over and over again that we are free from the rule of kings.

For days after being fired the second time, I found myself surrounded by a spiritual current. This time I followed the spiritual Light and Sound back to its source, and I tried to capture what I experienced in writing:

Wing's Breath

With wing's breath I took to the sky. Skyward…blueward…into the vast beyond. Outward…onward…where my heart beats sound and the worlds respond. On the trail of an arrow shot from God.

Through space and time I flew, where the play of man's mind unrolls. And the Voice of the Lower Worlds calls to me:

"How may I hold you?" it whispers, "you, whose heart has been pierced by the golden archer. What can I give to satisfy you? What garden do I own, what fruit can I offer that this burning from God's shaft might be lessened?

"The breath of God," it said, "the wing's breath. Only this may cool your brow. It is the song of the heavens, the music of the gods. Isn't it this for which the worlds were formed? So the eagles can soar and speak of IT, and the seeds may bloom for IT? Why else might flowers turn faces to the sun?"

Past my eyes flew the stars and the heavens, as the voice of the lower worlds faded behind. On, I searched, for the archer. To find the quiver from which this arrow was drawn and to return it home.

Then, his words called to me, echoing, and upon them I winged higher.

"Fear not," the archer said. "My arrows find their mark and deep into the heart they rush, never to be removed again. All pain is time's and all love is mine."

His love came clear and pure, and I plunged into its depths where only blue essence stirred. Then, coming to the surface, there all the reflections of mankind glimmered.

The archer's grace was like a soft wind reaching everywhere. Here stroking the grass, here rolling a fallen leaf and here tossing the child's hair. The breeze caressed all things alike, yet moved only what was free and light. Then upon its currents I swirled to the heavens.

Into the skies with him I climbed, to the mountain's height, where we looked across the world's far reaches.

"Yes, I am the wing's breath, the reed song, the call of the eternal in your heart," he said, resonating a deep chord within me. "Yet do not forget the long years before you knew my whisper. When you first heard my call, was it not the hollow wind through the trees, the lonely stars in space and the tear of desolation? Was it not the shadow of death and the dark night?

"Look across your world, for Life is also the wailing of a starved heart and a stream run dry, parching the earth. Like the natural disaster, the drought, or hurricane, or plague. It is the crumbling of life and the silent questions for those in their eleventh hour. For my arrow's been shot, and its shadow is felt, yet it has not pierced its mark."

Then, like the gale preceding the calm, the sky darkened and the winds whipped, uprooting what was sick and rotten. Old branches were scattered so the new could grow. All life was shaken, rattled and tested, so the film of sleep would be wiped from their eyes. Then a new star appeared in the heavens. The arrow had struck its heart!

"Now the little self flickers like a dying flame," said the archer. "Or bobs like a cork on the vast ocean of God. Or perhaps like a small vessel, crossing from port to port. What need is there of these when you have become the ocean? You have no movement which is not the ocean's movement, no heart which is not the ocean's heart.

"Can water of the sea be collected in buckets? Such water only grows stale. For the freshness you must enter in. Dissolve in the wing's breath. Lose your life for ITS sake and then you may quench your thirst with ITS love. It is pure and sweet, and lingers on the lips like a beloved's kiss."

The wing's breath swept all else away, and life now only dances across my face like the images on a mirror. I have entered into all things and found the secret is my own self. I am the wing's breath. I am the reed song and the wind of heaven. The call of the eternal is my own call, my own whisper. I am all things, for the archer has returned me home!

This must be the ultimate experience, I thought. This must be the great experience of God! Yet it was only a small step along the way. In fact, it was just the beginning of the voyage.

I had experienced what many others have known. Paul called it "The Top of The Mountain," which is when we see all of life clearly, as if we are looking out over the world.

Ralph Waldo Emerson and Walt Whitman wrote from this state of consciousness. They had reached the point of seeing the whole of mankind like a single consciousness, and knowing that their own voice was the very voice of that consciousness.

This was where my understanding of the emotional and imaginative fabric of the Astral Plane had been leading me. I had thought it was God-consciousness, or Self-realization, but it was neither. It was a glimpse of Cosmic Consciousness. And if it weren't for the guidance of the Inner Master who told me there was more...much more...I might still be there believing I had found the ultimate truth, and thinking I should be telling everyone else.

Some call it the Higher Self, the Inner Master, the Lord, Spiritual Guide, or Guardian Angel. These are all terms to describe a consciousness that leads us and watches over us. It knows the way ahead.

Rumi once said that all the oceans of the world cannot hold enough ink to describe the meaning of this secret. It means far more than any words.

I tried to explain the mystery of the Inner Master once to a friend, during this period of my life. I said it was like two mirrors face-to-face. The mirrors become transformed into endless hallways of mirrored reflections through each other. This was what I experienced between the Master and myself. As I looked into the heart of the Master, I found an endless reality opening up within myself, and it seemed as if an endless world opened up within the Inner Master, as well, that was leading me on to a great new world.

However, if I was to truly understand this mystery, I would have to take another step. I would have to leave behind the group consciousness, and step out once again into the unknown.

Truth

"Ah, young one," the Master said to me, bending closer and looking into my eyes. "You say Truth is light and gentle like the fleecy clouds on a spring day, but it is the fierce fire wind that pierces thy heart.

"It is the tumultuous, thundering roar that causes thy mind to shake in terror. The call of Truth draws Soul to horrendous heights, upon a barely worn path, frostbitten and alone. It stretches thy thoughts beyond the limits of the little self.

"And if you would have it another way, It will leave you hollow, only the echo of a song once sung.

"Yes," the Master said, nodding his head, "Truth is sweeter than any earthly nectar, and subtler than the flicker of a flame. Yet, heed these words: Seek all of it, or nothing!"

Yes, the Path goes on, ever onward, because it knows no end.

ANCIENT
MEMORIES

WHISPERS JOURNEY FAR in the endless worlds.

Echoing across the hills…calling through the valleys…stirring thoughts to dream and wonder. Breathed like a sigh from the worlds beyond. Shadows of an Ancient Memory…

Do they call to live again? Or do they call like aged spirit to die?

• • • • •

I WROTE THESE words in my notebooks after visiting some Indian ruins in Arizona. Images came to me of children dancing and playing upon the dust. Women with backs bent in work and voyagers with weary muscles from a too-long journey. The pictures seemed like more than just my imagination.

I was in a strange state of consciousness when I wrote the above words. I felt as if a part of me was suspended outside of time and this vision was calling out for me to see it. It came like a seed thought floating on the wind that awoke and sprang to life within me, playing out recorded images from long ago. Yet it also seemed like a part of my own life. Were these my own Ancient Memories bubbling up from my own subconscious? Or did they belong to the outer world?

I followed the experience further. I had the impression that this stream of consciousness was speaking out from the land itself and was calling out to be heard again. By listening to this long lost song, was I bringing it back to life? Or, by being conscious of this memory was I putting old patterns to rest? I didn't know.

I had read about the Third Initiation and how it related to the Causal Plane. It is a dimension where one can see the Time Track and read one's own past lives like a deck of cards spread out in an arc before one, or so I had been told. But what I was experiencing seemed like nothing I had read. This vision was coming through my own being. I felt like some kind of radio that was suddenly receiving signals that had been bouncing around the ionosphere for eons, yet the whole thing was playing through my consciousness as if it was a part of me.

I had studied everything I could about the Causal Plane and imagined that I knew what it all meant, but what was happening wasn't even close to what I expected. I thought that observing the time track would be like watching a movie or looking at photographs from long ago, and that I would feel detached about what I saw. I imagined it more like some kind of intellectual idea, as if I would suddenly be aware of the patterns behind the world.

I didn't realize that my own being would become a part of these patterns, or that what belonged to me and what belonged to the world would seem almost indistinguishable. I didn't feel like I was gaining new knowledge, as I expected, but more as if I was now part of a bigger mystery. The silent questions returned and I wondered who "I" really was. Was I separate from the world, or was the world just using me as a voice for its own message?

I had imagined my life as being under my own free will. I thought I had been making my own decisions. But now I began to have the feeling that my choices were not completely my own. Of course, I knew that our lives are influenced by the culture we are raised in, but now I was seeing it differently. Now I realized that the world itself, or something even larger than the world, was expressing itself through the lives of the people. I had been unconsciously playing a role in some larger drama beyond my own awareness.

I felt perplexed. But this wasn't something I could solve by thinking about it. You can't solve the question of your own Self by intellectual reasoning. I was going to have to learn what this meant by living it. But what was it that I was living? It seemed much larger than anything I had known before.

Visions like this one would come upon me suddenly during that time and bring with them strange feelings and images I couldn't remember from anywhere else. Then they would end just as unexpectedly. It was hard to let these stories hang in the air like they did, with unfinished endings and unanswered questions. But I had no idea what should follow. They just seemed to exist this way, like intercepted transmissions without a conclusion.

One day I sat down to brush up on a little writing. The keys of my typewriter had been silent too long. I thought I would warm them up a bit. I was expecting nothing, yet suddenly realized I was listening in on thoughts from around the world. I put down the words as they came into my awareness. Bit by bit, unfolding before me, I found a story crossing time and space.

Simultaneity

The sound of the flute came from over the hills. All my sheep, every last woolly, grew quiet and raised their heads. Otherwise, I wouldn't have heard it with all their constant bleatings and racket. It was a soft sound, yet haunting. Its direction...hard to reckon...perhaps from the hermit's cave...or from the northern hill. It could have even come from the forest. The wind might have carried the sound from anywhere.

· · ● · ·

I hear the call of the mountain god. The sounds of Bird and Monkey go silent and Earth trembles beneath my feet. I know the call, and shed my skin like Snake. My spirit dances with Wind and laughs in Dream. I smell Jungle Flower in all the air.

· · ● · ·

As I recall, we were in the conference room, the five of us, that is. Jackson was getting a beating from Tuberillo for blowing the last deal, when we heard this noise. It sounded like the whoosh of wind.

"Frank," I said, "your window's blown open!"

Frank jumped for his office door, expecting a whirlwind of papers to swear at, but everything was quiet. I don't know why, but it seemed awfully funny. Tuberillo had the biggest laugh. Frank just smiled. We didn't get much work done that day, but we had a pretty good time after that just shootin' the bull. I think it was one of the nicest days I had with ol' Tuber, because I saw he was a real person, too, under his gruff exterior.

· · ● · ·

I don't take much with memories, schedules and shit like that. Get it? I say live life day by day. Ya spend your mind on a clock and ya lose it. Get it? But that day there, yeah, it was a high one. I was jammin' with Johnny and Slips. I play drums. We were movin' nice and smooth. Slips had some far-out riffs, when Johnny—like that—drops out. Johnny's face kind of lights up strange, like he was hearin' somethin', and I get these weird shivers up my back. Next thing you know, we're playin' a new hit. Just like that! It blew our minds.

· · ● · ·

Oh, yes, I remember. I remember it well, for that was the day when the wind became soft, and the desert grew quiet. My thoughts turned calm, like smooth waters. Spirit Eagle called to me, but the sound came into me roaring, until death took me. My body slept, but my sight awakened. And I must see the hunting grounds, and I must feel such freedom, and I must know such secrets that leave me hollow now, until death may come again.

· · ● · ·

God winks and universes quiver. ITS voice rolls forth, the Sound, and all Soul is touched, all time, all space. What can be simultaneity but the touch of Truth?

What a strange experience, to be able to witness all of Time and Space in an instant!

I knew that whether this story was literally true or not did not matter. I had already learned that lesson, so I didn't even try worrying about whether this was True or False. But the odd thing was that when I tried to find the meaning behind this experience or to understand the feelings and emotion of what I had just written, like I did during my Second Initiation, I found my previous tools failed me. I could not see behind the veil.

124

Apparently, this inner experience was not woven from a fabric of imagination. It was not just a metaphor. This was some kind of reality at a different level.

As months passed by, I realized that the ground rules had changed again. The lessons I had learned couldn't unlock the mystery I was now facing. In fact, I sensed that there was no way to figure out the meaning of this new state of consciousness. I was simply going to have to live it to know what it really was.

This turned out to be the only course of action that worked. I would simply experience and observe. Gradually I became more familiar with this new dimension of life. Like getting to know a friend, the more time I spent with it, the more I began to recognize it for what it was.

I was becoming connected to something that reached across time— something that was a part of the very causation of reality. However, I was not prepared for dealing with all the new feelings and thoughts that began flowing through me. As a result, I suddenly found myself with all kinds of problems. I began struggling with a whole range of inner troubles and conflicts, but I couldn't separate out which ones were my own or what I was picking up from the world.

The Universal Teachings

Karen and I moved to Sedona, Arizona, a few months after leaving the Eckankar Office. We took a job as managers of the Red Rock Lodge. It was a great place to live, and we both enjoyed having work that wasn't full time.

Karen wanted spare time to develop some of her artistic talents, while I wanted to see if I could learn what it meant to be a writer. Managing the Lodge, especially during off-season, left us the extra time we needed to develop our skills.

About five months later, Karen found a job at Sedona's local newspaper, *The Red Rock News*, as a graphic artist. Shortly after this, a position opened up for a reporter at the News and I took it. We left the Lodge and found a nice little house for rent off a dirt road called Red Rock Loop Road, near Oak Creek with a view of Cathedral Rock. It was a beautiful home in God's country, as Sedona has often been named.

The newspaper work didn't pay much, but we both enjoyed it. I got

25 cents per inch for what I wrote. There is nothing like deadlines to force you to learn how to write on demand. It was quite a challenge at first, but was just the discipline I needed. My writing skills improved immensely. I also got out my camera to go with my reporting duties and learned how to use the newspaper's dark room to develop my own prints for my stories. I got paid $5 for every photo they printed. To help pay the bills, I took on freelance photography work and writing for other Arizona publications, as well.

One of the things I enjoyed the most with my new job was meeting the people of Sedona. It was a small town back in those days. As one of two reporters, I got to meet almost everyone: Managers of banks, museums, churches, restaurants and motels, as well as policemen, firemen and local artists. The town was filled with retired people who had interesting histories, including an ex-NASA scientist, professional musicians and some wealthy businessmen.

I loved the diversity and range of people I met. Almost all of them had a special story of their own about how they had come to live in Sedona. Everyone knew what a wonderful place it was. Being a reporter meant encouraging people to talk about the things they were most passionate about. The more interested I was in their stories, the more inspired they felt to share. I found myself asking questions to explore their lives, to see what made them tick. No matter who they were, they would open up to a complete stranger simply because I worked for the newspaper.

It was a strange feeling at first. Here I was a young guy in my early twenties, yet presidents of banks and retired scientists were talking to me as an equal. Local artists and actors who put on plays and shows in town all treated me like I was one of their own. They wanted to talk because I liked to listen, but they also saw me as representing the town, somehow, and they assumed I knew what was going on. So, they often prodded me for news.

It didn't take long before I felt like I knew the town and its people. I could see the group consciousness and realized I was a part of it. It's a shame that so few get to experience this sense of community these days. It gave me a whole new understanding about people and brought me back again to my life lesson.

However, it was actually something more than just the group consciousness I was starting to work with. I sensed it, but couldn't understand it at first. I began to glimpse how the puzzle pieces of the town fit together. What at first looked like a diverse spectrum of people was really an interconnected living social organism, with everyone depending on each other in subtle ways.

One of the things that made for a stronger feeling of community came from Sedona's location at the edge of a mountain range, far away from the nearest city. This isolated the town. Also, in those days, you could only—if you were lucky—pick up one TV channel, and the quality was terrible. So, everyone stopped watching the tube, and spent time talking with each other instead.

After returning from a day trip to the "big city" one day, I found myself filled with inner turmoil. Phoenix rattled me for some reason. It seemed like an overwhelming chaos of thoughts, feelings and desires, which I couldn't separate from my own. I felt as if I had been knocked from my orbit and was confused.

I went for a hike, taking my camera, hoping I could clear my head:

Vultee Arch Trail

The jumbled emotions and high-paced pressures of city life whirled within me. I knew these troubles were not mine, but that somewhere along the way I had picked them up. Perhaps a moment of sympathy or a moment of anger.

No matter, I hiked in Sedona's countryside for time to think. I drove down the long rocky dirt road leading to Vultee Arch Trail. My thoughts were upon an argument I had just started. It wasn't much, but it bothered me. It nagged me. I knew it shouldn't have happened. The road ran out—at least what was left of the road—so I abandoned mechanical transportation for foot power.

The sun eased its way toward the horizon. There would be little daylight left, but that didn't matter. The trail was clear. I began an easy steady stride that took me through the shaded pine forest. My feet padded across the soft earth. My thoughts wandered back.

Where did I pick these up—these strange tornados of turmoil? They certainly weren't mine. They fit me all wrong, choking me too tightly in some places, so baggy I tripped over them in others. But I can't recall anyone feeling comfortable in them. Everyone feels uneasy when trying them on.

The air was good to breathe. The exercise was good. I suddenly felt I had brought my problems to the wrong place. They didn't belong here.

It made me feel as if I were a carrier of disease in the Garden of Eden. I decided to abandon all such thoughts, and as I walked I relaxed.

A change took place. I began to feel welcome and heavy loads fell from my shoulders. My step became lighter and my pace picked up. As if some great sponge soaked off that other world, I faced the life around me with new notions of what might happen.

Here, this small worn trail made my walking easier. I thought of all those first feet that crossed here...virgin woods with no direction better than any other. Those feet laid a path any could follow. It was a well-laid path. No sharp twists, nice and smooth...undoubtedly created by happy feet. It reminded me of something.

I thought of the struggles those first feet had, and it reminded me of my problems. What a strange comparison! Could it be that forging new ways is the whole crux of turmoil? Those first feet could not enjoy the path as I did—not until they themselves were followers. Until they could forget where it turned and twisted; when they no longer worried if it might be leading them wrong.

The light that flashed off the trees seemed to answer in confirmation. I felt an added faith in this trail, for now I knew the spirit of the pioneers who laid it. Where it led didn't matter, since I knew it had succeeded.

A cool wind cascaded down from the mountains that I glimpsed through the clearings. The shadows lengthened. I passed pines tall with age...old stumps some ants had claimed...rocks and communities of wildflowers. They all seemed new to me.

I stopped suddenly when a buck and doe, with a bound and a leap, jumped across the path before me. They were gone on their own path seconds later.

Then it dawned on me. Nothing was a follower here. Branches pushed their way in unknown directions. Birds formed nests where no sign of nest was found before. Rocks formed shapes found nowhere else. It was bustling with builders and pioneers.

The trail pushed out of the pines and opened to a clearing of red rock formations. The cliffs glistened at their peaks. As far as I could tell, the path ended here, far from anything I knew. Miles in the wilderness from any man-made road, except for the trail.

Then I spotted Vultee Arch. So this is what brought those first feet out to the middle of nowhere. This red-stone bridge of rock was certainly an oddity, yet looked quite at home where it stood.

This arch had called pioneers to blaze the trail. So they had followed something after all; some inkling of a path before them. Some way, perhaps vague, but clear enough to follow.

The air grew chilly and the shadow lines rose higher and higher up the rock spires. I would have to return soon. I sat and stared through the valley where Vultee Arch Trail lay hidden below...thick with pines, and silent. The silence of dusk, like a sigh for the passing day.

I sighed too...then started back.

I was learning something here, or perhaps I should say that it seemed as if my body was learning something. I had spent too much time focusing on my inner problems and had lost touch with the innate wisdom of my body and Nature itself. I immediately felt the healing that came from discovering it again.

I began hiking up into the red rocks of Sedona more often. I climbed alone, far from the roads and deep into the desert mountains. During lightning storms and oven-hot days, I found the weather and elements themselves soaking into my body and filling an important need. It was as if my physical being was hungry for interaction with life. I had forgotten that the world of nature was a part of me.

I remember waking up from a vivid dream one sunny day, having dozed off in the afternoon. In the dream I had been reading ancient Indian teachings written upon the red rock mountain walls. I couldn't remember the writings when I awoke, but was left with a deep feeling that there was meaning inscribed upon the Earth itself. It was like a message imprinted from ages of men and women who had crossed the land. Almost as if the planet itself had absorbed the conscious lessons of the lives of those people and was now trying to give back this wisdom to any who would listen.

Do we leave impressions upon the world from the conscious lives we live?

I found a whole new insight after recording the following inner experience:

Prajapati

Bare outlines of a wooded scene filtered into view. My attention locked on and I found myself projecting into a most beautiful world. Trees of bright green, with leaves that flashed in the sun, lined a rushing river. The river filled me with energy and lightheartedness. It flowed with water of blue-green, the lightest hue, like none I had ever seen before. I wondered where it came from.

Then, looking up, I saw the white majestic walls of cliffs and mountains soaring high into the clouds. The rock face fell straight and smooth at least 1,000 feet. I instantly thought of the Hindu-Kush Mountains in Northern Tibet.

I flew upstream searching for some falls where the cold, fresh glacier water crashed from above. I seemed to remember where this might be. But I suddenly swerved right, traveling at a tremendous speed and only half catching images of the changing terrain.

Off in the distance, I saw a yellowy glow reflecting off the trees. As I approached, a campfire revealed itself. Yet, this was no ordinary fire. Its flames filled me with an expansive feeling, as if it could awaken all the secrets throughout the worlds. It was a mysterious light that drew me to it, and I knew exactly why the moth will fly into a scorching flame. I felt this same desire within me.

Like a magnet, it drew me on, and as I approached I noticed that no warmth came from this fire. It spread out only a feeling as vast as space itself. My vision became crystal clear from this energy and I knew that all things grew in harmony with this light. Its glow washed through me and eased all my tensions. There seemed to be a soft sound coming from the light, like a babbling brook, which brought relaxation and an increase in understanding. I reached out to touch it.

My hand felt something solid. I jumped back, startled, for the figure of a man stood now where the fire had been.

Bowing at the waist, he introduced himself. "Prajapati, at your service," he said with a smile. A merry look that sparkled in his eyes set me laughing at his gesture.

Here was Prajapati, the great Master who guides animals. Watching him before me was like finding the answer to some great mystery I had always longed to know. He walked softly to a stone, placing his hand on the smooth surface as if in some communication. Then he took a seat, pulling his knees up within his arms. He looked off into the distance saying nothing.

After a long period of silence, he turned to me and spoke in a voice that was clear and soft.

"Freedom is the law of nature!

"Nature exists on the breeze, circulating and touching all atoms. It is the call of freedom and the world is soothed by its song. Such shame that man lives and dies for civilization. If he put his faith in nature, I would show him his true kingdom.

"Man is heir to the throne, but his world is paced too fast. Whirlwinds of energy, like invisible tornados, dizzy the minds of billions. Where do they all hurry to? I have no idea.

"Yet I marvel at Man. Look what he has done! Man brought the smile to Dolphin. He brought softness to Cat. Loyalty to Dog. He has the gift of God!

"In days of old I walked openly with Man. Do you remember when we met in that glorious empire of Mu? That was the soft rolling land where all things grew without seed, for Life awoke spontaneously in the water and air. Cat was invited into Man's temples there.

"I stood by the side of fishermen in Atlantis when they built that great bond with Dolphin. Then, in the Northern land of Europe, shepherds led Dog out of the woods to tend their flocks. Look, time has whisked by since then, but what has changed?

"Everything in your world is your kingdom. It is yours to uncover and awaken, for you can see its True Form. No others can see it for you. Forget not even the smallest one by your side, and even Rock and Stone will await your shadow when day's work is done. Perception is your gift of creation!

"If you give freedom to all things, then you have the secret of nature. I can give you no more. Look to the Inner Master for all else!"

Prajapati stood up again and looked far away toward the horizon. His form gradually faded into a golden light, which grew and grew until there was no saying where it ended. This was truly his world!

I wrote this spiritual experience down as it happened to me. At first it seemed much like many other Soul Travel experiences I had had before. However, as I began trying to put into words what I had seen and felt, I sensed something coming through the article itself. I wondered if others might get something out of the story, so I submitted it to a small Arizona newsletter, where it was printed.

I would like to make something clear here, before going on. When reading my story, *Prajapati*, please understand that I am describing an inner experience. For some reason when these things are put onto paper, they tend to sound more miraculous and phenomenal than they really are.

First of all, Soul Travel is not the same as Astral Projection. There are a lot of people who confuse the two. With Astral Projection, it feels as if you are wholly and completely outside the physical body. The only connection between the two is usually a silvery tube that seems just like an umbilical cord. It is a tremendously exhilarating feeling, but also can be frightening when it first happens.

131

With Soul Travel, you generally retain awareness of your body. I often find myself aware of numerous things going on around me and inner experiences at the same time. It is more like an expansion of consciousness. With it comes a great feeling of freedom, but also a feeling of grace and protection, since it brings a connection to the wholeness of our being, Soul of Itself. Just like any experience, once you get used to Soul Travel, it seems natural and not extraordinary at all.

Back to my story: I received letters from around the world when *Prajapati* went into print. Somehow, news of the article spread by word of mouth and brought in requests for the newsletter from as far away as Europe and the East Coast.

Later, the *ECK World News* reprinted the article, with a drawing of Prajapati by Diana Stanley. More letters arrived.

I was surprised that it struck such a deep chord for so many people. I had thought it was simply my own experience, but apparently there was something else in it.

A Japanese gardener, who happened to read the article, stopped me one day in Sedona when he saw me interviewing a shop owner nearby. He asked about Prajapati: "Is he the same being as Pan, who takes care of plants and flowers?"

"I don't know," I answered.

However, as I listened to him and the stories he told about his work, I began to see what was happening. Here was a gardener who had spent his life with flowers, trees and plants, and he knew there was something taking place when he worked with them. He was having his own inner experiences when he attuned himself to the plant kingdom. Although he might never have thought of it this way, once he read the story it struck a note of recognition within him. It spoke to him.

So, I began to see that my story somehow belonged to the world and was not just my own.

I received insights and questions from dozens of people who shared their own stories, but there was one thing that bothered me. It arose from a question that continually came up: "What did Prajapati look like?"

I didn't know how to answer this. Wouldn't Prajapati appear differently to each person? Did he really have just one universal form or was he simply the guiding force of Spirit amongst animals? The problem was that I didn't want to share the personal aspect of my inner experience. I was only trying to share the portion of my story that might mean something to others. But this question was asking me to take my personal inner experience and give it out as if it was true for everyone. I suddenly felt very uncomfortable. I didn't know what to say, so I avoided the question.

After the article was reprinted in the *ECK World News*, it started all over again. Three or four more people asked me: "Is that what Prajapati looks like?" referring to Diana Stanley's drawing. Something didn't feel right about giving out my own inner experience of how he looked as if it were some kind of reality for the world.

It seemed too personal to share, and yet hadn't I already shared a part of my experience? I then began wondering if I should have written the story at all. I had taken something from a Soul Travel encounter, but had I also put words into the mouth of Prajapati as if he had spoken them to the world when it was my experience? I began having doubts. Had I made a mistake? Had I gone too far?

I felt like something wasn't quite right, but I couldn't figure out what it was. I asked the Inner Master for guidance. Not long after this I wrote the following in my notebooks. It turns out that the Outer Master would end up giving me a clue to the answer.

It was a December day and I was sitting in the lunchroom at the Eckankar International Office in Menlo Park, California. I was leaning my chair back on its rear legs when Darwin Gross, the spiritual leader of Eckankar came up.

"Hi Doug," he said. "Hey, I caught your story on Prajapati." His smile told me he liked the article. But just before he walked away, he turned and said, "By the way, that picture of Diana's, does it look like him?"

I nearly fell over backwards. Even Darwin is asking me what Prajapati looks like?

Diana Stanley, who happened to be at the lunch table with me, spoke up to say that she really felt Prajapati might look older than her drawing. "But he IS thin," she said.

Darwin nodded. He then went on to tell a story about a fox he'd seen a few days before, trying to cross a big four-lane freeway. The fox had been pacing back and forth, looking for a chance to race between the cars. Darwin could see the fox might not make it across, so he turned the situation over to Prajapati for help. On his way back, later the same day, he saw the little fox had been hit. Its body lay alongside the road.

"What happened," Darwin said, "was that this little fellow felt the warm light and safe protection of the Master, but he mistook it for a signal to go ahead. It's not an uncommon mistake."

I wondered if there was a message in this story for me. Had I made the same error in writing the Prajapati article? Are such inner experiences better kept silent? Rumi once said, "The line between truth and imagination has less breadth than a poet's thought." I began wondering how real the experience had actually been. Had I simply created the whole thing from my imagination?

Returning home that evening, I felt the presence of someone in our apartment the moment I stepped through the door. Looking around, I couldn't see anyone nearby, but the impression was still there. In fact, as it approached nine o'clock, the presence grew stronger and stronger. Finally, I realized someone was waiting for me in the inner worlds.

As soon as I sat down and focused inwardly on the presence, I found myself out of the body, face to face with Prajapati.

This time I took extra notice of his appearance; his sandy, almost silvery brown hair, his squarish face with a boyish charm, and his eyes, light blue, the color of the sky. His age was hard to gauge. He was smiling and seemed happy to see me.

Without any words, he beckoned, and we projected to the high mountains of Tibet, not far from where I'd seen him before. He led the way through a forest to an opening in a rock wall at the end of a wide valley. It was the Oracle of Tirmer. I recognized it once I saw it and had the feeling I'd been there before. The rocky wall around the opening was overgrown with moss and climbing ivy.

Prajapati led me inside, where in the back I found books and old pages of writing. I immediately began to study these and at once realized that they contained the same ideas I had written in the Prajapati story!

I then realized that my story came from some ancient teachings. This explained its universal recognition by so many others.

Reading through more of the parchments, I could see that these records were part of the ancient memories of this planet. They have been filtering into the thoughts and thinking of mankind down through history. This was the teaching that Prajapati had been trying to give me in my previous experience.

At this point, Darwin's story about the fox came back to me. Now I understood. Just like the fox looking across the highway, I had wondered about crossing that subtle line of becoming an authority on Prajapati. How could I answer for others how he looked, as if this reality was a universal truth?

The spiritual path is strewn with the remains of seekers who have tried to set themselves up as authorities on the spiritual teachings. It is a dangerous line to cross and few ever make it without succumbing to ego and vanity. Although I now had the inner assurance and protection of the Master that what I had written was true, this was not a signal it was any safer to try crossing that line.

Each person must come to these understandings for themselves. After all, no one really wanted me to tell them about Prajapati anyway. They were only asking because of their own inner recognition and their own memories of the universal teachings.

Once again, I had new spiritual laws to learn. Sharing stories from the universal teachings was not the same as sharing personal experiences. What are called "teaching stories" have deeper meaning than anything I could give them. Therefore, I had no way of knowing what the universal teachings would mean to others, and I had no rights to claim them as my own.

Trying to answer the silent questions of others, or trying to relieve their longing to know and see the spiritual worlds for themselves would be like setting myself up over others. This goes against the spiritual law that says each much discover these teachings through their own personal experience.

The world has thousands of people acting as authorities of spiritual truth. Pompously handing out sayings and divine principles like candy to children, they have missed the most significant truth. Even if we could read the Book of Laws with our physical eyes, such teachings mean nothing to us unless they become a part of our inner life. In other words, the real meaning of the universal teachings must become something we live and put into practice. They have no other purpose than this.

A Different Language

In case you were wondering, the reason I was sitting at the Eckankar Office, which had moved from Las Vegas to Menlo Park, California, was because I had taken a job working in the publications department there. Karen got a job in the office as well, working as a graphic artist. The general administrator who had fired me was long gone.

General administrators at the Eckankar Office didn't last long in those days. Even Paul Twitchell said in one of his talks that he couldn't find anyone to stay for more than a year or so. He called it a man-killing job. I didn't understand the reason for this at the time. It would be many more years before I would recognize the extreme difficulty that power creates for a spiritual path. What I had learned about the dangers of trying to become an outer spiritual authority was just the tip of a much bigger iceberg.

It wasn't easy leaving Sedona. Karen and I still think of the year we spent there as some of the most wonderful days we ever had. We weren't the only ones who didn't want to leave. Cyper truly loved the red rocks and high-desert land. She would go off into the mountains for up to a week at a time. When she returned, she would have this wild look in her eyes, having lived on her instincts in the wilderness. It would take her a day or two to return to domesticated life. I've never seen another cat who could shift from one state to another like that.

When Karen and I decided to move, Cyper was not happy at all. I knew she loved our home in Sedona. However, Karen was now pregnant, and with a little one on the way, we both felt that we needed some full-time jobs with a little more stability. I wrote to Darwin and told him that I'd love to come back to the office and work with the publications, especially with my new experience as a reporter and photographer. He wrote back saying he thought there might be an opening and he would be glad to see us again. It wasn't exactly a straight answer, but I took it as a yes. After making our preparations, it came time to leave, so I told Cyper that we had one week left. If she was coming with us, she should go out to say her goodbyes.

In a day she disappeared. Over the next week, Karen and I packed the boxes and got everything ready. An hour before we were supposed to leave, there was still no sign of Cyper anywhere. Karen couldn't bear the idea of leaving without her and wanted to wait, but I told her that Cyper knew what she was doing. Cyper didn't want us to move. She was trying to make us stay. She hoped that we wouldn't leave if she didn't come home. So I took a moment of inner communication to tell Cyper that it was her choice to come with us or not, but we weren't waiting. If she wasn't there in an hour, we were leaving her behind.

Karen said, "But maybe she can't hear you. Maybe she doesn't know we are leaving. She's only a cat."

"She knows," I said. The only question I wondered was: Would she choose us or Sedona?

We were getting into the car, with Karen crying because we were leaving without her, when Cyper walks into the yard meowing loudly and balling me out for being so stubborn. She told me about it all the way to California, and it wasn't through inner communication, either. However, I knew exactly how she felt. It was hard for me to leave Sedona as well.

When we arrived at the office, they had just printed my article about Prajapati in the *ECK World News*. It was a wonderful surprise and a nice welcome back. The jobs in the publications department were there as I expected, and so were a lot of our old friends.

Adjusting to our new life took a while, however. The Menlo Park area was crowded, compared to Sedona. Interaction with nature was difficult and we missed it. One day, Karen and I decided to get away. We drove up into the hills to one of the parks in the area. We parked Karen's blue VW bug and went for a walk. When we came back, we had a parking ticket. Apparently, you couldn't just park your car and go for a hike in California. It felt like we had crossed into a foreign country.

During our hike in the Los Altos foothills, we had an interesting meeting with a rattlesnake. We ran into it after rounding a bend on the trail. A group of people had stopped ahead of us. They were watching the snake out of curiosity and trepidation. The rattlesnake was lying there at the edge of the path. There was no easy way around, since the path dropped off on the left side with a cliff, and rose up the sheer mountain side on the right.

After stopping to watch for a few minutes I could see that it was best for everyone if the snake moved. But he seemed to be lying there defiantly, as if he liked being in everyone's way and he liked the fear he cast over people.

So, I stepped over into the brush and picked up a big stick, about the size of a walking staff. As soon as I did this a number of people looked at me with a worried look. One lady said to me, shocked and indignant, "You aren't going to hit it, are you?"

"No, of course not," I said.

Then I walked through the group of people there and stepped a few paces closer to the snake. He immediately started coiling up and hissing. I took the stick and banged the end of it straight up and down on the ground three times and inwardly told the rattlesnake that it was time to move. He was in everyone's way and it would be better if he moved off the path.

The snake raised his head in a dangerous stance and began rattling. The group all seemed to suck in their breath at the same time. I could see the people behind me wanting to stop me before we had some real trouble. However, I knew the snake was just bluffing. He was mad at me for telling him to move and was telling me so.

I then banged the end of the staff down again three more times, and once again told him inwardly that he should move off the path. He had no right holding everyone up like that.

He let out a big hiss and then turned away and began slinking off into the bushes. The group was quiet. They weren't sure what they had just seen. I turned to Karen and said, "Shall we?" and the two of us continued on our walk with the walking stick still in my hand. The rest seemed stunned, and confused. Banging a stick on the ground hardly caused the ground to move enough to scare off a snake. But somehow the snake knew what it meant. Was this some kind of language I had used?

Interactions like this with wild animals are hardly new, of course. For example, just north of Sedona, the Hopi Indians hold their annual snake dance, where the Indian dancers will grab up rattlesnakes any which way, dance with them and then set them back down again. They move in a circle with the snakes, suddenly stopping to pick them up and winding them around their bodies as part of the ceremony. They prepare for this sacred ritual by spending days fasting and purifying their thoughts. The snakes have never bitten the dancers as far as I've heard.

The Horse Whisperer is a book about a horse trainer who learned a silent language of movements and glances that allowed him to tame even the most troublesome horses. *Kinship With All Life* is a book by J. Allen Boone that describes his communications with animals and other life forms. There are many examples like these.

However, when I found these experiences coming to me at this time of my life, I found that there was nothing I could say about them. After the snake had left, there was nothing more to do than move on. So, I have never spoken or written about these things before. These experiences would just happen.

In Sedona I had picked up an understanding about this new language. However, even on the city streets of California I had a couple of the oddest experiences with animals.

I remember walking home with Karen from a nearby grocery store one day, when I noticed a pack of dogs following us and watching us in a strange way. They stopped to stare as we crossed the street to our cul-de-sac. The intensity of the way they looked at us seemed a bit odd, but I didn't think too much about it at the time.

After putting away the food, I thought I heard someone at our front door. I walked out into our living room to see a German shepherd pushing the screen door with his nose and making little barking noises. He sounded friendly, but it was the feeling I got from him that struck me as strange. I had the impression that he wanted me to come outside. It was as if he was speaking to me silently.

I went to look at him closer and he backed away from the door. He was acting as if he wanted me to follow him and he wanted to show me something. I walked back toward the kitchen and he once again started pushing the screen door open with his nose and barking. I wasn't sure what was going on. I had never seen this dog before, yet he acted as if he came to the house just for me. I could see it in his eyes. I laughed as I realized he was just asking me out to play.

I finally thought, well, why not find out what this was all about? So, I told Karen I was following the call of the wild, and headed out the door.

The dog immediately started leading the way. He crossed the main street to where the rest of the pack was waiting. He looked around to make sure I was following. He headed up a side road and around the back of one of the stores. The dogs all ran along, circling around in various directions, checking out different scents and objects, but generally following the German shepherd.

We then headed out up another street and continued on like this. At first I thought the dog's insistence that I follow him meant that he had something important to show me. But as we went along I realized that we weren't going toward any particular destination. We were just making the rounds. And I could see now that he wasn't treating me any differently than any of the other dogs. I was simply one of the pack.

I decided I might as well join the dog pack consciousness and go for the ride. What do dogs do when they run around town, anyway?

Well, they keep moving and they cover an incredible amount of territory. We were always moving in a kind of gentle lope, stopping for but a moment to smell something or to check out whatever had changed since the last time they had visited. Then, we would move on again.

There were of course the knowing looks amongst members of the pack as they noted changes in the environment and what they meant.

Leadership of the pack also seemed to change fluidly from one dog to the other, like a group of boys exploring new terrain. As one found something of interest, the pack would come over to see.

But more than anything, what I noticed was a whole new way of seeing and sensing the world. I can't even describe it. It wasn't anything I can put into words, but it was completely different from the way people see things. I was being given a glimpse of their reality, as if someone had given me a radio that listened in on their thoughts.

We kept moving in a gentle run and never really stopped, but the oddest thing was that even after an hour of this I didn't feel the slightest bit tired. My body had tuned into the consciousness of the dogs and it seemed as if I had this never ending stream of restless energy pouring through me that kept me moving. It was dog-energy, and I didn't want to stop anymore than they did.

After the second hour, I started worrying about how sore my muscles might be the next day. I remember this thought because it seemed like a strange human thought entering my mind. In fact, my mind was remarkably free of thoughts during this time.

By then, we had crossed at least ten miles of city streets. The range of territory we covered was amazing. Around the third hour, I found that we were back close to where we had started. I was starting to get bored, so I broke away from the pack, said my goodbyes and ran home.

My life as a dog was over, but I didn't feel winded at all. In fact, I felt like I could have kept running forever. My muscles never showed any soreness at all. It was the weirdest thing.

Another experience came shortly after moving to California. One day while eating lunch, I heard the gardener at the Eckankar Office complaining about a certain group of gophers that were chewing up the lawn. The gardener had tried everything he could think of, and admitted he had no other alternative than poison.

I cringed at the idea. I asked if he had tried talking to the gophers. He looked at me strangely.

"No," he said. "How do you talk to gophers?" he asked, with a doubtful look in his eyes.

"Well, you just talk to them," I said.

"Look," he said. "I've got to get rid of these things. They're eating the whole lawn up. I don't like the idea of poisoning them any more than you do."

"Well, can you give me a few days?" I asked. "I'll see what I can do."
He said, "Okay, I can wait a few days."
The following was recorded in my notebook:

Walking through the moist grass, I found the gophers willing to talk. They were perturbed. Here was Eckankar, they said, which was supposed to be all so wonderful, and they were going to be driven off by poison! If this was a true spiritual path, why wouldn't they be allowed to eat its lawn?

I laughed. I hadn't expected this at all. After I questioned them some more, it became clear that the gophers were attracted to the lawn because of the spiritual energy they felt. To them, eating the lawn was their way of gaining something from the path. I had the biggest laugh at this.

So, I explained to them that their spiritual growth would not come from what they ate, but from what they did. They weren't going to get any closer to God by eating the Eckankar lawn, but if they took on the position of working to protect the lawn instead, and gave up their own desire to eat it and took on a higher purpose of protecting the lawn, then that simple act would assure them of the spiritual growth they were seeking.

I had to hold this thought in my mind for a while before it seemed to sink in. It was quite a change of perspective for them. But after a while I felt a shift. They seemed to get it, and in fact they seemed delighted to serve a higher purpose.

I then realized that Spirit moves all creatures in their own way, and they have a true desire for spiritual growth just as many people do.

As I said, these were some pretty strange experiences. I know there aren't a lot of people who go around talking to gophers, at least not outside the funny farm, but the next day the gophers were gone and they never returned for at least the next two years I was there.

I had actually not talked directly to the gophers, per se, but talked to the over-soul, you might say, or the entity of the group consciousness. When I found myself working with the group consciousness, as I described previously, I found that animals, insects and even plants have a consciousness like this as well. However, with the lower species it is a little different.

While in Sedona I tried a number of experiments and finally found the trick of it.

For example, I started with some ants that were making a regular thing of crawling through the kitchen of our house on the Red Rock

Loop Road. This was not just a few ants, mind you, but a complete Conga line. I tried to tell them to get out. That didn't work. I told them that they were invading our home and they had no right to be there. They didn't agree. I threatened them. No dice. Finally after a number of different attempts I began to sense that they weren't listening to me quite simply because I wasn't listening to them.

That's when I realized that I was trying to talk to the ants as if they were individuals, rather than talking to the over-soul, or the group consciousness. In fact, the individual ants did not care what might happen to them. They only lived for the sake of the group. The over-soul, however, did seem to be listening and did seem to care about the colony. As I felt myself tuning into this over-soul, I too began to feel the care it had for all the ants as it watched over them. Once I was in communion with this entity, I began to get ideas of what to say. I explained that by honoring our home space the over-soul would assure spiritual growth for the whole colony. To bring grief to us, however, could bring harm to the colony as well, since we all receive back what we give. For the first time I felt a response of recognition, as if I had gotten through.

After that, the ants stopped marching through our house. We did see one once in a while, but never the chuck-wagon express that we had before.

One evening about a week later, when Karen and I were coming back from a moonlight walk, I noticed something odd: There were no moths around our outside light. The moths had always been there in droves on a clear night like that, whenever the light was on. The light seemed to draw them from miles away. I was wondering about this and what might have happened to the moths, when I turned to look across the street at the volunteer firehouse. The light was turned on there as well, but it was flooded with moths. That's when I realized that nature does listen and responds to the care we have for all of life.

I was learning how to work with the guiding entity of a group consciousness on a one-to-one basis. The group consciousness was no longer like some towering force outside of my ability to influence. In fact I could work with it just like any other person or friend. It was all taking place on the Causal Plane.

This realization unfolded into a deeper understanding about people when I wrote the following in my notebooks. I had started this article during my Second Initiation, but I could not quite grasp the meaning of it. So I set it aside, half written. I picked it back up after having the above experiences. I could finally understand this new discovery and the meaning of it.

Over-Souls of the Human Race

People say that all the creatures of this world have predators except mankind, showing the greatness of the human race. It's a nice thought, but man's rulers are just as real. These are the Over-Souls I am talking about; the entities who rule the cultural forces that control our lives.

These inner forces ride men and women just like people ride horses, steering us this way and that by popular opinion or social pressure. We overlook the weight of these influences because they are invisible to our physical eyes.

Ever since the industrial revolution, our war against these Over-Souls has become a fight for the survival of our individuality. The broadcast media and machines of production have turned our society into a culture of mass conformance. They have replaced man's individual inner life with unified emotions created like prefabricated houses.

How do we come to terms with these inner forces? How do we retain our individuality in the face of their apparent omnipotence?

It is too easy to say that the spiritual path is the answer, or that a spiritual leader can show us the way to freedom, as some groups claim. How is this different from being swallowed up by another group, a new entity? Therefore, it is the science of individuality we seek. That must become our study.

As individuals we can learn the art of speaking to these Over-Souls through our own heart. This is how to work with mankind's ruling forces and yet keep our individuality intact.

Although the huge corporations and institutions count hundreds of thousands within their fold, apparently outnumbering us, still, they are only one entity. Therefore, we can face them as Soul, one-to-one. Once we realize this, we are no longer outnumbered or overpowered by the gods that rule mankind.

For example, take the policeman who gains his power from the authority of the police department. When talking to him, we can speak THROUGH him to that ruling power. The police force is one entity, just like one being. The policeman must obey the will of that entity. Therefore, we can talk to this Over-Soul as one being to another.

People these days say that organizations, corporations and institutions are too powerful and must be stopped, but a definite change comes over us once we gain the reins of our inner imagination. We do not need to accept the image put upon us. There is no reason to feel overwhelmed by the largeness of these inner giants once we, ourselves, begin operating from the "largeness of thought" as Paul Twitchell put it. Then we can see these Over-Souls as individual entities and work with them like we might with a friend.

Coming to terms with these ruling forces is one of the main lessons of the Twentieth Century with its mass culture. As strange as it sounds, those in the next century will probably wonder how this problem even existed. They will have no idea what it means to be de-humanized by computers, how people can feel like a number in a system, or how terms like "human error" and "management efficiency" can be used to put individuals down under the thumbs of the corporate powers.

It is sad to see how television, newspapers and radio have created new cultures that do not come from the people, but are created by professionals. They have broken up our community feelings and the strength of our families because they are now pushed onto us from the outside. The change to our society has been astonishing. We now lock the doors to our houses and cars to protect ourselves, when we once felt safe without deadbolts and door-chains.

Without a feeling of social responsibility, people become more selfish. Marriages become agreements for individual pleasure. Building a strong family becomes secondary. The masses no longer are co-creators of society, but are now just consumers.

In this way, the Over-Souls have taken control of millions.

However, once we recognize that we each, individually, are inseparable from Life Itself, then our world becomes whole again.

We need not run from one culture to another or from one belief to another. We can work with all of them as if we were interacting with different people. We can deal directly with these influences as Soul and retain our individuality.

The whole truth being said here must be felt to be understood. Then it is as if the secret of life has been given to us. Like a huge wave, it washes away the struggles and mysteries we have made for ourselves, and opens us up to the creative impulse of Spirit; an impulse that springs to life only through the individual.

We are life itself. It is that simple. Ruling forces bow down to those who are true individuals, not the other way around.

It is interesting how this cultural problem has shifted in the last 25 years. Today we see citizen action groups and consumer rights movements challenging the power of large institutions. Most organizations now realize the importance of listening to popular opinion and criticism. I think this is a sign that people are learning to communicate with the Over-Souls.

At the time I wrote this piece in my journal, a change was slowly dawning on me. Up to this point I felt as if I was following my own path. But this changed and I found myself with a growing sense of responsibility for the whole of life. I not only could understand and relate to the Over-Souls of groups and organizations as if they were individual beings, but I felt in touch with all of reality. Individuality was leading me into a closer connection with the universal.

It seemed that, as a Second initiate, I had stepped off the path of humanity. I left behind the hold that the world had over me through culture and group consciousness. As a Third initiate, however, I began to see that behind organizations, institutions and other hierarchies there was a deeper and more eternal truth. At each stage, it was the Inner Master who made this realization possible. It seemed as if he was the force in my life that opened the doors to these secrets and guided my feet on the path to greater freedom. The subtle influence of this inner spiritual teaching consciousness, which I call the Inner Master, gradually became clearer to me.

Looking back, I can see another significant change taking place. The path during this third leg of the journey seemed to start narrowing down. I discovered that it became more and more important to choose my words and actions carefully if I wanted to stay aligned with Spirit and where it was leading me. Every choice I made became important, and I needed to choose consciously to continue following this inner teaching.

It is strange how the path seems to taper to a singular focus. I have seen students leave because of this. They could not go beyond this stage. They wouldn't give up the idea that all paths are equal and, therefore, there is no need to choose one. But for me, committing to just one became necessary at this stage. The path became like a razor's edge for a while, until it opened back up again.

This phase of the path reminds me of the man on his journey to a foreign country, who found himself facing a deep wide river blocking his way. He began searching for a way across.

Eventually, he discovers a small row boat tucked behind some bushes and decides this is a perfect solution. It is as if God sent him this gift. He gets into the boat and starts rowing across. Then suddenly he stops.

He starts to feel guilty, since this small boat is good for only one person, and as soon as he gets to the other side, no one else will be able use it to cross the river. Using the boat feels selfish. So, he turns back.

Searching further down the banks of the river, he sees a group of people building a bridge. "Perfect," he says. "This is the right way of crossing the water, since others can use it as well." So, he joins in their task and becomes a bridge builder.

Once the bridge is nearly complete, however, he begins to have misgivings again. After spending months in construction, the bridge no longer seems natural. It feels man-made, and not the way that God would have intended. So, he abandons the effort.

Wandering along the banks of the river, he finds logs that have washed ashore. "I'll build a raft," he says. "I'll use driftwood the river delivers. Nothing could be more natural. And I will attach a rope to pull the raft back, so that others can use it after me."

He works for weeks until his project is almost finished, when he once again feels something is not quite right. "The spiritual path is an individual path," he says to himself. "I need to cross the river on my own." So, he dives into the river and begins swimming across.

It soon becomes clear that this man will never get across. He is too caught up in ideals to choose one path and stick with it. Until his desire for the goal becomes more important than all his considerations, he will never cross the river.

It is strange how single-mindedness becomes a step we must take before reaching universal awareness.

This realization showed me the commitment I needed to make to the Inner Master. It became personal. Only after this realization could I see how this spiritual consciousness was leading and opening up the path for me. It was an inner current guiding me much the same way as Over-Souls guide animals and cultures. But there was a big difference: I was being led knowingly into a growing awareness that moved me out from under the influence of the Over-Souls. Even more importantly, the Master was showing me the greater role I could play in the universal hierarchies of life. I began to see how my own thoughts were touching and reaching out into the streams of creation that unfold the world. This came to me as a gift from the Inner Teacher once I made my commitment to help in the Master's work.

Dropping the Intellectual Mind

My notebooks up until this time were filled with threads of intellectualizing. I continued off-and-on trying to solve certain problems through mental analysis. It generally didn't work too well, although it did sometimes clarify my thoughts. I sensed that I was missing some very big secret, but this would only cause me to think more about it. I would try to use my writing as a sort of oracle to show me what I wanted to learn.

Through a series of experiences, including the ones I've described above, I gradually began seeing the mistake I was making. I had been trying to use philosophy to solve life's problems, but in fact I was only distancing myself from life when I did so. Life is something to live. By taking responsibility we become a part of Life. Life is not some idea or illusion to make disappear by a trick of the mind, as some New Age teachers have suggested. It is something real to live and care for.

The following story describes the kind of transformation this realization brought. The story is a mixture of fiction and real inner experiences woven together to capture the essence of what I was going through. It didn't exactly happen to me all at once, as in this story, but when the realization finally dawned on me, the impact was the same. There is no question at all that I was a changed person after this.

The Night Philosophy Died

A cold wind blew through my body as gray pillows of clouds cast their shadows over the figure of Rebazar Tarzs, who stood before me in the vastness of the Himalayas. His face was firm, his coal black eyes peaceful and serene. His words were short.

"Philosophy means nothing to those who have seen the higher worlds."

Then silence…cold silence that strained at me.

Why? My thoughts felt scattered, as if there was nothing to hold them together.

"But what about the higher worlds?" I asked. "The worlds of God?"

The ageless spiritual Master looked beyond me. "They are there for each to discover for themselves," he said.

This was the only answer I got, and it was the same reaction I received from the gray-haired Master, Fubbi Quantz, guardian of the Katsupari Monastery in northern Tibet. All the inner masters I knew ignored my questions.

Abruptly, Rebazar Tarzs' last words reached me, "I have nothing more to say to you until you are rid of the lower self!"

What had I done?

Totally dejected, I left, wondering what worse could happen. Where were the penetrating discourses on life I was used to, or the invitations to journey into the inner worlds? What had I done?

My philosophy felt riddled with holes. Somehow my life had become too confused. It haunted me and here, when I turned for help...only rejections.

It didn't stop there, either. I began getting a cold reception at home. At work, my job was falling to pieces. I wondered if I needed to look somewhere else for my income. Even my friends had nothing to say, and worse—I felt I had nothing to give!

It was as if the world had abandoned me and my inner self was in the midst of a raging storm. I knew something had to be done.

There was no one else to turn to for answers but myself, and knowing that I had given up self-pity the moment I began my search for God, I decided there was no other recourse but the spiritual exercises. By God, I would storm the higher worlds if need be!

If my life was falling apart; I would force my way in. I needed some answers!

Fortunately, it came easier than I expected. It seems as if I only had to start doing something for myself. Using the imaginative technique for Soul Travel, I found myself expanded beyond my body consciousness. I seemed to be in some strange nondescript realm, where the colors were completely purple-red of hue and nothing else of distinction existed.

Then a man appeared. His ruby red eyes flashed in the ethers. His dark wine colored robe flowed in the purple mist. "Tonight I kill philosophy!" he suddenly said, speaking to me directly. "In one fine slash I will cut philosophy to its minuscule size!"

(I later found out this stranger was one of a secret band, called the Rhanktor, whose job it was to maintain the centers of things. It is their belief that life tends away from its center and loses itself.)

I waited for this intruder to explain himself further, but after a few moments I could see he was waiting for me to respond.

"Why should you do that?" I asked. "I haven't asked for your advice."

"Hah!" he bellowed. "You scour Tibet for the presence of Rebazar Tarzs. You trek to Katsupari for a few words from Fubbi Quantz, and you tug at the coat strings of the inner masters for an answer. And now when you are handed truth you reject it!"

Thoughts returned of my troubles in the physical world. I remembered this was why I was here. It's amazing how soon one forgets. And it did seem he had heard of these Masters.

I decided to listen.

"When I speak about the origin of philosophy," he began, "then I also speak about its death. It is that simple.

"Man claims he is the creator of philosophy. It is childish stupidity! Philosophy comes from the elements. It can come from nowhere else!"

I listened and wondered, waiting for more—but that was it? How could it be? What did he mean?

Then I watched as he swung his arm in a wide circle and my vision began filling with symbols. At first I didn't know what they were, until I recognized them as the four elements: earth, water, air and fire.

They began mixing and swirling together in a cloud like a multicolored pool. Something was happening. Something seemed to be building in this energy vortex, when suddenly a shower of sparks came flying from the center, moving deep into space. I suddenly realized I was witnessing the creation of the physical universe!

Then, seeing deeper, there came images of farmers working fields; the earth element was shining in their faces. Pushing with their plows, the soil rippled furrows of rich dirt. Sweat stained their clothes and caked earth clung to their bodies. Their rhythm and steady plodding seemed the motion of the earth element itself. Working in the soil with their hands, their backs, their feet, somehow this soil became a part of them and their thinking.

And I could see a nation growing strong, with the stability and solid strength of this earth element.

But, it then started changing. The world I was watching began responding to a new element—water. I saw before me the streams and rivers rushing across the land where the men and women worked. The water element was there and it drew them. It beckoned them and they followed its call to the sea.

The waters pulled people out upon its rolling, fluid back and they came to like its motion, its restlessness. Their thinking and dreams became restless too, and they longed to travel farther out—to be lost upon this element that dissolved their heavy-rooted traditions. They drank from a new, far-reaching, ever-changing vision, the water element, and their philosophy changed and was built around it.

As the people traveled, I saw them meeting another element, always invisible, never containable. It swept across the seas and the land. Air left nothing untouched, and yet nothing could touch it.

No farmer could keep his farm from its raging storms, or hold onto its graceful breeze. No ship could stop its fierce winds, or travel without its helpful gusts. What was this element, air?

Men and women looked within, deep into their subconscious to understand—for that is where this element stirred them. Their moods rose and fell with the pressure changes of air. Their philosophy became like the weather, unpredictable and changing, rising high into the airy heights and deep into the misty valleys.

The world seemed to be woven from the threads of these elements; earth, water and air, and I watched as they swirled together in my vision. Suddenly, from their center, like a flame, came the fire element. The wonder of lightning. The sun's scorching light. Electricity, dazzling and sparking the minds of inventors. The power of the fire element surged like pure energy through the nerves of the nations.

Communication, projection and transportation changed the world. The houses came aglow with light, and it seemed as if their lives became lighter too. Traditional morals faded from mankind's philosophy, and with the sword of fire in their hands, people felt all things were conquerable. Everything could become known. The world's heritage and history, based on the previous elements, held no meaning next to this new power of the flaming fire element.

Now I could see where our world stood, and that the philosophies and thinking of the human race flowed from the elements. They grew from nothing but the elements. In philosophy there was nothing original at all.

My strange companion smiled at me. Then leaning forward, he whispered, "So you see, I have slayed the whole of philosophy in one easy stroke!"

"But what of Plato?" I asked. "I know little of the modern philosophers, but Plato and Socrates—I'm sure they found truth in the higher worlds!"

"And look what good it has done!" he answered with a wave of his hand. "The world still struggles to fight itself free of their great plans for governing people. Higher worlds, yes! They have elements of their own, higher in vibration, with their own philosophies...but no philosophy is worth one iota outside its own land!"

"You see?!! Plato should have left his vision where he found it!"

With that, the Rhanktor man vanished as quickly as he appeared.

Slowly, I found myself returning to the human consciousness. I sensed that my inner storm had passed, and all emotion had gone out of my struggle. I also felt empty, strangely alone. I realized how much philosophy had meant to me. Now it was gone forever. Wiped clean from my mind.

The world looked so simple now.

I heaved a sigh and looked out my bedroom window. I saw the trees swaying back and forth. A thin line of smoke curled up from a chimney nearby. The sound of cars and children playing came to me. My life was filled with these. Even the shadows and the silence—my world was but a tapestry of these elements.

What was philosophy, but emptiness? It now seemed to me more like a ruptured hole through which poured thoughts of escape, dead ideas and social conventions that tried to put Life in a box.

I suddenly felt whole.

I then knew that no idea lives unless it springs from within ourselves. No life is full, but from the light and sound of Spirit flowing out and flooding the elements of our world through our own work and effort.

I had turned to philosophy because I felt wounded by life. I wanted some formula to set me free from the whim of the world. I was afraid to let go and just be. I was afraid to just live.

But, now all that was gone and in the past. Philosophy lay limp and dead before me like a puppet after the hand is removed.

I filled my lungs with the air element and felt good. Then something came tugging my attention to the inner worlds. A moment later, the image of Rebazar Tarzs entered my vision. It seems he was waiting for me.

Humor danced across his dark eyes. "The seeker who looks only for Life goes far in the spiritual works," he said to me. "The man who is earthbound struggles with traditions of the whole human race. And so the epitaph reads: Under the weight of centuries, philosophy has crumbled. From the light of God, Soul will triumph!

"But listen to me. You are not going to convince anyone of this. They must find it out for themselves!"

The hold that philosophy had over me was broken. I felt freed of it, and the world now seemed a little less certain, but more alive and real.

Spiritual knowledge means nothing outside of the way we put it into action. I feel sorry for those who think they can study spiritual truths without practicing them. What can be learned from that? I think the whole of the Universal Teachings comes to us from living consciously, and can only be applied for the purpose of a more conscious life. Such wisdom should never be confused with mere intellectual learning, because true wisdom comes through work and experience.

I wrote in my notebooks:

Man spends too much time reviewing mind pictures. In fact, he is lost in them. When he looks at a mountain, he does not see the mountain. When he looks at a road, he does not see the road. Every day, when he meets with people, he does not see who they really are, but sees only his own ideas of them as bankers, children, friends, policemen, enemies, mothers and fathers.

This is the problem with intellectual ideas. He does not see God's hand behind these realities. He does not see Spirit pouring through each in a unique manner, moving in ITS Divine Way to remind all life of that which is beyond all conception.

The scientific approach of objective observation does not work past a certain point on the spiritual path simply because this practice requires splitting ourselves into two parts: One part is the observer and the other part becomes the object of observation. But this does not work in the universal consciousness of the Causal plane and above, because the substance of that world is all of One Mind. To understand It, we must become of One Mind with it. We must see FROM it, not think of it.

This is one of the problems our academic education has created for us. We have been trained in a form of mental knowledge that is separate from our own being. We think we are gaining in intelligence with such scientific and philosophic thinking, but we are also losing the wholeness of ourselves. This is why children and people who live simpler lives can often catch the meaning of the spiritual teachings faster than intellectuals.

For me, a person who loved science, mathematics and philosophy, the lesson was a difficult one. I had the mistaken idea that knowledge was somehow disconnected from what I did with it. As if wisdom could simply be given out or learned through academic study. Old habits die hard.

The Greatness Factor

About the same time that I had started writing my first article on the Over-Souls of the Human Race, as a Second Initiate, I had also started wondering about something I called the "greatness factor." It was not fame that I was thinking about, but the ability of some people to influence our world. They have changed things in a universal way. However, just like my article on Over-Souls, I could not solve what was behind the riddle of this greatness factor until I became a citizen of the Causal Plane. Then I realized that this is simply the way of life in that dimension.

This took a long time to sink in, and the understanding came gradually by exploring clues that seemed to hold hints. One of these insights came as I began reading about the life of Nikola Tesla.

At the time, very little was written about the man. He was hardly even mentioned in most books about great inventors or leaders of technology. So here was a man who history had forgotten and fame had bypassed, but he still had this factor that I was wondering about.

So I decided to make a deeper study of his life. It ended up in the following article I wrote.

Looking back, I can see that Nikola Tesla was one of the first people to begin working with the fire element. This just occurred to me after re-reading *The Night Philosophy Died*. The philosophy of our world changed as our culture began to feel the influence of this element. Tesla helped pave the way.

While researching this article, I was given permission to access Tesla's private notebooks and photographs of his experiments at the San Francisco Public Library, where a special collection on Tesla was kept under lock and key. All the quotes I used in my article are words taken from actual recorded conversations, lectures or published papers:

Nikola Tesla—Forgotten Genius

"Tesla," said Thomas Alva Edison, the scientist, "I'm not interested in your alternating currents. There is no future in them. You are wasting your time!"

This is an actual quote.

Looking back to that historical meeting, we can see how near-sighted "the greatest inventor of our times" appeared next to Nikola Tesla.

Tesla had, in one flash of vision while walking with a friend in Budapest, invented the complete alternating current system, which has brought in our mass production age and our era of electrical wonders. His system included motors, generators and transformers still found in every home and business today. Yet it took Edison and a team of researchers nearly twenty years to perfect just the single filament of his incandescent bulb!

Tesla's inventions not only changed the world, but with the stunning beauty of nearly perfect efficiency. Compare the Tesla generator with an efficiency of 90% (even today one of the best in the engineering field) to Edison's bulb, with an atrocious 5% efficiency. That means Edison's filament of twenty years work wastes over 95% of its energy!

Here, then is a look into the mysterious, strange and enigmatic life of Nikola Tesla.

In 1888, Tesla presented his alternating current system to the scientific fraternity. Three years later he began startling the world with what seemed to be electrical miracles. His 1891 lectures describe high voltage sparks, sheets of electrical flame and brilliant tubes of electrical fire that he thrust about like swords. Tesla then passed hundreds of thousands of volts through his body to light a lamp or melt a wire, to prove that high frequency current could be used safely.

Let's visit a Tesla lecture and listen in on a transcript of his actual words.

The small theater, seating perhaps 200, is dimly lit by candles and gas lamps. The audience is silenced in anticipation, as a tall man in a black tuxedo strides onto stage amidst an assortment of bewildering apparatus.

"As in nature, all is ebb and tide," he begins, "all is wave motion, so it seems that in all branches of industry alternating currents—electrical wave motion—will have the sway...

"We wind a simple ring of iron with coils, we establish the connections to the generator, and with wonder and delight we note the effects of strange forces which we bring into play, which allow us to transform, to transmit and direct energy at will. We arrange the circuits properly, and we see the mass of iron and wires behave as though it were endowed with life...

"Here is a simple glass tube from which the air has been partially exhausted. I take hold of it; I bring my body in contact with a wire conveying alternating currents of high potential, and the tube in my hand is brilliantly lighted. In whatever position I may put it, wherever I may move it in space, as far as I can reach, its soft pleasing light persists with undiminished brightness.

"Here is an exhausted bulb suspended from a single wire. Standing on an insulated support, I grasp it, and a platinum button mounted in it is brought to vivid incandescence.

"Here, attached to a leading wire, is another bulb, which as I touch its metallic socket, is filled with magnificent colors of phosphorescent light...

"Here again...I bring my body in contact...with the end of a wire many miles long—and you see streams of light break forth from its distant end, which is set in violent vibration...

"Is there, I ask, can there be, a more interesting study than that of alternative currents?"

To listen to Tesla's words is to be entranced by the power of his vision. And what vision he had! There is hardly an element of electricity, even today, which he did not foresee, predict, and even discover himself.

He invented every essential of modern radio before Marconi, radar 40 years before its use, and modern neon and fluorescent lighting. He demonstrated the first remote control by wireless, and discovered microwaves. He also discovered cosmic rays 30 years before they were "discovered," as well as X-rays. He created artificial earthquakes that shook New York City. He created bolts of lightning over 135 feet long. He began the "race of robots" and computers, and he discovered the principles of laser light.

Of honors, he received few, and the reason is simple. Tesla's inventions were too far ahead of his world. Man can only change so fast. He will reject what he is not ready for.

The question we ask, then, is: Was this man a superhuman wizard, as some have proposed? Where did his amazing ideas and inventions come from? And how with all his success could he be an unknown today? Perhaps this story can now be clearly explained. Perhaps we can now see the magnificent principles that Tesla used—and that we too can use these same methods in our own lives.

Tesla knew three things. First of all, he knew where his ideas came from. Secondly, he could SEE his inventions with his imagination before they existed, and third, he knew the process by which he could make these inventions a practical part of this world. There is so much to all of Tesla's life, we walk away in awe. But if we recognize these three principles, then we can also walk away with something we can use.

In all of Tesla's writings and lectures, he repeatedly stresses one single point, yet it is this same point which has been continually overlooked, ignored and even disputed. Thus, it is no wonder that Tesla remains a mystery.

"The recognition of the existence of ether," he said in 1891, "and of the functions it performs, is one of the most important results of modern scientific research...it has been a great step towards the understanding of the forces of nature and...it has been for the enlightened student of physics what the understanding of the mechanisms of the firearm or of the steam engine was for the barbarian."

So, it is the ether upon which he places such importance. The ether, which scientists now consider a useless superstition—and yet Tesla bases his whole understanding of electricity upon this one principle. Who is right?

Well, he knew something other scientists didn't. That when he shifted his state of consciousness to the state where he could see ether as a reality, then the whole heart of electricity became visible as well. Energy then turned into something he could feel and become familiar with. He could then see the characteristics of electricity that inspired his ideas for inventions.

Tesla knew where his ideas came from: "from a primary substance or a tenuity beyond conception, filling all space, the Akasa, or luminiferous ether..." Call it what you will, the fabric of energy, the element of electricity, the essence of light, but from this substance all his ideas and inventions sprang!

What Tesla did, then, and no one has yet given him this proper credit, was to open the doors of electricity for our world. It is indeed curious that up to this time scientists had tried again and again to make electricity a practical commodity with not much success. Edison's bulb, a few limited D.C. motors, and the telephone were about all that resulted. It was slow going. But after Tesla opened these doors and showed the vision he saw within the ether, we can see electrical inventions suddenly springing up everywhere.

"I am not an inventor," Tesla would say, "I am a discoverer of new principles." In fact, he felt so strongly about this that when he was offered to share the Nobel Prize with Edison for their electrical inventions, Tesla turned the award down!

He showed the world that all things have their own vibration, and by tuning into that vibration a building can be brought to ruins, a tube of gas made to glow, or a message sent around the globe. The key to all nature is that it always exists in oscillation—in alternating currents. This ceaseless motion of electricity surrounds us all and is a part of all physical things, riding on an ocean of ether just as waves ride on the sea.

Now we come to the most amazing facet of Nikola Tesla; his powers of visualization. His imaginative faculty was so vivid that he says he physically saw his inventions before him, and only when he reached out his hand could he tell they were not real. He would put his motors together, piece by piece, turn them on, let them run for a week, take them apart to see how the parts were worn—all with his imagination!

This was how he could produce so much in one lifetime, because when he built his test model he knew it would work the first time, and it always did. When he built his laboratory at Colorado Springs, he knew he might want to generate as much as a hundred million volts! He made no physical tests. He simply visualized his huge coil and every precaution he might need. When the lab was finally built and the switch was thrown, sparks up to 135 feet long flew out from the tower. Everything worked perfectly—except the power company that supplied Tesla's lab could not take such a surge in electricity. It burned out two generators! Tesla and his crew made all the repairs.

Tesla was not concerned with the mathematical formulas or theories. He said he would leave those to others more able than he. But he knew that visualization is always much more complete than theories. It sees things that formulas will never see.

As Paul Twitchell writes in his book, *The Far Country*: "...continuous imagination is sufficient for all things and all my reasonable plans and actions will never make up for my lack of continuous imagination." This is the second principle which made Tesla's inventions a success.

The third and final principle that Tesla knew, clearing up the mystery surrounding his life, was how to take what is in the imagination and make it a practical part of this world. This final principle has been overlooked to the detriment of countless good ideas.

Tesla had an unending flow of fascinating ideas, but he knew he could not simply go out and tell everyone. When he announced his invention of the "death-ray" (laser) which if aimed at the moon would produce a glowing circle only a few meters wide, yet bright enough for the naked eye to see on Earth—no one believed him. So, Tesla had to pick those ideas, and present them in a way that the world could accept.

Even then, Tesla had a tough time. When he stunned a crowd in Madison Square, in 1898, with his remote control of a model ship, everyone immediately thought of this as a powerful new war weapon, a wireless torpedo. Tesla answered this sharply: "You do not see there a wireless torpedo, you see the first of a race of robots, mechanical men which will do the laborious work of the human race!"

Tesla went on about his robots in an article printed in Century Magazine. "I propose to show that, however impossible it may now seem, an automaton may be contrived which will have its 'own mind' and by this I mean that it will be able, independently of any operator, left entirely by itself, to perform, in response to external influences affecting its sensitive organs, a great variety of acts and operations as if it had intelligence...In fact I have already conceived of such a plan!"

Tesla did not stop with big new visions, although he did propose such unbelievable ideas as lighting up the whole Earth's atmosphere as if it were one giant bulb—he was also the first to patent the household fan, and the electric clock. When he discovered microwaves he proposed the medical profession would find them useful.

In 1896, when he created a real earthquake larger than any natural recorded quake ever to shake New York City, he merely replied, "It was caused, quite unexpectedly, by a little piece of apparatus you could slip in your pocket." From there he went on to open the whole field of seismology, when he stated that ore deposits, oil fields and ships at sea could be located by the same vibratory means.

In every case, Tesla did not stop with his understanding of electricity or even with his inventions. He put them all together into a package that was a vivid demonstration people could understand. He gave it a touch of his vision, and he made it look so practical it had to succeed!

So now we come back to the question that has been nagging us—if he was such a success, why did he die penniless? Why is he almost an unknown today? Why was he never given the credit he was due?

The answer is a lonely one and a simple one. Nikola Tesla was a genius bringing countless wonders of electricity to a people who had just learned the word. He was using the principles of imagination and the previous unknown laws of ether currents to open a new field of thought and a new world. In return, he was granted the most beautiful visions of the future and more raw power than one man had ever wielded before.

Thomas Edison may not have compared to Tesla's genius, but he was one of the greatest organizers of men. He inspired a spirit of determination which brought success, so that all his workers cheered and said, "We did it!" Everyone else, meanwhile, pointed to Edison and said, "He did it!"

It is always the leaders of men who gain fame, just as it is the leaders and controllers of money who gain wealth. Thus, Tesla may have left this world penniless, but he was paid in the coin of another realm, and he left richer in spirit than many men will ever know.

After writing this article, it dawned on me how all the great advancements in science and religion, art and literature, and all the developments of mankind have come through someone. That is the only way such changes could enter this world. Everything the human race has produced comes first through someone inspired by a discovery within. This is how truth flows from the inner worlds into the physical, and I too was acting as a channel for this force, in a small way, by writing about it.

The saints and Masters who visit our world are the ones who open the doors of spiritual understanding. They each bring with them something different, a unique quality that becomes invisibly embedded into our culture. Now I could also see that it was not just the Masters, but that each of us brings some individual element into the world. We all add our own note to the symphony, through our life and awareness.

It is the self-recognition of this principle that transforms it into something meaningful.

Writing this article about Tesla would end up influencing my life in unexpected ways. Within a few years I would embark on a new career in electronics. I wondered if I could apply the techniques I had written about. Today I have over 20 patents, with 5 more on the way. My inventions have been used in over 20 million products sold. I just left my job as the Chief Technology Officer for a billion dollar business to help launch a business based on a new technology. I learned a lot from Tesla.

Looking back through my research notes, I ran across an interesting quote. It came from a book on Tesla's life, called, *Prodigal Genius*, by John J. O'Neill. I scribbled down the following words spoken by Tesla directly to the author of the book. It is interesting how his story so closely parallels what I was experiencing with animals at the time. No wonder Tesla's life seemed to resonate with me:

> I have been feeding pigeons, thousands of them, for years; thousands of them, for who can tell...
>
> But there was one pigeon, a beautiful bird, pure white with light gray tips on its wings; that one was different. It was a female. I would know that pigeon anywhere.
>
> No matter where I was that pigeon would find me; when I wanted her I had only to wish and call and she would come flying to me. She understood me and I understood her.
>
> I loved that pigeon. Yes, I loved that pigeon. I loved her as a man loves a woman, and she loved me. When she was ill I knew, and understood; she came to my room and I stayed beside her for days. I nursed her back to health. That pigeon was the joy of my life. If she needed me, nothing else mattered. As long as I had her, there was a purpose in my life.
>
> Then one night as I was lying in my bed in the dark, solving problems, as usual, she flew in through the open window and stood on my desk. I knew she wanted me; she wanted to tell me something important, so I got up and went to her.

159

As I looked at her I knew she wanted to tell me—she was dying. And then, as I got her message, there came a light from her eyes—powerful beams of light. Yes, it was a real light, a powerful, dazzling, blinding light, a light more intense than I had ever produced by the most powerful lamps in my laboratory.

When that pigeon died, something went out of my life. Up to that time I knew with a certainty that I would complete my work, no matter how ambitious my program, but when that something went out of my life I knew my life's work was finished.

Yes, I have fed pigeons for years; I continue to feed them, thousands of them, for after all, who can tell...

Everything Falls Apart

Just as it seemed that I was beginning to get an insight into the powers of the Causal Plane, my whole inner world began to unravel. It started subtly at first with doubts creeping into my thoughts. Something didn't seem quite right. It was an inner feeling I had. I had the sense that I was missing something important, but I couldn't figure out what the problem was.

Around this time I had a dream with Paul Twitchell that I entered into my journal:

Paul was very friendly and even helped me with the house work I was doing, while we talked. He picked up some dead light bulbs and shook them to make them work again.

"No person is transparent," he said.

I knew what he was talking about. I had been thinking that at times I found myself in a state where everything I did seemed right, as if some current was just flowing through me into the world. It was like being transparent to Spirit, and I had been trying to work to attain this state more often.

"Then, how does a person care for his responsibilities or the way he treats other people?" I asked.

"Exactly the way you just said it," he answered.

In other words, everything should be done consciously as a part of taking care of our responsibilities. These things should not be left to some inner force to take care of for us.

In my search for the greatness factor, I had thought that being transparent to Spirit was the underlying answer. It was not the people, themselves, who were great, but this spiritual current from the higher God worlds flowing down through them that brought something great into this world. This was my theory, but Paul's words showed me that I had something wrong. No one should try to be transparent to Spirit. We must always retain our individuality and responsibilities.

The more I thought about what Paul told me in the dream, the more I realized how often people turn to religion, spirituality and even philosophy to find a way out of responsibility. People hope that God will take care of them, or they can achieve wealth by thinking positively, or they can find the key to the mysteries of life through occult secrets. Some religions teach that becoming one with God solves all problems. Indeed, this is the very wisdom of the Causal Plane, and for the first time I realized this was also the illusion of the Causal Plane.

I had fallen for the oldest trap in the lower worlds. I had taken up the adventure of trying to track down the mystery behind greatness, when in fact this was leading me in completely the wrong direction. I suddenly realized that greatness had nothing to do with spiritual truth. It was a trick of the mind. I had thought that spiritual greatness was somehow different because it was not about ego and personality, but about the spiritual currents of creation. I could now see that creation, itself, was a blinding force built on ego.

I began to understand the problem I was creating. It was just like the lesson I had learned on the Astral Plane. Feeling as if I was on top of the world affected those around me and made them feel worse. Greatness had the same effect on the Causal Plane.

From the moment I began my spiritual search I was determined to make decisions carefully. I wanted to avoid the dangers of getting caught up in beliefs without verifying them for myself. I tried not to fall into egotism and spiritual vanity, which I had seen so often. I didn't want to have a single blemish, but I had been caught in an age old illusion. How could I have let this happen? It was a blow to my ego. Seeing this, I realized that watching my ego die was in fact a good thing.

Anyone who believes they can walk the spiritual path and not make blunders is fooling themselves. That's the first thing I had learned. I had been facing in completely the wrong direction. Now I realized how little

I really knew. I felt like a failure, but also realized for the first time that I was seeing things truly.

Everything in my inner worlds seemed to fall apart. What could I trust? I thought I'd been growing spiritually, but now I wondered if I had only been growing in ego and vanity. The depths to which this error reached shocked me. It was something that seemed to stretch across hundreds of lifetimes. It had become a foundation of my world. I had been following this illusion for a long time.

The people of the human race are often caught up in the streams of creational powers, generally unaware of how they are being used to play out a drama. I too had been caught in this trap, but now wanted to get out of it.

Trying to recognize these forces and to gain the meaning of the self-recognition of them is what changes us from mere pawns into awakened individuals who can change our own course and free ourselves from external powers. However, the spiritual path is not the path of greatness. In fact, it is the path of obscurity. The light of greatness entices us away from who we are into an adventure that belongs to the world, not to Soul.

Waking up is not easy because we must recognize how little we really know.

The following is a story I wrote at this time. It reflects the lessons I was going through. It starts out like the classic mythical adventures of good against bad, but don't be fooled by this. I thought I could look behind the age-old force of this world, as if to wrench the secret from the gods. But suddenly, the story turned more personal than I expected. It ended up hitting much closer to home and showed me the trap I had been caught in for ages. Just like my experiences on the path, I suddenly realized how little I knew and what a hostage to the fortunes of the lower worlds I had become. The lesson was not the one I expected.

The Jewel of Kali

Sleep was coming quickly as the last waves of my awakened consciousness were slipping out like an undertow into the ocean of spirit. Suddenly I felt an unmistakable tapping on my shoulder, and in a snap I was out of my body.

162

It was Glistar, a friend and spiritual traveler whom I had met one day in a way station, a crossing point between this physical world and the invisible planes. He had just returned from a journey into a forbidden area of the inner worlds on a mission to influence the acceptance of spiritual Truth in this world. He had been trying to alter the fate of how spiritual teachings have been treated on this planet. His clothing was made of a strange green cloth that had a shimmer of what seemed to be gold thread woven through it. His light brown hair was cropped short. His eyes were afire.

"Tonight," he said, breaking the silence, "we have a chance to see the jewel of Kali!"

Dark shadows ran through the room and a shiver crept across my consciousness. "Why such eerie greetings?" I asked.

"We live in a time when everything is breaking up," he explained. "A grand crime is ruining this world. Kali, the goddess of pleasure, has bought the souls of millions and is using them to extend her life. The innocence of this planet is being stolen!

"So, tonight, if Spirit is with us, we will penetrate the secret to her power—the Jewel—and perhaps influence the course of destiny!"

"But is it dangerous?" I asked.

"Of course it's dangerous. Even we are not outside her wiles. It could mean our freedom throughout eternity! But that won't stop us..." He made a step towards the window and vanished. I quickly followed, not wanting to lose him.

Leaves of images, like pages, flew past me suddenly. I felt the protective aura of Spirit swirling around, but glancing back...for a moment...a feeling of evil swept over me. Something dark and ominous followed. Then, just as suddenly, it was gone.

Movement stopped. We were crouched in the shadows of a headstone. The moonlight was dim. Its pale light swam across the cemetery. I looked out across hundreds of graves as far as I could see. The sickening feeling of trapped souls brought shudders across my back.

"These," Glistar whispered, "are souls that Kali has snared in her powerful web of illusion. Look!" He pointed to the center of the cemetery, where a black chamber flickered from the light of torches. "Her jewel is in there!"

Thoughts of Kali, the Hindu Goddess of destruction came in pieces through my memory. She is the idol of the sex cults and masochistic sacrifices. She is depicted with six arms, her hair is made of snakes, and around her neck hangs a necklace of skulls. She is the force of destruction embodied, yet so much of the world worships her without knowing.

She destroys, yet she is also the pleasure goddess. She is the embodiment of seduction, and the source of sexual desire. Therefore all life seems to come through her. She gives birth to life and then entraps what she has created. The entire world believes that finding the Kali is finding pleasure, and it is only she whom all seekers seek. All of this is her illusion.

Suddenly my thoughts were jerked back to the present and all my senses were alert. A dark shadow filled my vision again, but was gone so fast I wondered... what was that?

"The searchlight of Kali," said Glistar. "We may have been spotted. Proceed with caution."

Stone by stone we approached the dark chamber, crossing a strange world. It was a place without life. The trees had no leaves, the wind no sound and the earth was a cold chill. It was an abandoned land. Slowly we crossed it.

Just then, Glistar tapped my shoulder and pointed to the chamber. A black iron door was opening and out of it came the Kali. She was a terrible figure shrouded in black lace. Only her head of snakes was visible in the dim light. Music and the beat of a drum came through the door and pounded at the pit of my stomach. A hiss rushed out like the wind, cutting into my nerves with an electric current.

"She leaves to give her monthly offering of blood with the full moon" said Glistar. "She demands it of all women, for she cannot escape this karma, herself.

"Now is our chance, but be careful!"

Silently we slipped toward the door as Kali passed away into the shadows. The entrance was slightly ajar. When we walked in, only our footsteps echoed through the room. Inside was completely black, but for a dim glow escaping through a box. We both stared. My heart pounded harder.

"That box contains the Jewel of Kali," Glistar explained. "But take only a glimpse, then we must go. Remember, don't be fooled by illusion!"

He lifted the lid carefully and a bright light spread out from the box with a sound; a hollow sound, empty like a vacuum. It drew me closer. Then I saw what it was: a lotus flower with six petals of white, red, blue and changing colors that gleamed like an iridescent shell. Its light flooded me with pleasures that have slept for unknown ages within me. This was what I have sought all my lives. What all the saviors and all great men have longed for. This was it!

Then, a great force climbed up my spine and flared like fire in my brain. Glistar tugged at my shirt. "Let's go," he said, looking around as he spoke. "I've got a bad feeling..."

Blackness suddenly filled the room. A sickening feeling of evil penetrated and rushed through my being. I wanted to destroy it. I wanted to destroy everything just to get rid of it.

Then came the most merciless laugh. It was the Kali. Her mocking laughter rang off the walls and through the thick air of the small chamber. I couldn't tell where the sound came from. It seemed to be a part of the dark room itself.

"Glistar, we've . . ." I looked to find my friend, but he was gone. Kali's cackle spun me around.

"You look for your naive friend?" Kali's voice goaded me, echoing from every direction.

"Where is he?" I demanded.

"Look outside, idiot—a fresh gravestone stands!" Her howling exploded, and right then I wanted to rip her apart . . . all six ghastly arms.

"You can't do that!" I shouted. "He was a spiritual traveler."

She roared all the louder. "He was an egotistical adventure seeker," she said. "He has been after me for years and now I've got him." Her laughter reverberated throughout the chamber.

Then I saw again the box that contained her jewel: Her priceless jewel—her power and life source. I rushed at it and ripped the lid off. I wanted to crush it out of existence.

But as I saw its light, another thought hit me. "The jewel is the secret to her power," Glistar had said. It was that secret I needed . . . not to destroy it. Or else Glistar, what remained of Glistar, might go with it. It was the secret I needed . . . and I was going to have it!

The laughter of Kali subsided as soon as the lotus was uncovered. Light from the box spread out into the room and her awful shadow was gone. In the silence I heard a soft sound of feet approaching. I looked toward the entrance hoping to see Glistar . . . expecting to see Glistar at any moment . . . but instead a beautiful woman entered!

She was the most beautiful woman I had ever seen. Her tawny brown hair hung loosely over her shoulders and a small athletic figure, perfectly proportioned. She was dressed in a pure white flowing dress. It seemed too white for the room. Her eyes were big and soft, deep blue, and her face clear and vibrant.

Her warmth and beauty took me by surprise—in such a place—yet my first instinct was to challenge her.

"I won't leave this jewel until I've got what I want!"

She smiled and her eyes lit up, as if I had said the most endearing words.

"My jewel," she spoke softly, almost coyly, "is for any who would wish to know its pleasures. I'm glad you've come."

I was shocked and stunned. She was the Kali! Impossible! She was too beautiful.

"What have you done with Glistar?" I said.

165

"Your handsome friend left of his own accord," she answered. "He wanted nothing to do with me. But I'm happy you chose otherwise."

Her voice enchanted me and her eyes told of excitement. But, was she telling the truth? Was I being lured by her inescapable beauty? She seemed everything a woman could be...

Kali walked to me and softly took her jewel's lid from my hand. She was so gentle I couldn't object, and seeing her close made my heart pound hard. A growing sensation began to fill me...and I thought back to the black searchlight of Kali. Somehow it was similar, but now I both wanted and didn't want this strong desire.

"Let's walk in the moonlight," Kali said, lifting up my hand. "The moods of nighttime enchant me."

I said yes, but wanted to say no at the same time. The touch of her skin was like fire to my senses and something in all of this scared me. Was this my desire?

Kali's arm slipped around my waist and I hoped she would never let go. Her head leaned against my chest, while the moonlight shimmered upon her wonderful hair. The breathing of her small frame flowed through me...

Something deep within was screaming NO!!! Some deep part of me was crying out to be heard. Love is one thing but this was not me! Pleasures flooded my senses—but I was battling for my existence!

Her lips reached out and met mine and there was nothing, nothing in all the worlds that could resist. She was all desire, all pleasure, and any struggle was but the fire of her love. I was lost in her web, and yet it was all my own.

She was not quite something external any longer and this tugged at me deeply. It reached right into the core of my being. The Kali had become a part of me!

I was the Kali! She laughed and it came like my own laughter. I struggled and yet it was only her struggle. She was within me, a part of me—my own universe.

Suddenly the voice of the hideous Kali screamed. "You fool! You know nothing! You've the intelligence of a worm slithering across the earth. Dare you enter the chamber of Kali? Did you think you could escape alive?! The maze of Kali's illusions can never be thwarted!"

Yet who was she fighting but herself?

I felt the touch of her black shawl upon my skin and knew it was no lace cloth, but a web of illusion itself. And yet it was all MY illusion.

My illusion...it had always been my own illusion. The thought made me sick.

I had fought the whole battle against myself! All the ugliness—all the

166

lust—it was all mine. I had only externalized the whole thing because I couldn't face my own self. I felt my world crumbling and a deep sadness welled up within me.

How long had I been projecting my sickness upon others, upon the world, so that all of life became so filled with evil that I became the hero and white knight who was right every time? How long had my life been so diseased? I looked down a long dark hall of lifetimes.

My world had been hidden from my own eyes. Now I saw it clearly, like a ship that was smashed upon a rock and rotted. I had not seen my life for what it was. Like a tattered rag caught on a branch in a raging storm, my world too was tattered and rotten. I didn't want it any longer. I wanted a new life... but what?

The Kali, the desires and passions, held me no longer. They had entered my world, but that world was now shattered. I felt like water that no hand could grasp. Now there was but one force to turn to—one essence to live upon. The ECK.

Then I looked away from the lotus—for all that had passed I had seen within the lotus—and Glistar was there standing beside me. It was good to see him.

"The message is simple," he said. "We must each know the powers that influence us. We must know the truth about this world and the invisible worlds. To be unknowing effect is a criminal offense against Soul!"

I knew our adventure was finished and I felt tied to Glistar by some strange and secret bond that I couldn't explain. My life would never be the same. I wondered when I would see him again.

Then my thoughts went to Kali. It's odd, I know, but I imagined she was standing before me—and looking into the lotus I saw she was there in all her beauty and ugliness. But now she stood quietly, watching.

"Where is your power now?" she asked suddenly.

"It is gone," I said. "I have none, nor can I ever have it again. My world is crushed."

She laughed loudly. "It was but my world you ever had! It was but my power! And now you find only sadness in your freedom!"

"Not sadness, Kali. It is weariness. I must rest."

A smile flickered upon her face. "It is my job, young one. I have lived for eons to tempt this world with power. Upon power it grows only to be crushed at its pinnacle for the desire of me! Rome burned from my touch. Ancient Greece, Egypt, China, all crumbled in my hands. No great man has resisted my art. Look! Napoleon, Hitler, Alexander the Great—all were but my toys! Do you not want such greatness?"

"No, Kali. I am only a man. I work and struggle like any other. Seek one who is worthy of such a deadly game."

Her gaze looked to the horizons, searching. She would find another…a thousand others. She would lay to ruin other empires and plant the seeds of vanity by the side of every worthy idea.

"None can leave my grasp unless I will it so!" she said out loud.

Then she turned and looked at me. But was that fatigue I saw in her eyes? Was that weariness? She looked at me and seemed to show the ages across her face. I knew then what it must be like to live on and on in a world of daydreams and loneliness.

"Farewell, young one. I will rest too someday…"

Then I saw something I will never forget. She began fading away, vanishing from where she stood into the mist, when from her aged eyes fell a single tear.

A pang struck my heart, for within that tear I saw a small reflection of true yearning for God—the most beautiful facet of a seeker's Soul. However, I knew, perhaps for eons, it would glisten too deep. It would lay asleep beneath a wild force of illusion.

"Now," said Glistar, startling me, "you have seen the real Jewel of Kali!"

This is why the greatest teachers warn us to search first for God before anything else. The path unfolds in a way that is not obvious. It is not the straight line we think it should be.

Shortly after this, I was fired from the Eckankar Office again. Darwin had prepared me for this. He explained it wasn't because of anything I had done. In fact, a few months later he would shut down the *ECK World News* where I had been working. However, for me it all came at the right time. It was time to step away from the organization.

I had a friend who also worked at the office then who I could talk to about the changes I was going through. His name was Harold Klemp. We had been close friends for many years. He was one person who never got caught up in the outer commotion that so often runs through organizations. Eckankar was no different. The worldly plans of Eckankar and the excitement of celebrities, like in any organization, can draw Soul away from Itself, in the opposite direction of truth. Harold would often marvel about the far reaching effects of vanity, especially spiritual vanity.

I described to him my new realizations and he made a comment I will never forget. He said, "Doug, the thing that is different about you is that when you realize you are wrong you admit it. You are willing to turn around 180 degrees and go in the opposite direction. That's rare."

It was a nice way of telling me that I was indeed the fool that I thought I was, but at least I was smart enough to figure it out.

I made the decision at this point in my life to start over in my study of the spiritual path. I went right back to the beginning; page one, chapter one, you might say, and was determined that this time I would catch the meaning of the true spiritual consciousness. Somehow I had gotten the wrong idea about the path. I had lost the thread, but now realized I needed to throw away everything I thought I had learned to find the unadorned Truth.

I didn't realize it at the time, but this was exactly what I needed to take another step. I was turning loose of the organizations, religion, philosophy, and all the other worldly forces that originate on the Causal Plane. They paint a picture of greatness, but a greatness that belongs to the world at the expense of Soul.

Just when I felt like I was nowhere, I had in fact learned the lesson I was supposed to learn.

By this point, however, I knew one thing: I wouldn't even try to guess what the next initiation might hold.

THE SMALLEST
OF THINGS

THIS IS A LITTLE SKETCH of some daily episodes that occurred over a week to our family of four (counting four-legged members.) It started as an exercise to stop and look at each day closely, to see how life unfolds moment by moment. I quickly discovered that especially in the smallest of things I could see the presence of a hidden intelligence. It proved to me that the spiritual path is not really about the grand earthshaking experiences. Rather it is so tightly woven with Life as to be inseparable.

· · • · ·

TODAY IS MONDAY, and the event of the day that stands out strongest for me is that the relationship with my son has healed. He is only 20 months old, but he sure can get stubborn. And when he gets stubborn, I get frustrated. But I feel that I have learned something important now, because we are able to do things together and have fun.

His name is Levan, and he just came up to hand me his toy key chain. Now, why did he do that? I know now that I must keep asking that question: Why won't he play his harmonica if I'm looking at him? Why does he like screwdrivers so much (he carries them around for hours on end)? Why, when he bumps his head against a wall by accident, will he go back and bump his head a couple times on purpose? I wonder about these things. They are like little doors I can peek through to see another world.

When I understand Levan, I get along with him better. But I also want him to understand me. So, today we washed the car. He had one brush and I had another. He worked right next to me, but when I came too close he would push me away...you know, keep out, this is MY area!

This seems to be a time in my life when relationships with people are very important to me. I'm glad Levan is here. He helps me learn what it all really means. No one could plan a college course better. He is a real gift, because I don't have to go search the world for the right teacher or the right book. It's all right here in my life—all 35½ inches of him...

. . ● . .

Tuesday.

Well, I got a phone call today, in fact just an hour ago, and it was a real blow to me. Someone called up to say that a freelance job I was scheduled to complete was being cancelled. This was a $3,000 to $4,000 project, and I was just starting to believe the money was already in the bank. So, when I hung up the phone, it was as if someone just pulled a plug and my emotions spilled all over the floor.

You know, if someone picks up a tuning fork and hits just the right note, it can shatter a pane of glass. Well, it doesn't always take a big tragedy to do the same thing to our emotions. It can be that little incident with just the right pitch, and there go our emotions in pieces all over the floor. It's an easy time to go into a real slump and depression. But I wasn't in the mood for that, so I let the experience happen and float away—just like how they used to dump garbage off ships at sea.

Actually, now that I think about it, I was somewhat prepared in advance for this disturbing news, which helped me handle it better. This morning I was attempting to do my daily spiritual contemplation, where I try to lift myself up and out of the human consciousness, beyond all its worries and desires. It's usually like 20 to 30 minutes of clear view from the mountaintops to see how to live a little closer to life. Or many times I might meet the Inner Master and make a personal journey with him.

But this morning was like some mornings. I wasn't having any luck. I tried two or three techniques for Soul Travel that I knew, but nothing was happening. I only sensed a subtle feeling to take it easy, don't try to tackle the whole universe today. Take a little vacation, and take it easy.

So, when I got that phone call I immediately knew what this little message meant. I sat there watching my emotions spreading out all over, and I thought—heck, I'm on vacation today. I'm just not in the mood to let this bother me.

174

I thought: If I were out on an ocean cruise, on a real vacation, I would just crumple up that nasty telegram with all the bad news and toss it out to sea. It would look so little out there, like a tiny dot bobbing up and down on the endless waves. I would breathe in a nice deep breath of sea air and say to myself: Yep, it's a good day to be on vacation; a good day to take it easy.

So, that's what I did today.

· · ● · ·

Wednesday.

Karen, my wife, came home with an interesting story from work today. It turns out that a friend of hers, Relly, was cleaning out the office refrigerator, enjoying the job, when in came a younger girl. After this girl saw the fridge almost empty, she suddenly got worried.

"Where's my lunch?" she asked. "Where is it? Where is my lunch?"

Well, Relly, being the rather mischievous sort, said with a perfectly straight face, "Oh, we threw it out." Then she went on to finish with the refrigerator.

Suddenly, the young girl began shaking and looked around nervously. "Come on, where is it? What happened to my lunch?!" the girl looked scared, very scared.

Relly became concerned now, realizing something serious must be involved. So, she pointed to the opposite counter and said, "It's probably over there. We're just cleaning out the old stuff."

Before the young girl even got to the counter, she said nervously, "It's not here! My lunch isn't here!" She was pale and shaking. Then she added, as if the world had just crumbled, "My Twinkies were in there!"

A few seconds later, she spotted the bag, grabbed it and left the office. Karen and Relly just stared at each other. Karen said, "She wasn't kidding, was she?"

"No," said Relly. "Someone ought to take those Twinkies away from her!"

It goes to show you that your neighbor might be a strapping 6' 5" muscle-bound brute who's afraid of no one, but take away his Twinkies and he could collapse like a big baby.

Strangely, I had a little experience today that fits in with this. I went to get one of my many notebooks (ask Karen, she'll tell you all about them) from the shelf in our closet. When I pulled it out a box fell down behind it. It got me a little peeved because I just wanted to grab the notebook quickly and it was going to be a mess reaching into the back of the closet.

175

So, in the process of reaching for the box, I knocked another box off the shelf...and now I was mad. It really bugged me. So I reached down, planning to throw the whole nuisance back where it came from and stomp out of the room—but when I picked up the box the contents spilled out all over the floor.

I just stood there and smiled, because I realized what I was doing. I had started with this little bit of impatience, you know, and had a pretty good rhythm going, until I worked it up into a regular monster. Why, if I kept it up for another hour, I could have easily leveled the whole house.

I'll bet wars start the same way. We don't need peace treaties; a yearly laughter conference would work just fine.

· · • · ·

Thursday.

Two days have passed without a replacement for that job I lost on Tuesday. So I've decided that if nothing turns up over the weekend, on Monday I'll just go out and start something else. What is important is that I don't get caught in any inertia.

I think inertia creeps up on us more than we like to think. Even kids, those boisterous balls of energy get caught in it. What makes it so difficult to get out of is that we know what we should do, but we don't have enough desire to do it. So, it's better to watch out before it happens.

You should have seen the change my father went through recently. He's been stuck in a job he'd outgrown for the last few years, but felt his obligations to the family were more important. Two weeks ago he decided to find another job, and now he's really excited about the idea. He's got the vitality and energy I remember when he was younger. Most important, he's got dreams of the future again, and the creative flow to see them accomplished.

I ran into this strange creature, inertia, about three years ago. A friend of mine had been out of work for almost four months. He couldn't find a job anywhere and he was getting bored and apathetic. He asked me what I thought he should do, but I didn't have any idea. So I told him I would do anything—get in trouble if I had to—just to get moving. With some momentum we start getting a flow of ideas, what is right and what is wrong to do, but the ideas only come after we start doing.

I'll never forget the way he changed in the next few days. He packed up and left town, and the next time I heard from him he sounded like a new man. He was a very creative person, but just stuck in this inertia.

By the way, there are some meditation techniques that are quite passive

176

and can lead to real problems with inertia. I find that I have to keep changing my approach with my spiritual exercises to be most successful. Spirit, which is a wave of ideas and inspiration we can travel on, is continually shifting and moving. This keeps me out of the inertia band, generally.

·   ·   •   ·   ·

Friday.

Today I write the true confession. Yes, I have to admit, I have been deceptive. You see, just half an hour ago I finished writing Thursday. I've been a day behind since Wednesday. But today is really today. I have given up my deceitful ways.

I would like to keep these little daily sketches interesting, a little different for each one. I've begun to enjoy these evening chats. I stop to think about what has happened during the day and I find a completeness about it that I hadn't noticed before. Life really isn't all so mixed up actually. When you look at all the little things you see the true subtleties, like a golden thread, running through the smallest events.

Levan and I walked up to the park today. You have to use a system of propulsion to go anywhere with him. Otherwise he stops to see every leaf, puddle, or pile of sand. So we took a tennis ball with us today. What we do is throw it forward and then go chase it. Pretty good system, actually. We got to the park just before the big event.

The big event was the fire drill for the school next door. The fire chiefs were all out in uniform, with stopwatches no doubt. The buzzers went off and all the kids came out in such nice neat little lines. The chiefs watched carefully, but they didn't see what we saw—four of the boys just kept on walking right out to the swings in the park where we were.

Now, this got me interested. What would these boys do with all this freedom they came into suddenly?

What they did was probably typical. They got bored. They walked around feeling great for a while, bragging about their accomplishment, but then gradually realized that they'd done it. And now it was over. Nobody thinks about what they're going to do after they've gained their freedom. It just doesn't occur to us that that would matter.

Anyway, they got to thinking that the next greatest thing they could do was escape back in, without getting caught. So, when recess came, that was their big chance. Coolly and casually, like men of great freedom and worldly experience, they mingled with the innocent slaves. Back to the freedom of not having any freedom—and probably bursting to tell their friends of the Great Escape.

But I think they'll chance it again. Someday they will strike out again for this thing we call freedom. It's not the glory that draws them on, you know, but the empty vastness of freedom, which only they themselves can fill.

· · ● · ·

It is Sunday morning now. Quiet and peaceful, with the rest of the family still sleeping. I like this time of the morning. The silence seems to be warm and filled with new, emerging thoughts. I think of it as Spirit waiting to be shaped into another day.

I want to introduce you to the last member of our little family. Cyper is a four-year old, graceful, all feminine feline. She is black with four white mittens, a splash of white across her nose and a white diamond on her forehead. She has a long sleek tail and a wiggle to her hips that would capture any man's eye.

Karen says she is my sweetheart. Sounds like jealousy, doesn't it? But I must admit, though, that I love her. It's a bond of lifetime companions.

Cyper first made her conquest of me the day we brought her home from the animal shelter. She was all of five inches long, with the bluest of deep blue eyes. When I put my hand down, she waddled over shakily on her little legs, with a cute meow, and crawled up into my palm, where she snuggly rested her chin on my thumb and took her first nap. What can I say?

Cyper has gone into her second "kittyhood" lately and charges your feet from behind chairs and other camouflaged areas. Have you ever known a cat who likes to perch on top of shoulders? However, she knows some of my affection has gone to Levan for the last year, and she is a bit jealous herself.

Cyper has the responsibility of protecting our house from other cats, of course. But she also watches out for invisible critters, which you will see her scampering after once in a while. She is also an emissary of good will to some of our lonely neighbors.

I learned about her emissary mission a few years ago. Karen and I were on a walk with Cyper one day when an older gentleman spotted us. "Oh, is that your cat?" he asked. He explained how Cyper visited him every morning and what a nice cat she was. So, she'd been two-timing me . . . it was my turn to be jealous.

Cyper is the only cat in the neighborhood who doesn't wear a flea collar, except of course for a stray cat whom we nicknamed "Seaweed." That gives Cyper a good standing in cat society. The most respectable cat, to other cats, is the stray. They are professional cats that work full time, not part time amateurs like the rest. Since the stray doesn't wear any sort of foolish collar, a sign of domestication, other cats that don't wear collars are also elite. Even a big cat that wears a collar has to keep proving himself.

You might find it interesting that we have very little trouble with fleas, even without the collar. In fact, I think we have less trouble than anyone else around here, even though we live in what Karen calls the "flea-belt" of the country. A main street in town even carries the name, Avenida de las Pulgas, which means "Avenue of the Fleas" in Spanish.

You see, we have something of a truce with the bug population. While our neighbors are out poisoning, spraying, stomping and trapping bugs, we just escort one out the door now and then with a little reminder: "If you bugs respect our home aura, we'll respect yours, and Spirit will make us both greater." It takes a little patience, but the bugs do cooperate and seem to understand this Unwritten Code of Personal Space.

Looking back at my notebooks, I can see that my writings completely changed at this point in my journey. Somehow I had crossed into a new world. A world of stillness. A world filled with the presence of the moment.

Before this, I had been following some grand vision that seemed to be building and growing greater and greater. I thought the path would expand this way until reaching the attainment of God-consciousness. But suddenly, it was as if the growing crescendo had become a distraction. It was keeping me from seeing the path of Being. The mountains once again seemed simply like mountains, and the trees were once again just trees.

It was like discovering a precious secret; that Life lay in the simplest of things, in this moment of NOW, and in the presence of HERE. It had always been hiding there in the day-to-day happenings, but as if for the first time I saw how vibrantly it shined with Spirit. The world events seemed artificial and pale next to this nearness of Life. I felt strangely detached from mankind's unfolding play.

So, what would life be now? I had taken another step and was now working with the Mental Plane, the fourth world, but I didn't care what the books said about it. I felt like I had given up all ideals and simply wanted to experience reality as it was.

Like a wide-eyed child, I wondered: What would I find without all the drama of the world overwhelming the subtleties? What is life without all the bright lights and dark shadows? What purpose and meaning lay buried beneath the noise of triumphs and failures? The silent questions had come to lead me on again, and I followed like a devoted lover.

The Spiritual Hierarchy

I felt as if I had made a significant step toward a new realization, but I didn't yet understand what it meant completely. I was still subconsciously holding onto old dreams. Once again the rules were changing for me, and again it would take a turning point to make this clear. The following is an inner experience I had shortly after waking from a deep sleep. I scribbled this into my journal:

The clear night's darkness was only broken by our lighted procession winding its way through the black mountains. Our group of about fifty students had left the gray stone monastery on the Etheric Plane [a part of the high Mental world] where we had been studying, and we were now crossing, single file, the treacherous and hidden paths. We each wore a monk-style robe and carried a single lit candle, which gave the darkness a subtle star-like twinkle and seemed to connect us all together in the dark night.

We soon found ourselves approaching our destination, a huge cave of crystal embedded high in the side of a gigantic mountain. We entered the throne room one at a time.

Seated on a chair was a being, immense beyond all comprehension. His size was so great it was overwhelming, and I remember feeling the intimidation that his presence cast over the scene. In the room, everyone humbly bowed before this entity.

Within myself, I could only feel that age-old dislike for authority, which makes me burn at the sight of an individual holding his hand over weaker ones. Knowing what I had learned about the forces and powers of this world, I stepped forward to defy this king of the lower worlds.

I projected myself up and increased my own dimensions until I stood eye-to-eye with the Kal Niranjan, who is the lord of that world and all worlds below! All the worshippers in the throne room gasped, but Kal only smiled. Soon his laughter bellowed throughout the crystal cave. I then realized what a fool I'd been, falling for Kal's own trap of vanity. For all that I'd done was inflate my own ego.

I let myself return to size, yet still defiant, I spoke:

"I'll live my life like any man in your world, Kal Niranjan, and I'll take whatever you have to dish out."

But I left the room knowing full well the lesson I had learned.

As soon as I returned to the human consciousness, I knew what a fool I'd been to challenge the Kal. My words were no more than boasting and showed how little I knew about the things that filled my subconscious. Clearly, I had not yet completely learned my lesson from the *Jewel of Kali*.

Somehow I had swallowed and accepted the social idea that all beings are created equal and no one has any rightful authority over anyone else. This was a big mistake, and soon after this Soul Travel experience my life took a plunge until I could set myself right again with the spiritual hierarchy.

We are brought up these days on the teaching that the inherent spiritual rights of life are equal for all beings. The ideal of democracy has brought great freedom to the common man in our physical world. Therefore, we now believe that no one has any more divine rights than anyone else. Democracy makes a great philosophy for this physical world; however, I was beginning to see that this is not a truth that works on all the spiritual planes of consciousness.

The power of the spiritual hierarchy became real to me after I suddenly began facing strange trials and problems in my life.

First, my health fell apart. I found myself reacting to almost everything I ate. Then my childhood problem with asthma returned all of a sudden. I went for a medical checkup, hoping the doctor might shed some light on my problem. He said that I was the healthiest person he had seen in a long time. He could find nothing wrong.

At the same time, the last of my freelance writing jobs came to an end and I couldn't turn up anything to take its place. I interviewed for a number of editorial jobs. Everywhere I went my resume was well received, but they were sorry to inform me that I was competing against an ex-editor of the Chicago Tribune, or that they had been inundated by housewives who were trying any way they could to get into the workplace and were willing to take jobs at no pay to learn how to become an editor or reporter. I looked at my situation and could see that my career as a journalist had come to an end. I saw no future in it for me any longer. Meanwhile, months went by without a job, while working through the problems with my health.

I began visiting a nutritionist and started slowly eliminating the foods that were bothering me. For months I had to reduce my diet to only four different foods: chicken, egg whites, green beans and rice. It was certainly a strange diet, but it helped. However, I would still have asthmatic attacks from time to time that left me breathless and without enough energy to do much more than breathe. To fight for breath is a draining experience. I could barely grab a few fitful moments of sleep at nights, and this left me exhausted during the day.

My whole being seemed to be going through some kind of chemical change. I had lost the stability of my previous state, but had not yet found the balance of my new state. It was like trying to cross a bridge that was only half built, with no way of going back.

For the first time in my life I felt that I wasn't carrying my weight and not providing for my family. I remember going down to the unemployment office and standing in line to see about collecting an unemployment check. I saw myself standing there with dozens of homeless people and people on welfare and realized I couldn't go through with it. I would not let myself sink into a state where helplessness was my reality. I needed to work through this situation without asking for help. I knew that I could solve my problems and that it was my responsibility to do so. I left empty handed, but determined.

Immediately I realized this was the right course of action, and I suddenly saw how my struggles fit into a significant spiritual lesson that I was learning on the Mental Plane. The inner and outer issues were connected.

I was beginning to recognize that I had moved into a position of greater spiritual responsibility than before. It was now my job to work these issues without the help I had received in the past.

The strange thing about this was that while I could see the lesson I was going through, I couldn't put it into words. I sensed what it meant intuitively, but not in a way that I could verbalize. How could I explain this feeling that the inner worlds were no longer supporting me like before? What was the meaning of this change and the incredible feeling I had that somehow the world had forgotten me?

My life was starting over in a way. The center of my being had shifted to a new center. My past career and work experience couldn't help me.

What I had learned about my health no longer fit. My spiritual foundation from the past was also of no use. It was a whole new life and I didn't know where it was going to lead, but somehow it was up to me to make it work out. Somehow the answer was now more within me than in any outside laws or forces.

I decided to enroll in night school to take classes in electronics. It seemed right to start a new career in technology, and for the first time it dawned on me that my career had changed with each initiation.

My troubles were far from over, however. I immediately ran into issues at school. I sensed a problem lurking there as soon as I entered the campus grounds. Everywhere I looked I could see signs of an institution that forced students to follow their rules. It brought back some old grudges from my freshman year at college. I remembered my battles with this Over-Soul before and how unfair it felt. Now as both a physical and spiritual adult, I had no intention of putting up with this again.

No sooner did I make this decision within myself, than I felt an immediate reaction. It was as if the Over-Soul of the college had taken my decision as a slap in the face. I was surprised by the forceful reaction I felt in the pit of my stomach. The message I received was clear: If I wanted a degree, I would have to follow its rules. I returned fire back at the Over-Soul with almost exactly the same attitude I had against the Kal: I will not become one of your minions!

I swallowed hard, as I realized the pattern.

I went to register for the classes I wanted, but the registrar's office found problems with my residency files. It was a community college that required proof of California residence for enrollment. As I dug deeper, I ran into one road block after another. According to the state's records, it was as if I no longer existed as a person in California. I was a non-being. It was the strangest thing. Everything about me had disappeared from the state files. The odd feeling returned that somehow the forces governing the world had forgotten me. I was now a free agent, but I was also on my own to make things work out.

Next, the Registrar's office told me that if I wanted to get a degree I would need to enroll in all the basic educational classes, including English and physical education. There was no other way to get a degree. The Over-Soul was putting its foot down again.

By this time I could see what was happening. I held true to my stance that I would make my own future and did not need the help of any ruling force. I gave up plans for a degree and focused on taking the classes in electronics I was interested in. I decided not to get a college degree. I would make my way on my own. I knew it would be much harder this way, but I decided to put my fate in higher hands than those of this world.

The difficulties continued with school one after the other. As I thought about what was happening, I kept coming back to my challenge against Kal Niranjan. I had taunted him to throw anything at me he wished. I would take whatever he dished out. I began to see that perhaps there was a higher spiritual authority behind my experiences than I had realized. I then grasped the point I had been missing.

Yes, I had earned the right to stand up for spiritual freedom from these Over-Souls and gods of the lower worlds, but I still needed to honor them and give them respect for their positions. They too were serving Life in their own way. They still had authority over the worlds where they governed even if I was free of their control. I might be the citizen of another world, but I still needed to show respect for their laws.

I found myself thinking about Homer's book, *The Odyssey*, and what Odysseus was put through by the ancient gods of Greece. Images floated through my thoughts about the mythical trials of Hercules. I wondered: Could such experiences happen today?

I laughed at the idea at first, but the images seemed to fit the experiences I was going through. I then had an insight into these Greek gods of mythology: they were actually fictionalized legends about the Over-Souls. These stories were about the lords of the lower worlds. I found an interesting lesson in these myths that, suddenly, I could relate to. These lower world forces try to rule our lives completely, but the moment we take responsibility for our spiritual life we find ourselves fighting free of their control. They only have control over us because we have allowed it. Subconsciously, we accept their authority and believe that they have power over us, until the day we grow enough to make our own choices, consciously and unconsciously.

I discovered an interesting parallel to what I was going through, one day, after reading a book on the psychological stages of young children by Piaget. Piaget wrote about his study of children from their youngest age. He described how babies, first born, can't tell what part of the world belongs to them and what does not. They begin to use their hands and mouth first. They grab at things and put what they grab in their mouth.

Their hands and mouth become who they are. The things they grab are something else.

This is why young babies grab their own toes and suck on them like a toy. At some point, however, they begin to sense that these toes are also a part of them. They start to recognize the sensation in their toes and they wonder who it is that is grabbing them. Suddenly, they see that they are the one who is doing the grabbing. So, they come to realize that the toes are also part of them.

Later, when children grow, they go through a similar discovery. Piaget told the story of a young girl who talked while drawing a picture on a piece of paper. First, she tells Piaget that she is drawing a person. Then she decides to draw a lady—an old lady. Next she says that the old lady is a witch. Then she says that the witch is making magic and is trying to put a spell on her. Suddenly, the girl jumps up, screams and runs away from the witch who is trying to control her.

Young children at this age don't realize their own imaginations are creating these forces, since the experience seems like something coming from outside of them. Later, they begin to recognize that these feelings are also a part of them.

It is easy to see why primitive people would pray to the rain gods and the gods of the field, since their lives are dependent upon these outside forces that seem to act friendly sometimes, but can be angry other times. Today we view these beliefs scientifically and call this magical thinking. So we no longer imagine that there are personal beings behind these outside forces. We realize that when we start feeling this way that these are, in fact, our own projections. In other words, these projections are a part of us.

From this I could see the whole pattern of spiritual growth. It is all about the growing awareness of who we are.

We are continually learning, bit by bit, that the whole world and everything that takes place in our conscious life is spiritually a part of us. These ideas that the world is made up of powerful forces that control us is a belief we have accepted. We feel helpless facing these outer powers that seem completely out of our control. It seems as if someone else is grabbing our toes, or as if life is sometimes against us and sometimes for us. We can't see the pattern of our own life experiences, so we imagine that it is all random and our inner attitudes are insignificant next to the reality of the outer world. We have not yet recognized that this world view is all us.

Eventually, as I studied my own life more carefully and saw the lives of those around me, I came to see that there are in fact hosts of spiritual beings who control the states of consciousness of the world. The spiritual fates of the universe are in their hands, along with the evolution of life, not only on this planet but all the worlds below this one. They rank in increasingly greater and greater power, all beyond the reaches of the human race. However, they can only carry this authority until Soul learns to make its own life. Then, the silent questions come again, as we ask: Why are these things happening? What is the meaning of our life?

The purpose of the spiritual hierarchy is to manage the affairs of the world for those who have not yet awakened their own inner authority. Until then, the lords of the lower worlds have power over them. Once Soul has begun the journey home, however, it turns its affairs over to a different order, whose work it is to help us remember who we are.

I recorded an experience in my notebooks that gave me a clear illustration of this point:

I was in night class preparing for an electronics lab experiment, when I noticed the man next to me cheating on homework. He was copying answers from others and was trying to get a few from me, but I said, "No, I can't help you." I was surprised that a grown man would be so foolish.

A few seconds later I felt the slight breeze of someone passing behind me. Out of the corner of my eye I saw a white lab coat brushing by, but when I looked directly no one was there. I almost shrugged it off, but then realized what it meant—someone WAS there, but not of this world. I quietly slipped out of my body to get a look at who this was.

Sure enough, a man of stern features, wearing a white lab coat, was strolling through the classroom. He paused to look over the shoulders of each student, and it soon became clear what he was doing. He was looking for cheaters!

"What a nerve this guy has!" I thought. "What business is it of his?" Then it struck me that this was exactly his job. He was an enforcer of the inner laws, like some kind of policeman from the Astral Plane, and he had checked me out. I could then see that the brush of his lab coat was his message of approval to me. My ethics about cheating had passed his scrutiny. I had upheld the principles that his job was to enforce. He was patting me on the back.

Apparently, this surveillance is a part of the invisible side of our college system. Regularly patrolling the classrooms, these enforcers report to a higher authority than many people believe exists. Although my neighbor

186

might never know he'd been caught, those subtle doors, which are the opportunities leading to success, would now be closed to him. He would never know why and would wonder, "Why am I so unlucky?"

My words about the educational system have not always been known for their sweetness, but to now realize that the schools of this world are tied into the systems of the Astral Plane, and that these in turn bow before an even greater authority—well, I'm going to have to look at it differently from now on. Yet, I wonder how many professors realize that they must answer for everything they do, just as I must?

It suddenly became clear to me why certain companies fail and some succeed; why species go extinct and empires collapse. The actions and attitudes of every being determine whether they are working in line with the spiritual hierarchy or fighting against it. Whatever resists this invisible hierarchy slowly dies out, because what we know of as evolution is simply the result of a plan designed for the spiritual growth of Soul.

Therefore, to recognize the unfolding pattern of life and to align ourselves with it is to honor and work with the spiritual hierarchy.

My life immediately began straightening out the moment I saw the place of these Over-Souls. I had been rebelling against something I felt was trying to take away my own inalienable rights of spiritual freedom. But I had it all wrong. The lesson was not about fighting free of their control, since I had become free the very moment I was able to untie the subconscious knots that held me. Rather, this lesson was about learning to honor and respect these beings and the role they were playing. It was not about fighting against their authority, but finding ways to work with them.

Then the realization hit me: I no longer needed these gods to make or direct my life, but now they needed me. What a shift! Once I started working with these forces, life went easier and I found my world filled with the spiritual flow of creation. From this I could see there was a benefit in supporting these beings. I could try to go my own way, but it meant making everything happen for myself. It meant going the hard way. This too I might choose if I wanted, and as I thought about it I realized that this was the choice I wanted to make. It seemed to be an interesting one to try out; especially for someone who no longer cared about the success of this world and was happy with a life of obscurity.

Awakening the Subconscious

Shortly after these realizations, I had a dream where I found myself in a dark, unsettling world. I wasn't sure where I was. Off in the distance I could barely see the outline of a person standing, observing and taking notes. He seemed to be looking at things in my shadows. I felt uneasy about what he was studying. It seemed personal to me for some reason. I felt that he had no business seeing my private affairs.

As I approached the man, he turned around and I recognized him. It was Carl Jung, the psychologist. I suddenly understood what was going on. He was looking at the world of my subconscious. He showed me what he had been studying, and in that instant everything around me filled with light. It was as if someone had turned on a switch. I could see the subconscious world I had been hiding from. I recognized thousands of influences that had been ruling my life. I felt embarrassed by what I could suddenly see so clearly. I felt even more foolish knowing that others could see the whole mess as well.

Carl Jung said nothing to me as he stood there in my dreams. His recognition of the subconscious was enough to awaken this same consciousness within me. In the dream, he pointed at a few things but said nothing. It was simply his awareness that seemed to turn the light on for me. I said to myself in the dream: "Now that I can see, I can never go back to not seeing again."

It seemed incredibly simple and yet irreversible at the same time.

No longer was there any need for grand philosophies of life. I had no reason to look for religious doctrines or rules for right and wrong. The struggles I had been going through were because of what I didn't know and the things I couldn't see. The answer was simple: To see. But I couldn't see until I was willing to accept that it was all a part of me.

The spiritual path no longer seemed like something that reached way out ahead of me. It was no longer leading to some other world. It was now taking me back to myself, to seeing the whole of myself, which had been hidden up until now.

It felt as if a film was falling from my eyes. Life seemed clearer. Everything looked simpler. The idea of trying to attain some kind of greatness now seemed naïve and foolish.

That's when I realized that there are no universal laws to obey on the Mental Plane. Instead, we must decide what is right for ourselves. I had read these very ideas from Paul Twitchell's books, but I had never understood them like this before. What was it that changed for me?

I went back through my books and lessons to study them over again. My subconscious beliefs of the past had colored what I had seen before. I had only seen what I wanted to believe. I thought I had understood, but now I found myself understanding for the first time what Paul Twitchell had written. It was such a strange realization, because I had fully believed that I knew what he was saying before. I thought I knew what he meant.

For example, take this quote from Paul Twitchell's book, *ECKANKAR, The Key to Secret Worlds*:

> No person has ever gained spiritual freedom by a process of logic, metaphysics, reading or listening to lectures. Yet these are the methods that most of humanity attempts...
>
> This then puts us in the position of being the non-seeker. I have said before in this book that we should be neither for nor against anything, and that we should neither seek nor pursue the light and sound [of God] in any way. In other words, we practice the philosophy of no thing.
>
> This philosophy of No-Thing is what we must look for in the worlds beyond. If we project ourselves into the heavenly worlds with the expectation of finding the all, we will be disappointed. We must look to the nothingness of the SUGMAD [God] in order to become that which we are—a part of IT, and a co-worker of IT. This nothing is everything. The very paradox of it is puzzling, for when we project into the afterworlds there is nothing there except what we make. Therefore, we make our future and our pattern of life, and in order to do this, we must be emptied of everything that comes into our worlds, this region and those beyond. All teachings that we have learned must go and all things that we have learned about material and spiritual life must be emptied of our spirit and mind.
>
> No longer can we expect the worlds beyond to uplift and hold within the framework of what has already been established. We, the spiritual travelers, must recognize the hierarchy and know that it exists. We are, however, not responsible to anyone or anything other than the SUGMAD.

I thought I had understood this quote before, but I had not grasped the real meaning at all because it is a message aimed at the subconscious, telling it to listen to Soul. We must empty ourselves to see reality. There is nothing to seek. This is not a message the mind can understand.

Rumi put it this way in chapter twenty-six of his *Discourses*:

These words mean nothing except to the initiated! Beware! Do not say, "I have understood." The more you understand and grasp these words, the farther you will be from understanding them. Their meaning comes in not understanding. All your troubles, misfortunes and disappointments arise from such understanding. This understanding is a chain for you. You must escape it to gain anything at all.

Therefore, the only universal truth on the Mental Plane is that there are no universal truths. Paradox is not a contradiction there; it is a reality, because each truth is valid only in its own state of consciousness. This is not something the mind can understand, but it is a truth we can see and know.

Therefore, the only real source of truth was when the spiritual currents entered my life. That was the only meaning of truth.

The Simplicity of Discovery

As I let go of the world-ego, life became clearer. When I stopped caring about trying to make great things happen, I found myself stumbling upon discoveries that amazed me with their simplicity. I had struggled so hard to understand the mystery of life in the past, but now it seemed to open up for me by simply seeing what the moment was showing and where it was leading me.

For example, take the search I went through to solve my health problems. As I began to see that my body was made up of hundreds of subconscious patterns, I began to recognize that I needed to bring consciousness to these patterns. I focused my attention on my body's instinctive actions and I found myself healing and growing healthier.

I had a dream around this time that opened up a whole new way of seeing health:

Darwin Gross was giving a lecture and I was seated in the front row. He asked me to assist him. He said that his talk was about a new form of biology. Then he drew a grid on a blackboard—5 by 5.

Ascending in the vertical direction, from the bottom up, the rows represented the physical, astral, causal, mental and etheric bodies. In the horizontal direction, the columns represented the vital organs of the physical body, such as the lungs, heart, brain, liver and sense organs.

Darwin explained that illness or disease could begin at any point in the grid. It could then spread horizontally or vertically to a square next to it, such as a problem with a causal organ weakening the mental counterpart, or an astral organ contaminating other astral organs. The sickness could move either horizontally or vertically. If a chain of illness spanned across all five rows or columns, then there would be death. This is when the disease became irreversible because the bodies became shorted out, like an electrical short circuit.

Darwin then pointed out a problem that had started in my Mental body. Looking at it I could see how it was just like catching an infection in that body. I had been over-stressing that body, which made it vulnerable to the bug I caught.

At the end of his talk he showed a very ancient clay figurine he had borrowed from a museum. The figurine showed what looked like an old Mayan man, whose coat was parted down the front and spread aside by his hands—as if revealing his inner organs. On the man's chest was printed this same 5-by-5 grid, with symbols marking the rows and columns. From this I realized that this was a very ancient teaching.

I experimented and learned that through Soul Travel I could move outside of the physical to see all of my bodies. From that perspective I could see in a clear way where my imbalances were coming from.

One of the strangest discoveries of this time came from trying to unravel the mystery of my asthma. Since childhood I had been bothered by it, especially as the autumn evenings settled in. The dark, the cold and humidity seemed to set it off. It disappeared as I grew older, but now it was back.

I studied and watched the pattern of my breathing and tried to see what was going on. I moved outside of my body to see it clearer. A tension and feeling of panic seemed to be coursing through my nervous system, coming from subconscious patterns. It was as if I was trying to gulp the air. My physical body seemed to be begging for more, but something was wrong.

I tried to slow down my breathing, to calm down my lungs, but as I did so I could feel a deep sense of panic arising. My physical body fought against every effort to breathe slower. It did not want to relax. It was fighting for air.

As I watched from Soul, I found that I could redirect the instinctive patterns of my physical body. I directed my lungs to breathe slower, to give up their desire to grasp for another breath. My breathing completely stopped. My body was suddenly still. Calmness came over me. It seemed as if I should be breathing, but I wasn't. I could feel panic returning, but I set it aside. Soul was guiding the way.

All at once, like a switch had been turned on, I felt everything shift. My nasal passages drained and felt clearer than they had in years. My lungs cleared and my wheezing stopped. The asthmatic reaction completely disappeared.

After going through this process over and over again, I discovered that by reducing my breathing to almost a complete halt, if I could calm my body's instinct to gulp for air, my lungs and nasal passages cleared and the asthma went away. It was completely unexpected and the exact opposite of what the instincts of my physical body wanted to do. After a few months I was able to retrain myself to a whole new pattern of breathing.

I was reminded of this recently when someone asked me what I thought of a new cure for asthma that was circulating around the Internet. It is called the Buteyko Method, named after a Russian doctor who learned that over-breathing is a common cause of asthma. His practice is just now being tested by independent researchers and is finding fairly good results. Somehow I had stumbled into the same discovery.

Through Soul Travel, I could see that the only way I could slow my breathing was by moving the center of my attention. My center had been focused too high. It was just as Darwin had told me in my dream: The problem started in my Mental body and was spreading from the Mental to the Physical. However, the pit of my stomach also had a center of focus with a mind of its own. Once I let my attention center in my gut, my physical body knew exactly how to breathe. I had lost touch with my solar plexus. Now I could see that it instinctively knew what to do. My mental thought had taken too much control of my breath.

If I tried to control every breath consciously and tried to will my lungs to slow down, it was almost impossible. But if I moved the center of my breathing down to the pit of my stomach and trusted Spirit to guide it from there, I automatically calmed down and found a slower pace.

I learned from this that rather than just trying to raise my state of conscious as I had in the past, I also needed to lower it. Expansion of consciousness meant getting in touch with higher and lower aspects. I needed to return to a simpler life and to recognize the instinctive wisdom of my physical body. This was what restored my health.

Another interesting discovery I made during this time came after changing Levan's diapers. He had a bad case of diaper rash. Karen and I had tried various ointments, but nothing seemed to work. I had a hunch that there might be an herbal remedy. I looked through all of my books on herbs, but found no mention of diaper rash. I decided to follow my intuition.

I went to an herb shop and slowly looked through the dried herbs. When I came to a jar of dried raspberry leaves, something seemed right about it. It is hard to describe how the intuition works, but it seemed as if the herb had an inner form that matched what I was looking for. I turned to one of my herb books and read that raspberry leaves are a mild astringent. That made sense. They also had a pleasant smell and they were amazingly soft and fluffy, after the stems were removed. It seemed to fit.

I wasn't sure exactly how to use them, but because of their softness I thought I would simply spread a few leaves out in Levan's diaper. Karen and I were both amazed that something so simple could have such an effect. The next day his rash was almost completely gone.

After struggling for months, his rash disappeared completely in a few days. We used the herbs for a week, but then stopped and his rash didn't return for a long time. When we saw signs of it returning a few months later, we dropped a few more leaves into his diapers and the rash disappeared again. Soon, he no longer seemed to need the leaves at all. It was as if his body learned how to heal itself after that.

The leader of the day care group, where Levan had been going, immediately noticed the change. She asked what we had done. After we explained, she asked to borrow some raspberry leaves to try it on some of her other children who had serious rashes. It had the same results with them.

A neighbor of ours happened to be a nurse who worked with babies at a nearby hospital. As chance would have it, she began complaining to Karen and me one day about the number of babies who had developed severe diaper rash. She had tried every medication she could but could not get rid of it. I told her of our discovery. She looked at us with a strange look and said nothing. So, we dropped it.

The next day she knocked on our door. After another bad day with rashes, she asked if we had any raspberry leaves. She had to try something.

A few days later she came back to report that it was a miracle. All of the rashes were gone. She would go on to try it on dozens of babies. It worked every time. She was so impressed at how much better it worked than any medication that she mentioned it to one of the doctors in the hospital. She was nearly fired on the spot.

You would have thought she was practicing voodoo or something. I hope most people working in the scientific profession of medicine would see this as an opportunity for a new discovery. But the doctor reacted as if she had become a heathen and was committing an unholy sin. Some people cannot handle new ideas unless they come in a form they are accustomed to.

I found a job working for an electronics company around the same time, after I started taking classes in electronics. I began as a technician trainee. However, within a couple weeks I stumbled upon an interesting discovery.

It came while testing a radio frequency part known as an isolator. As I was testing and tuning these isolators, I noticed an interesting pattern based on where the wires to a capacitor were soldered. I started experimenting by moving the wires and solder point around until I got an intuitive feeling for what was happening. Following my gut, I found that I could remove one of the very expensive high frequency tuning capacitors completely, and the isolator worked better without it. It also cost a lot less.

I called the head engineer over to show him what I found. Rick looked at me and asked, "Why did you try this?"

I tried to explain, but could soon see that the path I had followed didn't make sense to him. I was following a hunch. There was no logic or rational thinking to what I had done, since I didn't yet understand the technology well enough. So, I was at a loss to explain it.

Rick stood there studying what I showed him and realized that there was a good explanation for the circuit change I had made. It wasn't at all what he would have expected, he told me, but he went on to explain the effect of what I had done. He asked me to try ten more isolators to see if the pattern was consistent. All of them worked better with my new change.

About a year later, I would stumble into a more baffling discovery. It came while playing around with some coax cables. I was observing the way that frequency filters can be constructed from various lengths of cable. I didn't understand the theory completely, but I found myself getting an inner sense of what was going on.

Based on this, I built a strip-line filter using thin sheets of copper suspended between two metal plates. The results worked better than the coax cable, but I wanted to see if I could improve it further. So, I began experimenting with the shapes of the copper strips and discovered that if I started the strip off narrow and then widened it at a certain point that it made a huge improvement. The lengths of the narrow and wide segments had to be exactly the right lengths for it to work.

When I finally had it optimized I called Rick over to look. He couldn't believe the depth of the filter notches from such a simple design. He went off to his office and came back in a few hours and admitted that this time he didn't understand why it worked so well. Even after digging through his textbooks, he could find no explanation.

We talked about it for days. Rick was clearly uncomfortable about being unable to figure out how it worked, but finally decided that it could save such a significant amount of money in one of the company's most popular products that it was worth finding out if we could put it to use. Between the two of us, we found a way to tune the filter by connecting a high frequency tunable capacitor to the end of the strips.

The new filter worked incredibly well and was easy to tune. It cost less than half as much as our other filters. Before we could start using it, however, we needed to run some duration and temperature tests to prove that it was reliable.

After a week of continuous testing under high power, we were just about ready to call it a success when one of the tuning capacitors burned out. We thought it must have been a bad capacitor, so we replaced it. However, a few hours later another capacitor fried. Then came a third.

The only thing that could destroy a capacitor like this was if the voltage was too high. But the capacitors were rated for many times the voltage we had in our system, so this shouldn't have been a problem. That's when Rick decided to measure the voltage at the end of the copper strips, where the capacitors were connected.

We discovered that it was about ten times higher than expected! That's when we finally understood what was going on. The shape of the copper strips was transforming the voltage to ten times its normal value. This finally explained why the filter was working so well.

The company applied for a patent on my invention. It was the first patent they had ever applied for, and my first as well. A year after this, I would make another discovery, resulting in another patent application. I moved from technician to engineer and began designing circuits regularly.

I've had over 20 patents issued since then, not counting those two, with each invention being used in actual products or new products that are still in the process of being developed. My intuitive approach might be unconventional, but it works. It still helps to have a good theoretical understanding, but studying the problem from other states of consciousness gives me a wider perspective and shows me solutions I would never have seen through theory alone.

I remember one engineer sitting down with me one day a few years after starting my career in electronics. He admitted to me that he first thought my ideas on a new design would never work. They made no sense at all. He thought there must be something wrong with me, especially when I decided to proceed after he had pointed out my problems. When he finally saw it working, he was amazed.

However, he told me this only after seeing this happen three times with new designs. He didn't understand how I did it, he said, but he had to admit that whatever I was doing seemed to work. It was one of the strangest compliments I ever received.

This is the problem I have with trying to explain the spiritual experiences of the Mental Plane and higher. There seems to be no way that others can understand it unless they've learned to work from these states. But anyone who experiences it can see the effects and the benefits.

There was nothing in these discoveries that seemed remarkable to me. They just happened at the time. It was like walking along a path and finding what you were looking for. It almost seemed like an accident, until I could see how to do this over and over again. I trusted my subconscious to find the way through the dark, you might say. I've come to see that it always knows which way to turn.

More Discoveries

During the time of my Fourth Initiation I gave up publishing my writings. I felt as if I needed to take a break from the cycle of my Third Initiation, which had been focused on patterns of the world. It had been a great learning experience, trying to understand the influences that speak to people, but it now all seemed wrong.

My long-time friend, Harold Klemp, had a growing influence over me. I met with him often in various classes that he taught at the time. I stayed after class and we would talk for an hour or two. His quiet manner showed me a new approach. He hid his awareness in a way that most never caught. It was clear to me he had a spiritual connection that was rare, but he avoided calling attention to himself. He came across as quiet and shy, yet beneath this appearance I saw an inner strength. He showed me a new way of living that revealed the subtleties of the spiritual path. There was something hidden in the every day world around us that could not be found in the spotlights. Most never saw its depths. Our eyes are too easily dazzled by bright lights.

Realizing I had been searching in the wrong direction, I began looking through my notebooks. I wanted to see if I could make out the path I had taken through my years of study. How had I become so caught up in greatness that I missed the simplicity?

I ran across a few articles I started writing years earlier, but could never finish. I couldn't quite fathom the lesson, so I just left the pieces half written in my journal. I sensed something important, but couldn't grasp it at the time. Now, they seemed to open up like flowers and show me what I had been looking for. The following three stories are examples.

In Search of Infinity

In 1874, Georg Cantor announced a discovery that upset and puzzled the mathematical world. He said that there is more than one type of infinity. According to Cantor, some infinite sets are greater than others. This might sound impossible to distinguish, but it's true, and Georg gave mathematical proofs to show that some sets are infinitely greater than other infinities—putting them into a class of their own.

Cantor described and proved the existence of three sets of infinity. Up to today, no one has been able to even suggest what a fourth infinite set might be. John E. Freund says in his book, *A Modern Introduction to Mathematics*, "It seems that our imagination does not permit us to count beyond THREE when dealing with infinite sets."

Our imagination may not, but with Soul Travel we certainly can!

We know infinity is the reflection of the endlessness of a world—or what in mathematics is called a set. Thus, our search for infinity inevitably takes us deep into the five inner invisible worlds—the subtle dimensions of life. To enter these infinite and unending realms, each with its own reality and its own set of laws, is to discover Infinity for ourselves. There we discover that there are actually FIVE sets of infinity and that these correspond to the five planes of creation.

First, is the Physical Plane, which is not much more than a scattering of clay shells. It is simply matter and chemistry held together by some electrical, magnetic, and morphological forces beyond our complete understanding, and so its infinity is simple as well. To mathematicians this is the infinity of all possible points. This corresponds to the infinity of matter in our world, which is made up of atoms, particles and points. In other words, this is the infinity of quantity, which describes the mass of this world.

Next comes the Astral Plane, with an infinitely greater infinity, called the infinity of emotion and imagination. This is a world of finer construction than the physical, with an added dimension of emotional, imaginative reality. Here, the world is more than clay. It is also filled with feelings, desires, instincts and imaginative forces that shape everything there. Mathematicians say that this infinity is the set of all possible straight lines, which corresponds to the emotions that move us from one point to another. This is an infinitely greater infinity because for every possible point there can be an infinite number of lines going in an infinite number of directions. Therefore, our imaginative senses see a world that is infinitely greater than physical reality, because any point or atom has an infinite number of possible directions it can go when it is infused with imagination, while physical matter can only go in the one direction that outer forces direct it.

The third dimension is called the Causal World, because the actual plan for all things originates here. It is finer still and much greater than the Astral. To mathematicians it is the infinity of all possible patterns, but to the spiritual travelers it is called the infinity of absolute truth. It is called this because in this state of consciousness one believes he has reached the absolute. This perception underlies the whole experience and structure of this world, so that nothing greater could possibly exist. No wonder mathematicians were stopped from discovering the next greater world.

What could be greater than all possible patterns, which is the same set as all possible "things" or "ideas" or "events"? It seems indeed that nothing could be greater.

When we cross into the fourth dimension, the Mental Plane, however, we immediately recognize that it is greater still. This is a strange dimension compared to the absolute reality of the Causal, for here contradictions exist out of necessity. The whole of mathematical proof is based upon the belief that contradictions cannot exist, but this idea is blown to pieces upon entering the mental world. Why? Because every viewpoint in this world contradicts every other viewpoint. This is why the Zen masters use the teaching of paradox to reach this state of consciousness.

This is the world of relativity, where every "thing" is relative to the person who observes it. In fact, it is understood here that no "thing" even exists outside of our perception of it. So this fourth dimension is the infinity of consciousness. It is symbolized by the set of all possible observations, because for every "thing" there are an infinite number of possible perspectives from which to view it.

Einstein showed that measurements are affected by our own state of motion or acceleration. Quantum Physics proves that observers are not something completely separate from what they observe. Therefore "things" are not separate from observation and consciousness, but are a part of it. This all becomes immediately visible on the Mental Plane, since there is no absolute truth there, only relative truth.

This world is the resting place of the mental body, which is at ease flowing from one viewpoint to another like the river. Fourth dimensional man can never be crammed into the absolute systems of the masses that live in the worlds below, for he knows that all truth is relative and each person has his own infinity. So, the whole mental world is the infinity of infinities. What could be greater than this?

Now it should be easy to see why so few have glimpsed the fifth dimensional state; because each infinity seems to be the final and ultimate infinity. But upon entering the Soul Plane, the fifth plane, all of this changes. One immediately knows there is more, always more, and Soul is just beginning its journey into the heart of the unending infinity called the Eternal.

We now find that Soul as the observer is one with the observed. All division, all duality has fallen away. Infinity is no longer something out there beyond us, but a living, pulsating essence of Soul. The individual has become the universal...the microcosm is now the macrocosm!

The mind cannot comprehend this. There is no way to symbolize it for mathematics. Soul is all and yet individual. It has no need for measurements or viewpoints, since in its beingness Soul is the all in all. Soul is all things and all viewpoints, and yet it is simply Soul and retains its individuality. Separation no longer exists, so infinity, which we have chased through the lower worlds, is suddenly a part of all things, all viewpoints and all beings.

Having now found Truth, why seek? Having become Truth, how can Soul seek? And yet the Masters say that there are many more worlds beyond the fifth plane. Beyond the formless and the nameless are the greater experiences of God, Itself.

Is this not the goal of our search for Infinity? Perhaps our search does not end here, but just begins...

What struck me more and more as I rewrote these articles was how subtle it all was. It was like suddenly being able to pick out instruments, such as a flute or violin while listening to a symphony and hearing it distinctly against the backdrop of the whole orchestra. This is the same way the five planes affect us.

When the instruments are all aligned, we feel good and in harmony with life. When they are out of synch or at odds, the tune turns sad, like a song of anguish or melancholy, as if something has been lost or forgotten. Our lives are like a subtle tone painting, vibrating to the sound of Spirit, flowing through these cloaks that we wear around Soul.

I wanted to pick out the flute from the violin—to see the many dimensions and how they were woven together, which is what led to this next short piece. The ideas came to me after reading an article in a local newspaper.

Types of Eaters

I have found a total of five types of eaters, none of which are new as they have all existed since man first swung a club.

1. There is the "fast food" eater. He tends to be a physical type of person with strong interests in his work and play. People who travel a lot often fall into this category, as well as those who always seem to be preoccupied by

some hobby, sport or business venture. Today they pick up a quick hot dog or hamburger, but looking back we find the old West cowboys were known for their can of beans, and the Roman soldiers ate their gruel.

2. There are the "gourmet" eaters. These tend to be emotional types, often with strong feelings. Most of all, they have an interest in what we might call the "art of the senses." Taste and aroma interest them as an art form. They are drawn to meals with more than one course, many garnishes and sauces, gravies and spices. All handled and cooked with the care of an artist.

3. There is the "traditional eater." This is a type of person who is generally interested in history. If not of mankind's history, then certainly their own family's roots and lineage. The saying "just like Mom used to make" comes from this group, as they are the upholders of culture. The traditional eater is also concerned with their families' position in society and what is happening in the world. The holiday turkey with a family gathering has much more meaning than a simple meal; it is a social and historical event.

4. There are the "food faddists." These people are often belittled, but that is because not many understand their highly intellectual curiosity. They are the followers of theories, often taking sides on a new idea, yet generally willing to change their position if the evidence changes their mind. They might try eating foods with fiber or become a vegetarian. But whatever their diet, it is more of an intellectual experiment than anything else. Thus, it is not surprising that these are the discoverers of new ways to eat, which someday become the traditional ways of tomorrow.

5. The last group is the "individualists." They generally have strong intuitions, which are not feelings but an actual awareness of what is needed in their life. They know their food interests go in cycles and some days it seems they can just keep eating and eating, while at other times they aren't hungry at all. But they know that too much of the food types that the other four groups eat will dull their intuitions. Therefore, they are apt to be the outsiders of today's eating establishments.

Now, there is one point here that I think is very important: No person is totally any one type of eater. We may find ourselves more strongly in one group at one time, but this always changes. This is simply because men and women are many-faceted beings. The food we eat is only a reflection of the varied levels and subtle needs that we have.

More and more as I wrote these pieces I saw that my attention was turning toward the viewpoint of Soul. That seemed to be the secret behind the effortless path I was seeing. It almost seemed as if the less I cared about making discoveries the more easily these new insights came.

Having started all over in my spiritual search and having thrown away everything I thought I knew, I saw into life in a different way. Now I could see how the world around us is changed by the way we perceive it, since the world is not something separate from us, after all.

Breaking the Bonds of Time and Space

In sports, it is common to hear athletes describe instants when time slows down, each movement passing like a slow-moving train. It may be a fast pitch in baseball, or a smash from the net in tennis, but the player watches it all moving by in slow motion while his thoughts and observations race far ahead of the action.

Space often seems equally flexible during moments of acute concentration. Sharpshooters describe feeling their distant target with their eyes, as if it were a hard point or a bead. Ballet dancers tell about their sensation of floating or flying through the air, with the audience often experiencing the very same feeling.

Such perceptions are written off by our scientific way of thinking as merely subjective and quickly forgotten. However, these are not flights of fantasy or imagination. These are real and recurring experiences. This statement alone should cause us to pause and take a closer look, because it is from experience and experience alone that we know reality.

Is it possible to break the bonds of time and space?

Through a careful study of consciousness and the practice of Soul Travel, I've come to a very different conclusion than modern day beliefs. It is my experience that time and space change for us the instant Soul leaves or re-enters the body, and this is a far more common experience than most people realize.

It can be a sudden shift in perception, such as the time in my youth when I experienced a floating sensation after jumping from the third story of a house. I had climbed into the partially built home with a couple of friends. We knew it was off limits, but enjoyed the adventure of exploring. I had reached the third floor with Bob, when a car pulled into the front driveway. Knowing we only had seconds to exit before being caught, Bob and I decided to leap out of the glassless picture window frame into the back yard. I felt suspended and weightless for a moment, flying through the air, as if I were temporarily a thousand miles away.

We then landed in mud so soft that our legs were embedded up to our knees. Bob and I watched each other half in panic, half in laughter, as we struggled and wiggled every which way we could to get out of the mud before we were spotted.

Those who practice sky-diving often describe the same sensation that I had experienced for a split second; a feeling of suspension as if you weren't falling at all. In that moment, Soul, the conscious self, actually sees what is happening from outside the body. This is what creates the experience of an expanded sense of reality. It might be for only an instant, but Soul, our true Self, experiences freedom from the restrictions of time and space.

Isn't this the state that draws thrill seekers on to risk their safety in order to experience this feeling of Soul leaving the body?

The science of Soul Travel is not new. Plato and Socrates spoke of it in their discourses on philosophy. The Ancient Egyptians knew of it, as did the early Sufi mystics, and certain Christian saints practiced it and wrote about it. Paul Twitchell gathered together a history and explanation of Soul Travel in his book, *ECKANKAR, The Key to Secret Worlds.*

Twitchell wrote:

"Many people have out-of-body experiences, but few recognize them for what they are, nor can they control these spontaneous projections. Soul Travel can become as natural as breathing, but it is generally a frightening experience for those who are not used to leaving their physical body and to viewing the world through spiritual eyes."

We naturally revert to our old states of consciousness after having such experiences, and we will even suppress memories of them when they don't fit our belief structure. However, the altered states can be so vibrant and real that they are not easy to forget.

There are many occasions when Soul will escape the body but stays nearby. Such incidents can be quite subtle if we don't know what to look for. Many runners have this experience, which brings on a euphoric state. Their body feels like it can run endlessly without tiring. Their mind suddenly clears and they find a new surge of energy. It often occurs after pushing past extreme levels of exhaustion, like breaking through a wall. This is when Soul releases itself.

We've been taught to treat these events as the results of body chemistry. Our experiences, however, tell us something different is taking place, because these experiences never occur in repeatable ways like chemistry would, nor does the clarity of consciousness seem artificial.

An electronics engineer related the following experience from his youth, when he found himself subjected to over seven times the force of gravity while flying stunts in a US Navy jet:

"When I was learning to fly in the Civil Air Patrol," he explained as we watched the Blue Angels screaming by overhead, "we went up with some Navy pilots in jets just like those. We were making barrel rolls and loops with over 7 g's of force at the top of our turn. The pressure was so incredible I couldn't even lift my arms, and my chin was pressed down to my chest. You know, many people can't let go of fear in moments like that, but when you do—when you let go, it's heaven. It's pure heaven."

This is the subtle experience of Soul Travel. It is that moment when all life suddenly stands out clearly in sharp relief. Our consciousness becomes heightened and our perceptions witness the overall view. This is a tell-tale sign of being outside the body; seeing from an expanded view with a detached feeling. It is the same experience described by those having near-death experiences. Many who go through this are so affected that they lose all fear of death.

The means and methods of getting out of the body varies so greatly that we wonder if we have understood correctly when we hear about them. There is the whirling dance of the dervishes, the sleep and dream method, the meditative technique, trance and sympathetic projection just to name a few. The later method often occurs in times of danger, which is why we hear stories of people who did just the right thing to escape disaster but have no idea why they did what they did, or those who see or feel their loved ones at the exact moment of an accident or death, even though they might be hundreds of miles away. The fact is that many people instinctively know how to collapse time and space once Soul leaves the body.

Anytime we change our life we are apt to have more Soul Travel experiences. This is because our daily routines build a rigidity into our perceptions, which makes the world seem solid and stable. But after moving to a new house, changing jobs or even rearranging the furniture, we find fresh viewpoints slipping in as Soul forms new reference points. Thus, there are times in everyone's life that can be called crossroads, when our whole world changes because of something we have learned.

Our sense of time and space also change, if we watch carefully. This is the result of a change in consciousness.

A whole country, or even the world, can experience an altered sense of time and space during great catastrophes or disasters. This is often followed by a feeling of confusion, like when an earthquake shakes everything we once thought was solid. Few people recognize they are shifting into a different state of consciousness, even though they will notice the feeling of time speeding up or slowing down.

Of course, the quartz crystals in our watches don't change states of consciousness very often. That's what makes their sense of time so consistent. But does this mean our sense of time is wrong and the watches are right? Do we reject our own experience of time because it doesn't fit with our image of reality that we've gained through scientific instruments?

There is a peculiar similarity, from what I've seen, amongst those who reach the point of breaching time and space. We often find they have a finely directed concentration. There is an effort to unite their feelings and thoughts in an attempt to push the limits of ability, or in response to a sudden change that captures and focuses their complete attention. There is also a certain detachment that overcomes any feelings and gives a sense of clarity.

The experience of leaving the body is a common one. Have you ever closed your eyes when lying down for bed and opened them the next moment only to find the whole night had slipped by? What then happened to your experience of time?

Can you remember when you were a child, spinning and spinning in circles until you fell dizzy to the ground and felt yourself floating? Isn't this letting go of your reference to space?

Have you ever felt yourself falling in a dream, only to wake with a start? Isn't this Soul coming back into the body?

It is our concepts of time and space that are shattered when we move our state of consciousness. Most people, however, reject their own inner senses the moment they return to a stable reality. Thus, the whole event goes unrecognized.

Once we experience this altering of time and space, we often try to seek it out again. We desire that feeling of freedom when the world is no longer inanimate, but seems filled with life and energy. This spirit of life is a discovery that comes from leaving the body.

For those who don't look closely at the moment-to-moment events of their daily lives, Soul Travel sounds like an impossibility. But if we simply accept our experiences for what they are, we see those small instances when the bonds of time and space are broken. It is a very natural event, and only after thinking about it does it boggle the mind.

What fascinated me about this subject was discovering how our beliefs about the world can prevent us from seeing things as they really are.

When I looked to my direct experiences, I realized that I did not sense time the same way that a clock did. For me, time was continually expanding and contracting. Why did it change like this, I wondered? I soon found it was tied to movements in my state of consciousness.

That was when I realized that my previous concept of time had come from a culture that lives by clock-time. In fact, as I looked around me, I saw that our world displays "the time" and tells us over and over again "what time it is." We need to wear watches and have clocks everywhere—because otherwise we would lose track of "time."

This, however, is the world's time. It isn't my inner sense of time, or for that matter anyone's actual personal experience of time. So, this suggested there was something much more interesting about time.

In other words, our changing perceptions of time are valid. Time does vary greatly, because we change our levels of awareness from moment to moment, and time really is different in different states. So, the real reason we latch onto mechanical timepieces or electronic clocks is because they act as artificial stable references in a wildly fluctuating sea of Time.

This is what I meant by breaking the bonds of time—I was no longer tied to world-clocks for my personal experience of time.

I found the exact same thing unfolding with my concepts of space. I noticed that in some places space seemed more spread out. This struck me first in Las Vegas, when I discovered that my sense of distance was completely wrong. A mountain range that looked to be a few miles away was in fact 40–50 miles away. It wasn't just the atmosphere and drier, clearer air. The whole sense of space was more wide open, and it often felt as if the desert itself had a completely different sense of space than New England, where I grew up.

If I accepted my senses and perceptions and what they were telling me, then space itself was not the same everywhere. Why? Well, because states of consciousness vary from place to place.

Modern science has taught us to distrust our inner perceptions. Scientific instruments are considered more reliable, and thus our culture has adopted a belief system about the reality of the world that is not our own. We have taken the experiences of machines and lifeless matter as more accurate than the senses of living, conscious beings.

What a strange predicament.

Just like the clock on the wall fools us into thinking we know what time it is, so too our mind fools us into thinking we are learning more and more when we are in fact wandering farther and farther away from who we really are.

206

Daydreams

This seemed to be a point in my life for rethinking my goals. What I had thought was most important was no longer the same. My inner self took pause for reflection.

I remember the back veranda of that gray stone monastery on the Etheric Plane. I visited there often. A Master by the name of Lai Tsi instructed me to sit quietly and rest. He showed me a chair where I could sit and watch the magnificent sight of the shimmering ECK flowing into the lower worlds. It was like silver dew blowing down from the high mountain peaks that mark the border between the Soul Plane and the high Mental worlds where I sat.

Strangely, I felt as if the guardians of the monastery were treating me like a convalescent. I didn't understand this at first. However, as I watched the sight of pure Spirit, like a silver mist, entering the lower worlds, I found it washing away deep levels of negativity I never even realized lay within me. It was soothing and relaxing, and brought a healing from the deep scars of desire that pull the mind and emotions of mankind in every direction. I was weaker than I knew from these passions of the mind. The presence of the life force coursing through me, as I sat there resting, soothed the wounds and washed away all traces of these subconscious storms.

One of the most interesting spiritual practices I learned there came when Lai Tsi handed me a ball of energy and simply said: "Look at this."

It was a ball of spinning energy, light blue and silvery like the mist of Spirit, but there was something about it that drew my attention. My mind became fascinated by the energy. I wondered what it was I was seeing. Suddenly I realized it was a giant atom of this world, and within it was the very mixing of Spirit and matter, like some ceaseless movement of creation taking place before my eyes.

As I studied it, my mind seemed to melt away. All the concepts and mental constructs I had picked up seemed to drain out, as if a plug had been pulled. It was like seeing the very first moment of manifestation, the very first instant when Spirit turns into matter. My mind was mesmerized by what I was watching, yet I found myself dissolving in its energy at the same time, since I could feel that I was a part of what was happening.

Lai Tsi knew my mind needed something to chew on, since it was still driving me like a taskmaster that I couldn't stop. I can see this in the articles I wrote back then. There is a mentality about them. The mind still had its grip on me and didn't want to let go. But this atom of creation that Lai Tsi gave me began to undo the stream of mental dialogue babbling away within me. Now I understood where this sense of silence I was feeling was coming from. It was the hush of my own thoughts.

I can see now that these rivers of thoughts were not really mine. They belonged to the world. Just like my story of Vultee Arch Trail, I had somehow picked up this churning of the mind from the bodies that I wore in the various planes. Once freed of those bodies, the mind seemed to empty itself and find the stillness of Soul.

These bodies are so tied to the world and our families and the groups that we are a part of that we lose sight of our own Self. This is not a sign of weakness, but is simply the nature and construction of creation.

My notebooks show some of my thoughts at the time:

Karen and I were returning home after work the other day, talking about each other's experiences. She said, "I was telling Pat that we took Levan to see Sleeping Beauty and do you know what she said? She said, 'You've got to watch out for that sexist stuff!'"

"What? Walt Disney is no good?" I said.

"Yeah. You know, with the fair young princess and the prince coming to rescue her. Pat really thought it was terrible. And then Fran said the same thing. She said, 'I was raised on that junk and even to this day I haven't gotten over it.'"

Pat and Fran were bothered by the same predicament we are all in: our inner bodies are shaped and formed by the worlds that they belong to. Sometimes the emotion, our Astral Body, becomes trained so that we can never enter a relationship without "that junk" coloring the picture. We get frustrated because we don't want to play "the game" but can't help it.

I think we all want to be ourselves. We want to be Soul.

Sometimes our inner self feels like it is being squeezed by the big institutions, or trapped by our families or jobs. We want to climb out of these limitations, but there seems to be something insurmountable, something blocking us. I think we often get frustrated because we confuse our astral, causal and mental bodies with Soul.

Soul alone can keep order and truth in the inner bodies. Soul is like the stream, which crosses the rapids, crashes over falls, and is tossed and tumbled, yet it still flows onward. The water itself is never harmed.

Once Soul discovers It can wiggle free of these bodies through Soul Travel, It finds that It wants to experience more and more of life directly as Soul. In the process, Soul learns that most of what had bothered and troubled It were the problems of the bodies It wears, not of Soul Itself.

One of the wonderful things about being a parent for the first time was that it gave me a chance to look back at my own life and understand what was really going on as I grew up. It is amazing how children absorb the patterns of their environment and accept them into themselves. They pick up the social consciousness of the culture they are born into even before they can talk. Their own dreams become shaped unconsciously by their families and the world itself.

I found a deep sense of peacefulness and restfulness settling within as I felt the pieces of my subconscious falling into place. Watching Levan grow seemed to illuminate things within myself. I paused as I witnessed them. They awakened long forgotten patterns.

One of the things I noticed was that as soon as I began unraveling some of the tangled threads of my unconscious, my daydreams began to change. Daydreams play a huge role in the lives of children and shaping their lives. I gave a public talk on the subject. The following are from my notes:

Of all the things the spiritual path has changed in my life, it has changed my daydreams. I find once more the free and happy reverie I knew in my youth. The seriousness has faded. Now my daydreams flow out and seem to have no limit. I enjoy them.

My daydreams have changed in ways I never expected. They give me more feelings about life right here and now. From far off in the worlds of "what might be," comes a rich enjoyment, humor and love for my life the way it is.

It reminds me of a daydream I had as a kid. I imagined seeing a pool of water, clear blue, with beings standing around looking in. All these beings were gods, and what they saw looking into the pool was life on Earth.

Now the way my daydream went, these gods got bored. After all, there was nothing they couldn't do, nothing they didn't know, and to them life on Earth was a challenge because you had to forget and give up all your godly powers!

So, every once in a while of eternity, one of these gods said farewell to the gang. Down he came into the Earth world, where he would be born. He would then struggle and fight, hate and love, and after his life ended, back he went to the pool where he had a good laugh about the whole game. The other gods would be there and I can almost hear their conversation still:

> "Oh, and that time you went to war...(hearty laughter)...You were so serious, sweating it all out...And when that bomb blew up, did you ever get out fast!...(more rib-poking chuckles)...What a show!"
>
> "It was great! I thought it was so real. And it was my whole life. Why...(more laughter)...it was ME!"

Back and forth the joking would go about the whole affair. But the whole point of the game and the only way one of these gods could win was if he realized he was a god while still living on Earth. This was the goal. To shake off the illusion and the seriousness and remember who you really were.

This was a daydream I had. Somehow it came to me or I made it up, but it stayed with me a long time. It changed the way I felt about life. You know, I really didn't believe it—it was just a daydream then and I had no idea how true it really was. But it was a great daydream game to play, because the way I figured it—I'd already won. So, I could just watch everyone else struggling and fighting, never knowing they were gods too.

With daydreams, it doesn't matter whether it is true or not, all that matters is what it means to us. That's why in daydreaming we often come into close contact with our inner selves. So often our daydreams are true glimpses of the invisible worlds within us.

It seems curious to see thousands of people with the same daydreams. Have you ever seen that? It is always carried on with such seriousness! Instead of giving up my daydreams, I have watched them grow and I've seen them getting stronger. Strong enough to take me through the day, and strong enough that my attitude remains positive no matter what happens.

It wasn't long ago that I found myself at work struggling through a task. I was trying to drill out a hundred metal pieces about the size of my thumb. I was not using a great set-up, though, because after the fourth piece the high speed drill press suddenly jammed in the metal and nearly jerked the vice clean out of my hand.

It scared me. The damage this machine could do made my body shake. I walked it off for a few minutes and then came back to the remaining 96 connectors that were left. I continued, but with every connector I wondered, would this be the one? The drill will jam...the vice will spin out of my hands and…nothingness, blackness and pain. My imagination saw it all. 95 connectors left to go.

My battle with the machine became clear. The war was IT against me. The end was death or 94 more connectors. But then it dawned on me that the machine was winning! My fear was growing and I was accepting it.

This is when an old folk song came to mind: John Henry. I thought about John Henry, the steel driving man. No machine could whip John Henry. He drove steel spikes, one with each blow. I began humming the song, John Henry, and then I thought—why I'm a steel driving man too! I've got steel in my blood, my grip is like iron, and machine, you'd better watch out because if you couldn't beat John Henry, you haven't got a chance now.

And, you know, those last 93 connectors were actually fun. It turned my whole day around.

With daydreams I have the legal license to believe anything. It doesn't have to be true or realistic. It can be the sum total of what I most deeply want to believe, or something I've never even imagined before. It's my own world.

I still hear people these days who say that daydreaming is dangerous and damaging to indulge in. Perhaps these people have some reason for spreading fear about the creative and constructive outlet of their deepest feelings. But the fact is that we as human beings have a need to be what we are in the fullest sense. This is the whole point. We are far more than what exists here in the physical body.

Not long ago, I started feeling sick at work. I tried to stick the day out, but I finally had to head home for some bed rest. Yet, it wasn't so bad, because I found I'd been too busy and needed some catching up on my daydreams.

I began to think about the offer I had before me: the opportunity of God-consciousness. Somehow, long ago in the misty past, I made some step which led me here. What had I done? How have I become who I am? What awaits in my future? These were the silent questions that came and sent me off daydreaming.

The amazing thing is that I immediately began feeling better. It made me stop to wonder if that was the very reason I had gotten sick in the first place. Maybe I'd better schedule some good daydream sessions more often.

Our daydreams don't need to be held to a rock of reality. We can cast off, raise anchor, and journey into the heart of life. To its very pulse. Our dreams are totally for our enjoyment, and they are real in a way not known by this world. They can bring strength and health into our lives, and they are all ours. They belong to us alone.

As I dropped my worldly concerns, and as the concepts and belief systems I had been living with fell away, my inner self felt freer and closer to what was real. I believe we all need to spend time in a space that doesn't make sense to us. We need some craziness; we need to lose our minds, in a sense.

I called this daydreaming in my talk, however, there is more truth to it than most people recognize. Unfortunately, the world seems to be strapped to its chair of "reality" like a prisoner. This prevents many people from seeing the miracles of consciousness taking place every day.

Speaking of daydreams, here's a story I wrote around this time. I never published it, but wrote it because it seemed like a great ride and seemed to capture so many of the things I was learning. Mixed in are some very real inner experiences I had, just to make the story more meaningful:

The Cloud of Unknowing

Suddenly she was before me. As real as could be. But her face was filled with fear and she was calling for help.

"The cloud," she said. "The cloud is coming. Watch out...oh, it's here...Help! Please help!"

I sat bolt upright in bed. "Jeniff!" I said. It was Jeniff. It had been so real.

I looked around and shook myself. Her face and image were still swimming through my emotions, but what had happened? Was it a dream?

The quietness of the house came to me and calmed me down. But I couldn't shake the vision of Jeniff. How could I reach her to see if she was okay? It wouldn't be easy since I had no way of contacting that strange race known as the Space People. They visit whenever they like, but they arrive via direct projection of Soul.

What had happened?

I got up and put a pot of water on to boil. A friendly fly came buzzing in to see what was cooking, then headed back out into the other rooms. Jeniff was in danger. I knew it.

A cool breeze blew across my back and I spun around to see Maylan, the Spiritual Master of the Space People, standing in my room.

"She has been taken prisoner on the planet Pragnon," he said.

"What?"

"Three nights ago," explained Maylan, "Jeniff left aboard the spaceship Actuon. She went to Pragnon to study in the great library of the Winged

Spirit. The Masters are most interested in that library, for it contains some of the most complete records of the invisible worlds. The Masters themselves have had a hand in its contents.

"But only moments ago we heard from the Actuon. They say that all of Pragnon was engulfed in the "Cloud of Unknowing"—the Searlings' most formidable weapon. They have tried repeatedly, but have been unable to contact Jeniff. We can only conclude she has succumbed to the Searlings' trap."

"The Cloud of Unknowing!" I said. "That's what she meant when she said, 'The cloud is coming.' I saw her in my dreams just before you arrived."

Maylan nodded. "You've been in her thoughts," he said. "She spoke of you just before leaving for Pragnon."

"She must be saved, Maylan," I said. "What can we do?"

"The danger is imminent, but we must visit Pragnon and retrieve what we can of the great library, and we must help Jeniff and as many others of our people as can be found."

"But why are the Searlings doing this? What do they want with Pragnon?"

"They are pawns of the Kal Niranjan," Maylan explained. "The king of the lower worlds has deceived them into thinking that their huge empire must grow to cover the entire galaxy. They are driven by what they believe is their destiny to control every world and establish their superior way."

"But they must be stopped," I said. "Jeniff must be saved."

· · ● · ·

"Are you ready to leave?" Maylan asked.

I nodded.

Maylan sat in the chair next to mine. "Follow me closely," he said. "We are going to travel via the time track. I don't trust those Searlings. They might be watching Pragnon's spaceports, so we will enter that world quietly from out of its own past. Now, stay close to me!"

A picture loomed up in my mind and crowded out all other thoughts. The urgency of the situation focused my attention. It seemed black and empty, yet it drew me like a magnet. The awareness of my body faded slowly like a candle burning out. A feeling of Maylan nearby was all I sensed. But this was something amazing. This was not like anything I'd experienced before.

We were nowhere, yet somehow there was motion. A motion without direction and without order. We saw glowing lights like fires far below us, scattered out in the blackness. They were like energy fields surrounded by a dense black nothing.

Somehow there was a passing, a changing, but I don't know how. There was nothing to compare anything to. How big were those lights, I wondered? Were we inside an atom? Were those the suns of worlds and universes? There was no way to tell.

Then we began drawing near one of the lights. It grew in size as we approached it, until it loomed huge beyond all proportion. Now I could see it. It was in fact all time and space, and we were entering from outside it! Like stepping from out of the air onto the edge of a cliff, we felt the ground beneath our feet. We were suddenly standing alone on the streets of some strange city!

It was dark and I could not believe what just happened. Maylan looked calm and curious, as ever. The black shape of a tree softly rattled its leaves behind him. We both turned around to see where we stood, but at first even the air entering my lungs seemed a strange sensation.

We both noticed the stoop of a city house, not far from us on the unlit street. We stared at it. Soft sounds from within told us it was occupied. But I could not help staring in disbelief. It was all so different, so totally unreal. Something in my subconscious was having a hard time accepting it all.

"Jeniff lives there," Maylan said softly, pointing to the house.

"She LIVES there?" I asked, confused.

"Yes. She remembers nothing of her true past, as she is a victim of the Searlings' trap. But be careful, all on Pragnon have been caught. Only we are free from the Cloud of Unknowing. At least for the moment."

"What do you mean?" I asked.

"We must be careful. Check your every thought. Let no image slip by that you have not checked. Nothing must pass our inspection. Only our training in the spiritual worlds can see us through what we now face."

Then I thought of Jeniff. How could she have been trapped? What did this Cloud of Unknowing do? Was she hurt? I had to know.

I checked my thoughts and sensed I was too sure of myself. I needed more caution. Yet I had to see her.

"Maylan..."

"Just be careful," he said. "And remember, this project may fail without you, but Spirit is all that is important. Sacrifice all else for Spirit.

"As much as a man thinks he knows; that much he does not know. Remember!"

I walked away from Maylan, trying to feel calm. Trying to remember how I last saw Jeniff. Trying to sense what was going on.

214

· · • · ·

My hand reached out and knocked on the hard wood door. I waited, listening to the sounds of this strange new world. There was an odd mechanical groaning sound far off, which I wondered about. Then the door opened and she was there!

It was Jeniff. "Oh, there you are," she said. "I thought you might forget."

"Forget?" I asked.

"Oh, you have forgotten! Our dinner with General Hafkish. How could you forget? He is the Military Commander of Pragnon, and we must be careful..."

I could only stand there amazed. It was true. She had forgotten everything and now was living out some other life. What had happened?

"...What has me worried," she continued, "is that Hafkish has no tolerance for people he does not like..."

Something was racing within me to understand what was going on. Then the thought occurred to me: How did she know me if she'd forgotten everything else? Who did she think I was?

"...And he did not hesitate to organize a formidable army..." she went on.

Then suddenly I realized what I was missing. I could hardly believe it. By coming to Pragnon via its own time track, Maylan and I must have created our own history, our own past. We actually had a history here and it existed in the minds of everyone else!

I was looking at Jeniff as she continued to talk. Somehow I'd become a part of her intimate life in this strange world. I could see it in her deep blue eyes and the sound of warmth and concern in her voice. Her light brown hair fell across her shoulders. She was a beautiful woman. There was a certain thrill to be in this strange adventure with her.

She stopped and paused when she saw me watching her. "What is it?" she asked.

"Sometimes I think, Jen, what would I do if you were in danger? I'd risk my life to get you back."

I hoped it would jog her memory, but instead she reached her arms around me and rested her head on my shoulder. We hugged and then kissed.

Well, this isn't going to be too bad, I thought. This mission isn't going to be bad at all. Yet still, I thought of Maylan's warning: To keep aware. But of what? What was happening here? Could I just tell Jeniff the truth?

Suddenly she gasped, frightened, and I saw her face go pale as she stared out the window. I looked immediately, but could only see the

215

bright moon and the empty streets bathed in its light. Yet far above the streets, hanging in the air, I detected some huge mass moving slowly. Slowly it moved across the moon.

"Oh, that cloud. That horrible cloud." she said. "I don't know why, but it always upsets me."

I watched it, and indeed there was something chilling about it, something ominous. I could feel it, and for a moment, the very moment it covered the last of the moon and the streets were plunged into a deeper dark, I felt it reach out and sweep through my consciousness.

"Ugh!" I said, recoiling from it. I looked away. Then the thought came to me: This is the cloud! This is the cloud I know something about. But what was it?

"Jeniff. This is the cloud. There is something about this cloud."

"What do you mean?" she asked.

"There is something I know about it. Something I wanted to remember. It was important."

Jeniff looked at me confused.

"It had to do with you and me." I tried to explain. "It was important and was about your safety. Oh, how could I forget?"

"I don't know. But why do you look so worried? It couldn't have been THAT important."

Was it that important, I wondered? How could I have forgotten it if it was so important? Yet there was something about it that nagged me. I just knew there was something.

* * * * *

My thoughts wandered from the conversation between Jeniff and Hafkish, the Military Commander of Pragnon. What was it about that cloud, I asked myself again? What was I forgetting?

"...And we've got a good lead on that fellow, Maylan," Hafkish was saying in his husky voice.

"What's that?" I asked.

Hafkish turned to me and nodded. "They are calling him an ECK Master, as if there were such a thing. Someone needs to show the people the truth about him. He is raising people's hopes and breeding ideas of individualism in them. Now, that would be a good story for you. You know, people hold a lot of value in the stories you write for the News."

There was something about Hafkish that I could never trust. I always knew I must watch every word I said around him. His habit of holding his hands below the table when he talked didn't help, either.

"What I write may not be something the Pragnon Military finds so appealing," I answered. "After all, I can only write the truth as I find it, you know."

His dark eyebrows furrowed a look of consternation, and the scar that crossed his forehead became even bolder. He spoke softly, the tone of his voice telling me he didn't like being disobeyed.

"Don't you realize the trouble all of Pragnon is in? Our world has come close to the brink of destroying everything we have. People have panicked from fear of this sudden chaos, which has come upon our planet. If the Pragnon Military hadn't stepped in, there would be no order at all. Some things are luxuries in times like this. Some things must be set aside, as distasteful as it might seem."

"But what about the people?" I asked. "When they go to our library of the Winged Spirit, they read those books. All those books, Hafkish, telling about how we used to live so recently. Suddenly it's like we are another people completely and don't know our own selves. What happened to us? Have we changed so much that we've forgotten who we are?"

"That library is one of those luxuries," said Hafkish, gesturing with his hand as if he were flipping some useless garbage away. "Until this confusion has eased we are closing it down."

"Don't do it!" I said, feeling myself slipping into something dangerous. I could see my feelings were too strong, but I had to go on. I needed to say what someone must say.

"The people need to know. They have to know. What you say about the chaos may be true, Hafkish, but don't hide the truth. That's not the way. You'll bring us into a civil war or a revolution. Help us learn the truth. That will ease this confusion. Our fear comes from what we don't know."

I looked to Jeniff wondering if I'd said too much. She returned a look of deep concern.

Hafkish leaned forward. "There is no place upon this planet for that library, and people like Maylan have to go. It might mean revolution, you're right. We are preparing for just such a problem right now. But someone could prevent that. Someone like you could tell the people that everything possible is being done."

A shudder ran up my spine when I realized what I'd just said, and instantly I felt the desire to back off—to leave well enough alone. But was it too late already?

Abruptly, Hafkish stood up from his table. "Think about it," he said. "You can reach me anytime. I'll see my lines are open to you. Now, if you'll excuse me, I have business to attend to."

"Thank you," I said, and we left.

. . ● . .

"His whole life is based upon forgetting what happened," I said to Jeniff as we walked out of the huge Military Command Center. "Hafkish wants to forget everything and he wants everyone else to forget. But I want to know. It seems so close, like it's on the tip of my tongue. Who are we, Jeniff? Why are we here? I know there are answers to these questions."

But as I looked to her, I could see she was worried.

"What can we do now?" Jeniff asked. "You can't follow Hafkish's suggestion and we can't put him off forever. Sooner or later he's going to know, and then..."

"We can go somewhere else," I said. "It'll be all right. This life, it doesn't seem like my life anyway." And hearing my own words, I realized how true that was.

"But where?" she asked.

We both walked along quietly, wondering. What were we here for anyway, I asked myself? Why were we living in the city? Where were we going with life? And what was this feeling within me, these worlds within worlds and strange memories?

We would have to leave our home and our friends. My career with the Pragnon News was finished. I could see that. Yet, strangely, I didn't feel a sense of loss. There was something else I wanted that was more important. There was something else within that was moving me. It didn't seem to care about being a writer or having friends or a home here in the city. There was a destination, a goal, that was pulling me toward it...What was it?

. . ● . .

We sat at the table in a small food shop, enjoying our meal. It was good to see Jeniff feeling better. Her smile was warm. Indeed, I felt good too. It was a relief to be far away from the City of Pragnon. I was reaching for another of the green skinned fruits with orange centers called yovuls, when the owner of the shop came by, asking if everything was satisfactory.

"The food is wonderful," said Jeniff.

"Oh, thank you," he said, looking pleased. "Are you traveling?"

"Yes, from the City," she answered.

The round face of the owner bobbed up and down. "So many just like you. There must be hundreds every day leaving the City. We can hardly find rooms for so many in our small town. You are lucky you came early in the day. Later, we will have to turn people away."

"Why are they leaving?" I asked.

"They grow tired of the City. Its games and pressures." The owner shrugged. "You would know better than I. Many say they wish to get closer to nature. To see the land where the yemel tree flowers and to hear the music of the birds again. We may have little here in Fenn," the owner laughed, "but birds, we have plenty."

"And good food," said Jeniff, as the owner moved on to greet others in his shop.

For a long time I thought about what the owner had said. The people walked by the window where we sat. The streets of Fenn were busy, but something about what he said disturbed me.

"Jeniff," I asked, "why are they leaving the City? The City of Pragnon, which has been praised by so many down through history? We had no choice, but they do."

"Don't you see?" she said. "Nothing ties them to the City anymore. They know it has been their home, but they cannot feel it. It isn't natural to them, and this feeling is there every day from the moment they wake and go to work. Even when they return home. Who are they? They don't even know.

"I think they want to forget, but it's hard to forget when surrounded by so many others they know and a life they don't feel is theirs. They like it here, away from all that. Nature doesn't ask you to remember. Only to live moment to moment. To be yourself."

Her words painted a picture of these people, their lives somehow shaped and formed by something they couldn't understand. Weren't we the same, Jeniff and I?

"Then these people," I said, "are leaving because there is something within them. Not in their books or their homes, but within themselves. They've tried to forget, but they can't and now they wander all of Pragnon looking outside of themselves for what is within them."

"What else can they do?" asked Jeniff. "What keeps us from knowing our own selves? Why is it such a mystery, as if something locked it away from us?"

Her words stunned me and sent echoes through the depths of my consciousness. Locked away from us. The image stirred a sudden and deep awareness.

"You're right!" I said. "It IS locked away from us. Something IS keeping us from remembering."

"But what?" Jeniff asked, looking into my eyes.

I shook my head. "We can't remember and we can't forget. But..."

Something was beginning to come through my subconscious thoughts. It was there—this faint dawning of a light.

"But...but something IS clouding our..." I stopped short when I heard my own words. "Clouding..." I said again, and looked to Jeniff. "Jeniff, something is CLOUDING our..."

Suddenly a distraction outside of the shop drew our attention. People seemed in a rush, pulling their coats tight against a stiff wind and three couples burst into the food shop to get inside. The streets of Fenn were suddenly clearing.

"What is it?" I heard someone ask. "What's going on?"

* * ● * *

I looked out the window and saw it.

"Jeniff," I said, "look!"

"I don't want to," she said.

"But look," I said. "That cloud, it's doing something."

The cloud was low to the ground and as it passed towards us, over a tree, I could visibly see the leaves and limbs go limp. A dog and two cats went scurrying down the street. Birds were flying in every direction away from the cloud.

Jeniff gasped, then looking at me her eyes grew suddenly wide. "That time," she said. "When the cloud came. Do you remember what you said? The cloud threatened our safety..."

"Yes," I said slowly, gripping my hand into a fist, "that cloud is doing it! I know it. The cloud is doing something to this whole planet. It is making us forget."

The stillness and silence was heavy as we watched the dark cloud coming toward the shop. It seemed too incredible, but it was true. I knew it. And then I realized that I'd known it even before the cloud first came.

"As much as a man thinks he knows; that much he does not know," I said. "Jeniff, someone once told me that, but now I know what it means."

A silence settled over the shop as the cloud approached. We watched it moving slowly, like long fingers caressing everything it covered. Inching along, leaving behind it the touch of unknowing. Wiping out all memories and drawing a dark veil across the consciousness.

I'd known about the cloud before it came. The thought tugged at me. And I'd known much more. The answers were there...if only I could remember...

220

The night had been dark...yes...and I walked up and knocked on the hardwood door, and I knew about the cloud...I knew about the cloud even then...but someone else was behind me...someone was with me!

Images spun. I could feel myself reaching through the veil. Through the dark void. Deeper, looking for the shadow of that man...his face...his voice...

Why were we there? Why had we come?

"Sacrifice everything for Spirit," he said. Spirit! I could see the moment blazed before my eyes. How could I have forgotten? How could I ever forget that!

"Jeniff," I said. "He was there. Maylan, the ECK Master was there."

"What?" she said.

"Before our dinner with Hafkish. We stood outside. We both knew about the cloud and we came to save you. Jeniff, that is the Cloud of Unknowing!"

The shadow line of the cloud covered the other side of the street and gradually moved our way.

"Let's get out of here," she said.

. . • . .

No sooner were we out the back door, than we spotted him.

"Maylan!" Jeniff shouted, seeing him first.

She ran into his arms with a whelp of joy and an embrace. My love rushed out to both of them, and the resonant vibration of the Sound Current lifted us all.

When Maylan looked to me it was the gaze of the Master, his eyes deep blue pools with endless depths, and all the scales fell away from my eyes. There were no more doubts, no more questions.

"This life has never been mine and never will be," I said.

Jeniff then turned to me, a warm love in her eyes. "I was lost in the illusion of unknowing," she said. "If it weren't for your bold heart and courageous risk you took, I'd still be there." She came over and kissed me.

Only the gust of wind brought us back to the present. We all looked to see the cloud still approaching.

"Are you ready?" Maylan asked. "The Actuon awaits us." He pointed up over his head. I looked to see its faint star-like twinkle.

. . • . .

221

Later, aboard the Actuon, after helping sort through what Maylan had retrieved from the library of the Winged Spirit, I talked to him alone.

"We've had no trouble with the Searlings," I said. "What happened to them?"

"It seems," Maylan said, "they simply set the Cloud of Unknowing running and left. I suppose they'll be back later to pick up the pieces. Pragnon was once a peaceful planet, but the future seems to be one of many wars, unless enough people awaken to who they really are."

"But the Cloud of Unknowing, how does it work?"

Maylan smiled. "Now that's a part of the psychic arts you don't need to learn. But I'll tell you this: They have taken advantage of an old weakness in the human consciousness.

"Mankind has always had this great desire to forget. Like a recurrent amnesia. Over and over people are born into different lives, always forgetting who they were before and who they are now. It is the wish to start over, to live a new life, which is good.

"But look at the history of your own planet. Lemuria and Atlantis are only myths now. And every conqueror has done his best to burn every record of history to start history over. Even today, your world lives under the illusion that it is the most advanced civilization yet. Their amnesia is a boost to their vanity, and the Searlings know all too well the art of building vanity into their prey."

I walked to the window and watched a miniature Pragnon with its three moons fading into the distance. I saw the thick cluster of stars behind the planet and listened to the low distant hum of the air vaporactors aboard ship.

"It's interesting," I said, "the very pitfalls and barriers that Kal places in our path can be the stepping stones we take into the higher worlds."

Maylan nodded. "That is why Life, or God, or whatever you want to call that Ultimate Reality, allows the negative force to exist in this world. It is for our unfoldment and no other reason.

"Wherever you walk is holy ground," he continued. "This is the key to the immortality of Soul."

As much as I thought I knew—that much I did not know. This was the essence of the lessons I finally learned during this time.

Up until this point, I thought that I was making progress spiritually, but suddenly I realized this was an illusion. There was no progress— there were only different states of consciousness. There was no higher or lower, no better or worse. There was only the rightness of what I was doing now, not some grand plan or final goal.

There was something very deflating about this realization. I could no longer see myself as the white knight fighting the battles against evil. The path of Truth was no longer greater than any other path.

Nothing was right or wrong by itself—it was only when Spirit, or the ECK, supported a thing that made it right for that moment. It had nothing to do with the thing, the form, the concept or the name. The truth was that there was no truth—there was only Spirit.

I now understood why some teachers have said that no conceptions about the spiritual path are real. It is not what you imagine it is, no matter what you think. There is really nothing to study or learn. Rather, it is a matter of unlearning all of our mistaken ideas. There is no grand final goal of spiritual attainment, because we can only be ourselves.

This is why some of the greatest mystics only describe what the path is not. Paradox is not a sign of error or mistake, but is a necessity of reality itself.

Perhaps this is why we like to forget. We enter new lives, new jobs, new relationships and we forget where we've been and what we've done. To see it all is to see that life itself is a contradiction. The things we believe in today were things we fought against in our youth. The very things we criticize others for doing, we end up doing ourselves.

Perhaps we forget because the paradox and the contradiction from one moment to the next is too much to comprehend. But now, I could see that it was revealing something much greater. The causes I had fought for were not important, but following the element of Spirit in the moment was. There really were no rules or philosophy of life to live by, no secret teaching that revealed the mysteries of the world—and yet there was.

It was something so real and immediate that any name you gave it could only mislead. Any way of describing it, could only distract. It simply is what it is. In this paradox is the greatest of all discoveries.

I'm not sure I am describing this well enough to explain, but what really struck me was the meaning of the present moment. There was a Presence in the here and now. This is what kept me coming back to looking at the very things that were closest to me in my life.

I had written about Levan, my job and so many other things that filled my world. I decided to write about the person who was closest to me. I wrote this for Karen:

223

Sometimes I Forget

Sometimes I forget the countless moments after moments
   she has flowed into my life,
      like some clear water mixing with mine.
   It is hard to believe there was a before…

Our struggles were so hard at times that I forgot
   the firmness of life that has shaped our sharing,
      and like two vines we have climbed the same tree.

Two children we began,
   running free
      with no one to stop us.
   We breathed the mountain air,
      splashed the river's water with each other,
         and only the Mahanta went where we went
         and knew what we knew.

And we were wed in His presence
   with the morning music of the first bird's song,
      and the first rays of sun.
   Then our secret whispers were laid on Sugmad's Throne.

Ever-deepening, ever-widening, the years and Spirit have formed us
   like two trees with bases joined,
      yet seeming independent from above.
   And look,
      a nest now placed between our juncture,
         and this little one who likes to climb about our top-most limbs.
   Such words and thoughts we've had about this one!
      His boldness!

And we search for a moment's rest in our day.
   Together.

Sometimes I forget the countless moments we've had,
   our struggles and adventures of the past,
      but not the present,
         not this moment now.

It does not pass unseen.
   Too full is it of the secret thoughts
      we have never put into words,
     and our dreams and spiritual experiences.

Like limitless fortunes entrusted to a peasant,
   I guard them closely,
      for I know they issue from Sugmad's own vault.

The love she gives, teaches me.
   Her smile and laughter charm me.
     The sharing we have changes me.

These are the precious jewels I never forget.

In the present moment—right beside me—was the greatest treasure. In the smallest of things, were the greatest truths.

I might sleep and I might forget. I might revolve upon a wheel of finding and losing myself, like some dance of life, but even this game that Soul plays no longer disturbed me. It was as if Spirit had grasped me and would not let me go.

Now I saw what was happening. As the great drama of the world fell from my eyes, I saw the struggles and burdens as a testing. All the lessons and experiences were merely the firing of a kiln.

Creating a work of art is one thing, but to be, myself, the clay in the hands of Spirit was altogether different. I could only wonder at what was taking place within me.

This is what I wrote in my notebooks as I pondered this:

My Own World

May 25, 1981

It is strange after all this traveling throughout the worlds of God that I would come to just living my own life. Being of my own world. Nothing has quite prepared me for this.

Caring for society, working for a job, even providing for a family—I've been trained in all of these. But my own world...

It is in a bit of disarray. It needs sorting out... ideas and feelings put in their proper places. For example—this idea about "the world out there"—I still find it so easy to see it as the universal world, everybody's world. Now to discover that my own world is much larger...and even encompasses that "world out there," I've not been prepared for this.

I've been prepared to just be a part of it—not the whole thing. I still look for some authority, some final word to decide, "you must do it this way." But there is only silence. Especially silence. There is more of that than anything else in my own world.

What is at the heart of my world? What is it made of? There are islands, far and remote, within me that I have only dreamed of. How can it be so endless?

I look at the top of this page and I see a date written there. It is strange—a part of "that world out there." A mark that this paper might belong to some other reality than myself. But these words I write, they echo out of distant caverns...beyond time. From where do they originate? I long to see that great vortex of Sound, resonating the atoms of all worlds—my own world is but a part of IT! That is truly the universal reality.

I feel this moment now. It telescopes from the heart of IT. How can even words be put upon paper in this manner? How can one speak of this? There is true laughter rumbling throughout the planes of God. It is the laughter of one who would ask such questions—as if there were an answer.

Have I been prepared for this—that there might be no answer? That on and on the silent questions might roll, like the endless toll of a bell? The endless crashing of the waves...the endless wind...there is no answer for these. Why should I have thought there was an answer?

My own world. It is what it is. And I am what it is.

As mystics have said, the spiritual path is a journey alone to the Alone.

I had somehow left the world behind. To walk alone seemed to make every pain, every struggle somehow different than the world's pains and struggles. It was like entering immense and endless worlds...all for the joy of it...but it must be enjoyed alone.

Like the children who had escaped from the schoolyard, in my story at the beginning of this chapter—how many of us turn away from this freedom of aloneness because it is too much?

Threshold

The night winds waver in the shadow of the ECK,
And the Mahanta's voice whispers,
   "Your footprints cross the land today, dear one,
     "But they will fade.
     "Where, oh where is Soul?"

And deep within I feel
   The swirling currents, changing course.
Like a tattered curtain in the breeze,
   I take my leave.

"Ah, dear one," He calls to me.
"All is gone. Look!
"That which was your life is no more."

And my tear
   of Love
     Falls gleaming
By the threshold of Soul.

In my own time it came, in my own way. Sooner or later, Soul had to make that step, leaving all else behind to return to the Soul Plane, the fifth world, Soul's true home.

RETURNING
HOME

I FOUND MYSELF on a long white road approaching the throne of the great Sat Nam, Lord of the Fifth Plane. The light flowing from this being was almost too bright for my spiritual eyes. I instantly recognized his warmth as deeply familiar. Everything about him struck me as Truth, for his love was Life Itself flowing out into this world and downward to sustain all the worlds below. Now I knew why it was said that Sat Nam is the first complete manifestation of Truth as one travels the high road toward God.

I bowed deeply, to show my respect for the great Sat Nam.

Laughter came from Sat Nam, seeing me bent at the waist. "Come," he said, "look up. Let me see your face. I have awaited your return. I have watched your struggles and searching, as you dreamed and wondered where life was leading you.

"Ah, yes, the negative force has worked its miracle, for you are now the awakened Soul, ready to take residence in this fifth world. Welcome home, dear one.

"Through the ages you have lived and died, only to be born again. Yet with the passing of each cycle you have changed, growing stronger in your connection with Life, until your clear voice could be heard here upon my throne. When your call reached me and touched my heart, it was I who instructed the Master to return you home.

"Come closer. Feel my love. It will now be with you throughout eternity. Soul exists because of God's great love for It. Take this understanding with you back to the Physical world, for it is the light that dispels all clouds."

Sat Nam's eyes flared bright and tremendous warmth poured through me.

"Feel my love and accept it, for it imparts the imperishable spirit of this world. You are above all duality now and know the permanence of this eternal realm."

The great Sat Nam's eyes closed and I suddenly heard the most wondrous music. The brilliance of this being was indeed the light of this world and his heartbeat was the rhythm of the sounds I heard all around me.

Standing there before him, I knew now I must pick out my own way from here on. Although I was filled with the presence of Sat Nam, this was but the beginning of the journey. There were yet the Invisible Worlds of the sixth plane, the Endless Worlds of the seventh world. On and on it goes into the heart of God.

Sat Nam's eyes opened again and his deeply resonant voice reached me.

"You were like the fallen leaf carried everywhere by the wind of the lower worlds, but now you have returned. Your home is now here where Spirit awaits the attention of Soul to manifest the unmanifested.

"These are the worlds where all life is without form until you as Soul recognize what you will be by your own law. You must choose your own way and make your own path to reach out and transform Spirit on every plane. In this way you consciously express the light of this world.

"You have stepped beyond the worlds of Creation where every experience was pre-made and no action or thought was original. Do not look back. Let the Light and Sound enter every atom of your being. It will change everything you touch, for you will be transformed by It.

"The silent questions have brought you to this realm and they will lead you on further into the higher worlds. All Soul is drawn to my heart to learn the truth of Itself, which I impart when the moment is right.

"Never again will you find true rest or comfort in the lower worlds. The birds have their nests and the foxes their holes, but he who has awakened can never find shelter in the wilderness of Soul.

"Now, go where you will, be what you will and have what you will. This is your destiny in the worlds of God."

· · • · ·

AN INCREDIBLE FEELING of being welcomed home filled my steps for weeks. I'd experienced nothing like this. It was not an emotional sensation, but more as if my vision had cleared and I finally saw what had been around me all along—that I was home. My inner worlds seemed to be celebrating, as if something significant had taken place.

About this time I also recognized a pattern I'd never noticed before. A new centered feeling of balance filled my inner being, and I realized that in some way I was riding on a spiritual current given to me as a gift. It was like a greeting of love bestowed on guests.

Looking back, I remembered something similar with each of my previous initiations. The first few months were always filled with grace, where everything went right. I would look out over all of life, seeing from the top of the mountain. At first I imagined the accomplishment was my own, as if I had solved some mystery and was freed from the worries of the human consciousness. Then I would slowly slide back.

Nothing evokes the desire to know more than having just grasped the grand view of Life Itself, only to find it slipping through your fingers. Now, however, I could see the initiations were a gift showing me a glimpse of what was possible. Once I could see the goal, I knew what to work towards. I might struggle for years to earn my way back to that view from the top of the mountain. It meant studying within myself to see what was holding me back. What did I need to learn? What did I need to let go of to regain that state of consciousness?

Therefore, when the gift came with my Fifth Initiation, I realized what a generous greeting it was. I didn't take it for granted this time, but watched and listened more carefully than before.

The thought then occurred to me that this state of grace was like having a temporary free pass. In a sense the doors were opened to me for a limited time. So, why not take advantage? Why not go to Sat Nam, the Source of Life in this new world to see for myself? This was what led to the above experience.

Through the wisdom that pours from Sat Nam's presence, I realized that I must now make my own way and live by my own law. So the question was: What would I do? It was my choice, but which way should I turn?

What caught me by surprise was the sudden realization that there was no longer anything to follow. There was no right or wrong, nor anyone who could tell me what I should do. The Path was wherever I walked.

I never knew how spiritually immature I had been. Suddenly all of my requests for guidance were coming back at me as if Life was saying: "What are you waiting for? Do you expect someone else to make the Path for you? Make it for yourself!"

I scribbled the following thoughts in my notebook:

The turning point in our spiritual life comes when we can start to make an effort beyond what is given to sustain us. To give more than is given. To decide, act and know of our own self. To be!

It is a spiritual statement. It carries with it the meaning of the spiritual Masters and their purpose in this world. It explains the fellowship and intercommunication of Soul.

It is a different world, this world of Soul. It takes time to become accustomed to it. It takes silence and patience, and it takes a close study and alignment to the inner guidance. It takes boldness to live as an individual making one's own decisions.

For the first time I realized how much I had leaned on the Master up to this point. He had been the Inner Teacher who I could look to for guidance and a sense of direction. He had been for me the Path Itself.

Something was now changing between the Inner Master and my Self. I realized that it would no longer be the same going forward. Perhaps, it is only after we lose something that we can see how valuable it is. While still feeling unsure about standing on my own feet, half way between the lower Path and my own law, I found a deep feeling of gratitude for everything the Master had given me.

It was this sense of wonder that drew me on to learn more about the meaning of the Inner Master. What really was He? I had thought that He was Someone beyond myself reaching out His hand to guide me on, but as the Path vanished and the responsibility became mine to make my own way, I realized I knew very little about the meaning of the Master.

The following is an article I wrote while exploring this subject. The opening paragraph came from something Paul Twitchell had once written.

The Masks of God

If the people are Hindu, he has appeared as Krishna, Buddha, or Vishnu, so they would know him. He is Zeus to the Greeks; Jupiter to the Romans;

Ishtar to the Babylonians; Varuna to the Aryans; Jesus to the Christians; and Allah to the Mohammedans. He has appeared to all in every age of this world since its creation. As the vehicle for God he has come in the form to which the people are most accustomed and by the name familiar to them.

These are the masks of God. The one timeless power guides and protects whoever may contact It in every age, yet we know no more of It than our own limited understanding. To see Its true form, to personally experience It in Its unlimited reality, we must remove the masks of God to look beneath.

No outer path, no holy book, no metaphysical formula can show It in Its full force. We must find for ourselves what is the truth behind all life. It is a personal journey.

"I have been asked what I mean by 'The Beloved,'" Krishnamurti, a spiritual teacher who spoke out against the need for organized religion, told an audience in 1927. "To me it is all—it is Sri Krishna, it is the Master Kuthumi, it is the Lord Maitreya, it is the Buddha, and yet it is beyond all these forms. What does it matter what name you give?"

Krishnamurti freed himself of the religious images that hide reality. He had pierced this veil. Yet, fifty years later, he admitted honestly that he still had not solved the mystery.

"Some element is watching over..." he said. "Something is protecting...It would be speculating to say what. (What we know) is too concrete, is not subtle enough. But I can't look behind the curtain. I can't do it. I tried with Pupul Jayakar and various Indian scholars who pressed me...Is this something which we cannot discover, mustn't touch, is not penetrable? I am wondering. I have often felt it is not my business; that we will never find out...We are trying with our minds to touch THAT."

Our minds cannot fathom God in its true form, for Mind creates mirrors and masks that hide the true reality. Like a computer searching for the source of its own intelligence, Mind can only generate more and more theories that reflect upon itself. Soul Travel is the solution to this impasse. Meeting the God force on the inner planes leaves no doubt in the mind of the seeker, for it is a direct experience of Soul. Unless we free ourselves of the human state, we have not gotten beyond our small range of personal reality. We have not yet touched the universal.

"(The) figures of my fantasies brought home to me the crucial insight," Carl Jung, the psychologist, recorded in his autobiography, "that there are things in the psyche which I do not produce, but which produce themselves and have their own life. Philemon represented a force which was not myself. In my fantasies I held conversations with him, and he said things which I had not consciously thought. For I observed clearly that it was he who spoke, not I. He said I treated thoughts as if I generated them myself, but in his view thoughts were like animals in the forest, or people in a room, or birds in the air, and added, 'If you should see people in a room, you would not think that you had made these people, or that you were responsible for them.'"

Jung reached beyond the conscious mind to understand the law of the unconscious—a greater world than our personal opinions and narrow theories can imagine. There, thoughts and feelings exist of themselves and we are the visitors that experience them. How did Jung come to this discovery?

"Shortly before this experience," Jung explains, "I had written down a fantasy of my soul having flown away from me." According to Jung, this was a significant event, because Soul is our connecting link to the inner worlds. Therefore, if one has the experience of Soul leaving, said Jung, this means that it has withdrawn into the inner worlds where it gives life and visible form to an ageless reality.

With Soul Travel as his key, Jung explored further, opening the way from within, but could never quite open the final door. He had many experiences, but where did his insights come from? Who was Philemon? What was this force that was leading him? Jung continued to search for the Reality behind the mask.

"Psychologically," Jung continued, "Philemon represented superior insight. He was a mysterious figure to me. At times he seemed to me quite real, as if he were a living personality. I went walking up and down the garden with him, and to me he was what the Indians call a guru...In my darkness I could have wished for nothing better than a real, live guru, someone possessing superior knowledge and ability, who could have disentangled for me the involuntary creations of my imagination."

Why are we, like Jung, so unwilling to accept our experiences for what they are? Why do we only go so far in our understanding of God, and then stop?

At times it seems too hard to shake free of our beliefs. We cannot forget the opinions of the world. Everything rises up in our imaginations to keep us from using the keys that we have. We are afraid that our fictions of reality will crumble, leaving us with nothing, yet this crumbling, this falling apart of everything we've been taught is the threshold to truth. This struggle, this dark night in our lives is the shadow before the inner gift arrives.

It can be the presence of the God power, an unexpected spiritual experience, a sudden new awareness. It might be simply a feeling of love, or protection. It is different for each, but it is as if we have crossed some invisible line and found our lives are changed. We find an inner guidance leading our steps, yet here too we must see beneath the masks of God.

"While I sat in the cathedral this morning," wrote a young boy in his diary, Easter Sunday, 1886, (and later published anonymously as *The Boy Who Saw True,*) "I was wondering about a lot of things to do with God, even though mama would say it was very wicked, because she is always telling us it's wrong to question what we are told. Then suddenly I saw Jesus, and he said, 'It is never a sin to think, my son, but it is not always wise to tell one's thoughts to others.' And he smiled that lovely smile of his, and was gone. So now I've been thinking all the more, because if Jesus says it isn't wicked to think, I don't mind what anybody else says."

The next day a similar experience came to encourage this young boy to see behind the masks of God. Once again Jesus appeared, and said, "Be not troubled, my son, for that which the multitudes believe to be true is only the faintest shadow of Truth, and much of it is not the Truth at all."

This boy had no preconceptions about what he saw. He had that wonderful quality of youth to accept and recognize the love of God that poured through this being he called Jesus. Yet, he was soon to learn the truth about this, as well. On November 25, of the same year, he wrote the following:

"Wonders never cease! Fancy, I've been wrong about Jesus all this time, and I found it out yesterday. But I don't care. Whoever he is I love him just as much, and if he asked me to crawl on my hands and knees to London town, I'd try and do it to please him, though I know he'll never ask me to do anything so silly. Anyhow this is what I heard him say yesterday, 'My son, be not sad if I tell you that I am not Jesus, but another one whose name is of no consequence, but who has been your teacher through many lives...Bear this in mind, my son: it is not what ye believe but what ye are that weighs with the Exalted Ones, for They look into the heart and not into the head to find the shining jewel.'"

Behind all things flows the river of life. Out of the heart of God it comes to bathe the world and soothe it. Thus the Godman appears in every age to find those who are ready. He can take any shape. He could appear to one or many in contemplation. He can appear as a thousand or even a million different forms to a million different people at the same time. Yet, he is always the one that links up Soul with the path to God.

Each know him by a different name, yet often he walks amongst us, unrecognized. We can try to glimpse him beneath ancient images, but we will only find him in his true form on the inner planes through the direct experience of Soul. Then, through his words, we hear the sound of God.

Within his eyes we find the light. We then can travel with him as Soul into the higher worlds of reality.

Only Soul, our higher self, knows when it is time. Only Soul can recognize the call. And when the moment arrives, only Soul of itself can remove the masks of God.

As the Path before me disappeared and as I discovered the secret that Soul, Itself, is the Way, I found something unexpected beginning to occur. My whole concept of a spiritual teaching began to dissolve. The doctrines and principles had captured my attention for years. They had drawn me on, but now I could see that they were not the path at all. They were simply doorways.

There is no use in following a spiritual teaching, no matter what kind, unless it is to open the doors and step through. Yet, up until this point, I had been so caught up in the doorways that I failed to step completely through them. I had been sitting there by the entryways of the Path, admiring them. I was lost without those doors, it seemed. They made me feel safe and secure knowing that they were there like eternal rocks that I could turn to when the entire world seemed in chaos around me. But now that was all gone.

It felt like I was Toto pulling back the curtain on the *Wizard of Oz*. I was looking behind all the doorways of religion, or whatever you want to call these sacred images. The moment I stepped through and left them behind, was the moment I realized that Soul, the higher Self, is the source of all these symbols of belief.

Belief

Any image can become a religious channel, bringing down to the worshipper the blessings of their God and Heaven. And once it becomes a religious channel—whether an idol, a holy book, a mystical symbol, or a prayer—it seems to take on a strange and ecstatic power. To look into the picture of some Saint or Master brings a presence that can dissolve conflicts within and merge us into some greater essence that seems beyond the grasp. No one should stop here, however.

Beyond this point only Soul, freed of all ideas, can travel into the heart of Truth. Yet Soul must go on without Father or Mother, without creed or prayer book, without family or friends—except that secret Friend, that invisible guide, the Eternal One, who stands at the entrance to the myriad dimensions, the worlds unending within life.

Not one place of worship, not one idol's face looks the same after being seen through the eyes of Soul. All these religious images that the people of this world hold so dear are but doorways. Why stand before the door waiting, listening to the wonderful music from the other side?

> The door opens if you know the knock,
>   and your heart unlocks
>   to let Soul fly free.
> Beyond the hall of mirrors
>   that words can weave.
>   Beyond what you believe that you believe.

Even to use names like Path, or Soul, or God, was to talk about images that are merely doorways. Reality of Itself was something much closer to our own being—something inseparable. Not some Other or external essence, but simply Self. Not a limited self, but the completeness of Being.

I now began to see how the meaning of Truth had unfolded for me. First, it had been the world of physical facts. I needed to stay objective about reality, as if Truth could be discovered outside myself. Second, came the grand ideal of World Truth, which was the aim of mankind that I found in the Cosmic Consciousness of the Astral Plane. This is the Truth that our best leaders capture and the world can recognize.

Next, came the image of something Absolute that life is founded on. This is the deeper Truth that we can lay down into divine laws and principles, as many religions have done. I came to see this Truth firsthand on the Causal Plane.

Crossing into the next world, Truth suddenly became Relative. It applied to the moment, the situation, the specific purpose and goal. Each had a Truth, and Truth could only be found in this way. The idea of an Absolute Truth dissolved away.

In the high Mental worlds, sometimes called the Etheric, Truth changed again and became No Truth. It seems there, in that world, as if there is no such thing. There is nothing at all. One gives up the hope of searching for Truth or looking for Truth because there is no-thing, only the stillness that is empty of all form. Thus, at this level, trying to search for Truth leads us away from reality rather than towards it.

Now, however, Truth had changed again. Now I could look back and see that all of these previous ideals of Truth were simply doorways leading me on, stage by stage, back to Soul. There was indeed a purpose and a goal to these doorways, but their true meaning was only known after passing through them. Therefore it became clear that Truth was not something of itself, but was a reflection of Soul to remind us of ourselves as the true source. Truth leads us not to learn something new, but to remember something we forgot.

Mirage

2,500 years ago, the spoken word was the only means of communication. This shaped the whole perception of truth for the people of that time. Great storytellers were the wise men of the day, because they passed down the knowledge of the people from generation to generation. History was no more than its oral tradition, and even religion taught that all life was created by the spoken expression of God's Word.

Truth was judged by how it was expressed through speech. How did those words touch you? What did the subtle inflections of the voice reveal?

By the time of Socrates, the written word had begun replacing speech as the basis for truth. Socrates told his students how he feared that should man depend upon writing, his Soul would become forgetful and would see no more of life than what was before his eyes.

In many ways he was right. Today history is no longer felt and remembered as something that courses through our veins, our hearts and our minds with the echo of ancient words. Today history is recorded and studied. It is considered true if it can be supported by written evidence. Facts have become the basis for truth. The irony is that we only know this truth of what Socrates said because Plato recorded his words in writing.

Man's idea of truth is like the mirage of the desert—a trick of appearances shaped by his means of communication. Yet, he always assumes his idea of truth is the right one and all others are wrong, because he does not realize he has other eyes that see more clearly and more directly.

Today the sands are shifting once more as the written word is being replaced by images as the basis for truth. Now we believe it if we see it on TV. The old ideas of truth based on the written word are starting to crumble. The Bible, now, at best seems like a good story, not the written record of God, and the classics of literature nourish us no longer—which is why our educational system of today is in such turmoil, since the whole basis for its truth is changing.

And so man follows a mirage in search of eternal truth, never realizing he stands upon that sacred ground wherever he goes. His footprints are blown away in the wind. He looks back, but history cannot help him. He looks ahead, but his new city has not yet appeared on the horizon. He has wandered too far from nature. Heaven is closer than he knows.

What had changed that I could now see this all within my own Self? What had caused this miracle to occur that I could now find the light of Soul lighting my own path and, in fact, could now see that Soul had been lighting the Path all along?

The following is a note from my journals:

Recognition of Soul by the Master is all that the Master gives us. This awakens the recognition of Soul within Itself. The Master, then, is the welcomer of Soul back home to Its true Self.

The outer path vanishes because it becomes our Self.

I had a series of dreams during this time. In the dreams I would find myself walking a few steps behind the Master. Suddenly he would stop, turn around and say to me that he didn't want me following behind him any longer. There would be a moment of confusion and then I would see that he was asking me to walk beside him. This happened repeatedly before I realized what the Master was saying. In fact, for a long time I rejected these hints, thinking that it was the sheer creation of vanity, but eventually after getting the message over and over again, I listened. It was time to work WITH the Master in creating the light of my own path.

This culminated for me during a Soul Travel exercise with the Master, when he said to me,

I am only a fellow traveler like you. I cannot be your Master, or the Master of any other Higher Initiate, because you have now reached the point of establishing your own reality. This means your own law, which you must create consciously under no outside influence.

I was not only awakening to my own law, but now I could also see and understand the Master for who He was. I began, then, to realize that

I was somehow tied into this inner teaching matrix in a way that I had not known before.

Following is a story I wrote during this time that illustrates some of the changes I began going through with this new understanding:

Visitation

I paused for a moment and listened. What was it? The cool breeze rattled leaves along the walk while I waited, listening. Then it came again. A sound in the wind from far away…a child crying…It echoed within me.

Back in my room, I lay down in bed. I could still hear that sound…like a whisper. For some reason it tugged at me, pulling me out of my own small world into something bigger. Like slipping out of an old heavy coat, I left my physical body behind. The new consciousness I occupied was much like being in a dream, but I was totally aware of where I was and what I was doing.

Instantly, I flew through the walls of my house, out over the trees and down into the valley. I saw a small, two-story white house with a neat lawn and well-kept front yard. Some dolls and a bucket lay abandoned near the front steps, as if some game had been suddenly interrupted. I flew in through the front door and paused at the base of some stairs.

I felt a strange embarrassment, as if I had walked into the wrong house by mistake. "This is someone's home," I thought, "what am I doing here?" But something urged me on, and I flew up the stairs into a small bedroom. I hovered in the air near the bed where a little girl lay, her face buried in the pillow. She was crying her heart out. She was sobbing like the whole world had forgotten her and she was all alone. I could see it with clarity and could feel the emotions as if they filled the air around her.

While I hung there witnessing this private and personal moment, I tried to comfort her with my presence. A sympathetic surge of love rushed out of me.

Suddenly she stopped crying. She lifted her head from the pillow and turned toward me. Her eyes widened, but her gaze was strangely focused as if there was something she was trying to see. I could only wonder what it was that had suddenly caught her eye. Then, looking down at my own body, I could see myself clothed in a robe of white light. I looked like an angel!

Instinctively, an urge grew within me, and reaching my hand out toward the little girl, I heard myself saying words so thick with emotion that tears came to my eyes and a lump to my throat: "You have Bunny," my voice said, "and you have me...You'll never be alone."

She must have heard or understood, because she turned and reached for her little stuffed bunny rabbit. She hugged it close to her. Then, as exhausted as she was, she lay there watching me as she slowly drifted off to sleep.

This story is actually a mixture from a number of inner experiences. Some were Soul Travel journeys, where I found myself in the homes of other people without any intention of doing so. There I witnessed some very personal moments. When these experiences first happened, I thought I had made some kind of internal error that brought me to the wrong place. But after awhile I began to note that I was simply there to bring some detached awareness and sympathy to the people involved.

I had not planned these visits, yet I began to realize that my inner awareness was being moved to help others inwardly. It felt, indeed, as if I were standing beside the Master and helping with His work. This idea itself was a pretty hard one to accept at first. However, I found others describing similar experiences as mine. After dozens of these cases occurred, I finally began to accept that there was some reality to the idea that I was involved in some way with the inner matrix of the Master.

It was around this time that I ran across a little book in a rack of used books, written by C. W. Leadbetter, called, *Invisible Helpers*. He had written a number of books for Theosophy, however this one jumped out at me because in it Leadbetter suggested that the majority of cases where angels are witnessed by people in danger or in need are actually the result of advanced spiritual students who live on the physical plane providing help.

The idea that most of these cases could be from physical beings took me by surprise. It was not what I expected at all. This sent me on some inner travels to see for myself what the truth of this was. As you will see, these experiences also contributed to my article above, "Visitation."

After my exploration, here is what I wrote in my notebooks:

After reading Leadbetter's book, *Invisible Helpers*, where he says the majority of these cases should be credited to physical students who have attained the Astral Plane, I decided to see for myself. After zooming about in the Astral skies, creating a wonderful scene filled with colors, I realized that my Astral body needed more exercise like this. I had been away too long from this world.

Slowly I found myself descending to a wonderful city filled with Persian style buildings with spires and ornate planters with trees in them, everywhere. After walking down the street a-ways I came to a small stand where a line of people stood waiting. I got in line and began studying a tall board with about a dozen columns. Each of the columns represented some category, which I didn't understand at first, and they each had a descending number of lights lit. Some columns had more lights than others and one column in particular was very long. I wondered what this meant and then realized, as if someone had answered me, that the lights represented people on the Physical Plane who were about to die. Some were nearing death in a car crash, others through a sinking ship, others from disease or murder or war.

The booth was set up for those who wanted to assist as Invisible Helpers. I chose one from the longest group and realized it represented a small black boy about to be lost in a fire. It brought tears to my eyes. I went down into the Physical as an Astral spirit, to stand as his guardian as he crossed over. It felt good to be of assistance like this and know I was cushioning this little boy's experience of death.

However, I think Leadbetter was wrong, since out of more than twenty to thirty beings standing in line, I was one of only a few who were still living in the Physical. Most seemed to be Astral volunteers who were helping in this way. I could tell the difference by the vibrancy of the light from their bodies.

I've been back to that board to help many times. I have also shared this with others and found many experienced soul travelers have been able to visit this place and experience helping others cross over at the time of death. In fact, most soul travelers I have met find themselves assisting others in dealing with death—whether it is helping those who have been left behind, or with those who are actually crossing over. However, I believe most help comes from the inner worlds.

What I learned from these experiences, more than anything, was that I needed to help others inwardly from time to time. This was somehow the Law of the Soul Plane: I was not separate from everyone else, and the pains and needs of others were a part of me that I needed to respond to.

I didn't feel the need to help others inwardly out of a desire to be a good person, or because I liked feeling like an angel or invisible helper, but because it felt as if I was helping a part of my own Self. Something in my Self needed to do this.

This showed me that living by my own law, as Soul, was not something separate from the rest of Life, because Soul was a part of all the worlds. It was not just my soul, but all of Soul.

Following is a piece that showed me in even greater detail, whether I wanted to admit it or not, that I as Soul was involved with what transpires in the worlds of God. The changing tides of the inner worlds are often invisible to us, but this showed me that my struggles were not just personal problems after all, but were also part of something much larger.

I wanted to record the Soul Travel experience while it was still fresh in my thoughts. So, I sat down with Karen and taped this dialogue:

The Dying God

DOUG: I was lying here trying to do a spiritual exercise, when I saw a book in my inner vision. It was a book about the stars and the moon, showing the different phases and what they each meant. It looked interesting, so I decided to focus on the book as my spiritual exercise to see what was there.

The book showed why such a strong mystery has been attached to the phases of the moon and the stars. Each of these periods has a mystical meaning associated with it, because these meanings are actually a part of the reality of the moon and the stars on the Astral Plane.

I thought this was interesting. So, I began to look at things on the Astral Plane a little closer. I went to look at a tree there and it looked just like what we might call an enchanted tree, because it had a meaning embedded in it. I picked up a crystal there and I could see that hidden within this crystal was a mystical truth. This crystal was actually the holder of something...I don't know quite how to describe it...a spirit...a life...an energy...

KAREN: Is this why some people are attracted to crystals on the physical plane, because they sense this astral thing about it?

DOUG: Exactly. But as I studied closer I could also see that a lot of this was an illusion. People on the astral believe that everything there is filled with meaning, but a lot of this is their own creation. They think the mystery is external, outside them, but it is partly the creation of their own imaginations.

That's why the world seems so natural there, because it is an expression of the subconscious belief of the people who live there, just like we see in our dreams. So their search to find the mysterious meanings in nature, which seems quite common there, is really a search to find their own projections and understand them, like we might try to interpret our dreams.

I then discovered that there was a group on the Astral who were also seeing what I was seeing. They are like the scientists on that plane, and their discoveries are making a huge change there because they are spreading the word that group imagination is the source of these mysteries.

They have uncovered some of the steps of creation and are now starting to use it consciously. But as soon as they started shaping the Astral world consciously, the magic of nature began to die.

For example, they have learned how to make living trees, but these trees have no special meaning in them. It's as if they are empty. I saw these little man-made glass bubbles, which are something like crystals. They do have a meaning in them, but it is all the same meaning because they are mass-produced. I saw hundreds of them in shops and stands along the streets, where people sell them.

So, a question crossed my mind: Are the scientists killing something? Actually, I think they are. I think they are getting at the very life pulse and nerve center of the natural world there.

The scientists on the Astral are coming into the secret of how Astral creation comes into being. In the past it all happened naturally, which means unconsciously. In fact, the whole creation comes from Soul, but since Soul is unaware of its own powers, it imagines a god who is responsible. Therefore, Soul also creates the Lord of that world, Jot Niranjan, unknowingly. Jot Niranjan, then, becomes the source of the natural life there.

Due to the discoveries of the scientists, however, it seemed to me as if this Jot Niranjan is close to death. You always think of these gods of the lower worlds as if they will live forever, but this being seems very close to dying.

As I was seeing this, Jot Niranjan came to me and said, "You can be the awakener. You know the secrets. Just think; you can awaken all the mountains, all of nature. They can become awake again. All the trees can be awakened, all the lakes and rivers and oceans can be awakened and come back to life again, and man can return to a life in harmony with the devas (nature spirits) and nature."

I said to him, "I didn't come into this world for that." It seemed to me as if he was proposing the role of some kind of savior.

Jot Niranjan wondered how I could turn down such an opportunity. I said, "Don't you see? This battle would never end."

"Yes," he said, "but I would support you. I would give you my own powers."

KAREN: You'd be like Jot Niranjan II...

DOUG: Yeah. (Laughter.) But he couldn't see that he was fighting something inevitable.

I said to him, "Look. Look at yourself. How many years have you been fighting and dying for this? You can be free of this too. Why worry so much about it?"

What it comes down to is that most people don't want to go back to the old ways, so they are going to follow the scientists. That is going to become their new reality. I said, if that's what they want, why fight them?

Jot Niranjan sees that the world doesn't want it the old way anymore—the way of nature—but he still thinks that people would never walk away from such beauty if they knew what they were going to lose.

So, I began to wonder, if the Astral is changing like this, and the changes on the Astral affect the physical, what does this mean for the future of the physical world?

It seems that everything will become more artificial. The natural life will gradually die away. Science will be forced to find new ways to keep the world alive, to make up for the lost vitality of nature. The devas will die off and, therefore, the fruits and plants will become weaker and weaker. So, man will have to use his sciences to produce new fruits and grow new vegetables. You can already see this happening in the world with new practices of agriculture weakening the land.

In a sense, science will set up a new god on the Astral in the place of the old Jot Niranjan. This new god will not be one who supports unconscious creation, but only conscious creation.

KAREN: But the scientific replacements are never as good as the natural ones.

DOUG: I agree. They never seem as good.

KAREN: I mean, when you get some of those square tomatoes, they taste like flavored Styrofoam.

DOUG: I know. But as science grows, it will have to learn to do better.

Already we can see the products of science are slowly killing the forests of the world. The seas are so huge they haven't been damaged much yet, but they are coming next. The fresh water is already contaminated across most of the planet. It all comes down to the fact that the devas are dying. Not just because of the pollution, but because the people do not look to the spirit of nature. They don't depend upon the devas anymore. Now they have science and technology.

247

I realized, at this point that I, myself, could live in that old age of the devas, or in the new age of science and technology just as easily. I could live in either world. So this change is not as bad as it looks.

After all, this world is a training ground for Soul. By becoming more conscious of our creations and no longer giving up our power, unconsciously, to the world—we grow and learn. Once we know the laws of nature—which are unconscious creations—once we know them consciously, then we can use them and why shouldn't we?

KAREN: Is that what the physicists are doing here in the physical, when they find that their observation of a particle changes it?

DOUG: Exactly. So they are coming very close to making these discoveries. Little by little they are discovering the laws. They can now rule electricity, which before was an unconscious part of life. Things were filled with electricity, but now it is harnessed by man.

KAREN: So you are saying that these things are not going to be an expression of the inner worlds anymore, but are going to be an expression of the scientists?

DOUG: Not exactly, because we have to remember that what the physical scientists are doing is still a reflection of what is taking place on the Astral Plane, because the same thing is happening there, too. People are taking control of their unconscious creations. They already have the secret that it is their own projections that create the mysterious power of creation on the Astral world, so it is natural that in this physical world people would discover the laws of nature and learn how to use them.

It is just that few realize what is going to be lost in the process. For example, what is going to happen to all these religions, like Christianity, Islam, and all the rest that are based on the old laws?

KAREN: You mean the religions are going to die too?

DOUG: Yes. They are based on the old laws and ideas—the unconscious creations and the worship of them.

KAREN: But these religions never empowered the people to realize that they could change things.

DOUG: Right. By inspiring worship of the unconscious creation it gave the priests more personal power. But these priests have been preaching belief in a god that is now dying. This god is being killed, you might say, by the knowledge of conscious creation. On the Astral plane this is literally coming about. It's not just a metaphor. But it isn't all good. Many other things are being lost as well. For example, as the devas die, the wild animals of the world will die.

KAREN: You mean they become extinct?

DOUG: Yes. And the vitality of the land will die. This is all because this being, Jot Niranjan, is dying, and all these devas derive their power from him, you might say.

KAREN: Is this just the nature spirits, or is this the devas in the church as well?

DOUG: Any of the religions that look to Jot Niranjan, the Creator God, are going to change. You see, when Jot Niranjan dies, all the devas die as well, and all the knowledge they knew dies with them. This is why philosophers are saying that God is dead. They are talking about the Creator God.

Man needs to survive, so if he can't get it through the nature spirits then he is going to have to do it himself. In a sense he is now on his own. So he will have to make whole new breakthroughs in science. But first we are going to feel the loss of vigor, because our health has been based on our connection with nature. It is not just clean air and water, but the energy of wildness in nature that comes from the devas.

There aren't many places of true wilderness left anymore. Technology is taking over the whole planet. It is going to force mankind to learn a lot more about the secret laws of nature. He is going to have to take those forces, which in the past were unconsciously giving him life, and will have to use those forces himself, consciously, to survive. In this way, the human race is being forced to grow up.

Something is dying and yet something is being born at the same time.

I can relate to those who feel the pain of this planet. Thousands can sense her suffering just as if it were their own pain. I too have had such sympathetic ties to nature since I was a child. So, the offer to save her, to awaken the spirit of nature again, was something I understood. It spoke to me. But this inner experience showed me something grander and more complete was taking place. These changes are part of the evolution of consciousness.

In other words, life on our planet is entering a new cycle, as it has many times before, and with this comes a new balance, a new worldview, and a new opportunity for growth. Still, it isn't easy giving up the old ways of seeing. We grew up in that old world. We understand it, and the new technological marketplace seems cold and somewhat foreign. There is sadness with letting go, and we can see many fighting hard to keep their childhood dreams alive. However, even though we may not want to hear this, the coming changes are inevitable, and there are greater opportunities for spiritual growth when cycles change.

It is amazing to look back at this experience I recorded over 25 years ago and see how dated it is, and yet how prophetic it has become. Scientists now report that our planet's ocean reefs and rain forests are struggling to survive. One third of all animal species are predicted to become endangered in the next century. Global warming is now a part of our daily news.

Scientists have stopped trying to grow square tomatoes to fit better into shipping boxes, but they continue to experiment, and their new varieties are getting better. However, traditional heirloom tomatoes still have better taste, disease resistance and production. The problem is that new genetically engineered strains of plants are spreading far beyond the fenced land where they've been planted. Farmers now realize that they cannot restrain new genes from modifying crops everywhere, and there is now a mad dash to preserve the seeds of original plant life before they disappear completely.

Watching this unfold showed me how changes in the invisible worlds cast their shadows on the physical. Many of our struggles on earth are simply reflections of changes taking place in the subtler dimensions of the higher worlds. It also makes clear to me that our source of life is a spiritual one, and if we can learn to align ourselves with the shifts taking place, we have the chance to participate consciously in evolution.

Our physical forms are intimately tied into the fabric of nature. We will always feel a strong connection to the life of this planet because our genes are intermixed. Our bodies are tied together into a larger organism. The outward breath of plants is the source of oxygen for our inward breath. Our breathing outward feeds the forests and oceans. However, as Soul we are entwined with higher worlds as well. Soul lives upon spiritual currents. Truth is our spiritual breath. The inspirations of our lives come from within us and draw us on. Therefore, we are involved in two evolutionary cycles: One is changing our consciousness; the other transforms the life forms of earth. Both cycles have influenced us subconsciously for ages. We are now being offered the opportunity to awaken to and understand the way we are tied to all of life, both inwardly and outwardly. This is a priceless gift.

Old wells run dry because new rivers of life take their place. Our folk songs are disappearing and our sense of community is fading, but we now have a freedom of individual choice that we've never known before.

Our children's children will never experience the incredible mystery and power of true wilderness, but it is easy to see that our youth of

250

today are drawn by the technological age. They can now connect to people across the planet. They cross cultures and thousands of miles with the touch of their fingers. It used to be that you could drive around and see where families with children lived, since they were always playing outside. Not anymore. Kids today are growing up in a new world, with a sense of discovery that reaches out through the miracle of electronics.

There is sadness in seeing old gods die, and many religious battles today are merely desperate attempts to stop the world from changing. It is not always easy to recognize death as part of the evolutionary cycle, especially shifts in consciousness that affect the way we feel. However, letting go is what connects us to life and the growth of the moment. This is where we find the miracle of a changed consciousness—in the meaning of life as it is right now.

The changing world takes place because this is how Soul learns and grows.

Truth

Go on, if you dare,
But truth will change you
Again and again
Until it has left wrinkles
Upon your wrinkles.
And your tears have drowned
Away the ocean.

Then what is left to change
When all the idols have lost their name?
Only the ocean's tide upon the sand.
Only this ocean beating,
Leaving its trace upon the land,
So that you can see as life sees.

I could now recognize that Soul's understanding of Its Own Truth was more important than any idealistic missions to save the world. The spiritual teachings that come from the Soul Plane, therefore, are not actually for the world, but are for the individual who is ready to return home to Soul, Itself.

This was not exactly a new thought for me, but it was a new understanding. It meant that the forms of the teachings didn't matter. They were merely doorways. What difference did the color of the door make, or its shape? It was not about popularity or consensus, but individual self-awakening and revelation.

Key to the Sixth World

I turned from the great Lord of the Sixth World and looked across the vast desert of Akara. I could see that the rest was up to me. I must make my way alone.

Momentarily I looked back to the lower worlds and, indeed, it seemed like everything depended on what I would find. Then, I realized: this was the universal vision of this world. Whatever I might see, do or experience is a manifestation of life in this world, and thus Soul is no longer broken into parts but is only that great light of Life.

I now held the key to the spiritual worlds, yet what was this key? What should I do with it? I sought only God, but which way should I turn?

As I looked across the far reaches of the desert, my vision kept turning back to what looked like a great sun setting in the distance. My spirit picked up as the resounding vibrations within me confirmed that this indeed was my goal. My feet began treading their way through the sands of golden atoms.

It seemed like eternity crossing the desert, but as I drew near, the sun grew more and more brilliant before me.

Suddenly I realized: This was no sun, but a tremendous tree that was issuing this light! Its brilliance spread out in all directions along with a silent sound resonating in the air and the golden atoms beneath my feet. Any feeling of solidity was gone and for a moment I knew all that I was experiencing was tied into an endlessness of reality, and this tree stood rooted at its center.

This is the Tree of Life, I thought to myself, and as if I had spoken, a Voice whispered from the leaves of the tree:

"I am all you believe me to be, for in this world your belief is an act of creation and there is no other existence. Therefore, out of the great feeling of your heart I have been manifested from the spiritual ethers. My roots are the insistence of your belief hidden beneath the golden sands of your own projection.

"Can you believe there is no reality but what you create out of the God power? No beings in all the worlds below this one can accept this truth. They reject their own godhood. Thus, because of God's great love, IT has established the lords who create the worlds below this one, for Soul to accept Their Will until Soul is ready to gain the spiritual key of the Sixth World.

"Create! Use the God power and fill the world with ITS manifestation. Be the co-worker of God and hold no other reality before God. In this way the stream of God power flows down through this world into the worlds below. You must create the idea of God and you must prove the existence of IT, for IT has no other way of manifesting.

"Can you accept this? Have you shaken off your limitations of mortality?

"You have sought all the dreams of God, but now they are reduced to nothing. You must see beyond the mirror of God if you are to take your place amongst the citizens of this world.

"The great pain you suffer is the loss of your dreams, for you wonder how you can live without the dreams of God. So, create! Use the God power and make your dreams the reality you always wished they could be. Manifest further and further the reality of God, until you cannot distinguish your own awareness from IT."

I had taken another step, for you see, this chapter is not just about the Fifth Initiation alone, but the stages of Self-Realization. The Sixth world and Seventh are deeper aspects of Self-Realization. The Eighth Plane is where God-Consciousness begins to emerge, with the Ninth being the first complete stage of God-Consciousness.

These, of course, are all names and terms, and they hardly mean anything to us until we know their meaning from personal experience. In fact, they can either be doorways leading us to a greater understanding, or closed doors that only get in our way.

This is the problem with all forms of the spiritual path. Every religion and every teacher treats terms differently. For many they are vague or even contradictory. However, once I reached the Sixth world I could see that none of this mattered anymore. It was only what I made of Truth. It was only the manifestation of Truth through Soul that had any meaning.

Looking back, I can see my writing changed significantly at this point. Of all the pieces I had written so far in this chapter, none had been published. They were too personal and seemed to me too bold to share. I had published one piece during that time—an article called, "A Meeting With Rebazar Tarzs," which I've included in my book, *The Whole Truth*, so I have no need to print it here. However, even that piece seemed too revealing, so I submitted it under the pseudonym of Dan Stryder.

I felt cautious about sharing my understanding of Self-Realization. I didn't feel comfortable with the idea of setting out a truth that was my own for the world. However, a growing feeling was pushing me to start publishing again.

I wanted to be sure I understood what the meaning of this inner desire was, so I studied it for a long time before acting on it. It was mixed up with old feelings of wanting to be popular or achieving some kind of success, which I had to sweep away. I realized that this was not what I wanted as a motivation any longer. So, I needed to consciously remove those immature urges before I felt comfortable writing for publication again.

One of the reasons for my extreme caution came because I had only a few years before witnessed the fall from grace of my dear teacher, Darwin Gross. I had looked up to him as my guide for many years, but he had lost his balance and of his own free will stepped aside, passing the leadership of Eckankar onto Harold Klemp. That Harold would be the next leader of Eckankar didn't surprise me at all, since I had expected it for years. However, the difficulties that Darwin had gone through as a public spiritual figure etched a deep lesson upon my consciousness about the dangers of illusions and the importance of doing only what was true and necessary, spiritually.

Even though the path of publishing spiritual writings seemed to be strewn with land mines of vanity and delusions, still there was this growing necessity in me to create Truth as I knew it. Not a World Truth, or an Absolute Truth, but just to create as a way of manifesting truth.

Underlying this all was the realization that everything I thought I knew about the spiritual path was vanishing before my eyes. It no longer seemed real anymore. All the principles of the path were but temporary doorways, not the eternal truths I had once thought.

The silent questions returned once again, and I asked inwardly what was real? What was the path? What did it all mean? Now I realized that it was for me to create the answers. It was for me to establish what was real and to manifest it for myself. There was nothing outside of Soul to lean upon any longer.

So, the answer for my own spiritual growth was to write and try to put into words some trace of Truth; to create and manifest Truth as a writer. I needed to do this for Soul.

It had to be Truth I believed in and it must also be universal. It had to reach to the core of Soul, and could not be separated from life as if it were something external. I needed to express some essence of Self-Realization, and it must be hidden just as all Truth is hidden within Life.

The exercise of trying to create such a truth through writing became my spiritual practice for the next few years. It leaves an interesting record to study, but more importantly at the time it became something that filled me with a deeper understanding of the spiritual teachings than I had ever known before. With every choice of words, I learned something new about the path I was manifesting within myself. Writing became both an act of self-recognition and an act of creation.

At first what I wrote was simple. I wanted to show Truth as it lay hidden within life all around us. Something that could only be seen by looking closely and listening carefully.

Following is the first piece I wrote during this period.

The Coins of God

The coin lay there, half covered with dirt, far from where its owner intended it to be. The coin had taken its own path, setting itself free from the course of mankind, and now lay abandoned and tarnished with age. Its face bore the image of another time, another civilization, as if some bit of knowledge had been forgotten and lost by the world.

Waiting…perhaps for a new generation, a new age when it would be understood and valued for what it was.

Someone had a plan for this coin, but the coin had escaped that plan. Now it lay there closer to reality, closer to itself, surrounded by the silence. Unseen and alone, the coin now belonged only to God. The rain, the sun and the earth—only these know where the coins of God lie.

Coins have long represented an image of wisdom in my dreams. Therefore, lost coins from another time were to me like ancient truths.

However, this coin was also a symbol of something more: It was a reflection of Soul. We are all like forgotten coins that only belong to God. We are only truly known by God.

In a way, all of our life is symbolic of inner realities and inner truths. Our everyday life can be interpreted like a dream, because the things that enter and leave our daily experiences are also reflections of greater things.

255

Therefore, the spiritual teaching is something that can hardly be described. It remains hidden and yet is revealed by self-awareness. It contains paradoxes because it is both universal and yet unique to the individual.

I was learning a new language—this language of formless spiritual teachings.

The Boy and the Sea

A young boy sat on the edge of the wharf, looking out over the gray water. His legs dangled free in the air, kicking back and forth. This was the place where he sat every day to listen to the sounds that the wind carried and to watch the way the waves danced. The sea was his friend and he came to visit, just as he visited the geese in Mrs. Thatcher's yard and the seagulls behind Mr. Danver's Fish Market.

But the sea was different. The sea seemed changed every day, and yet somehow was exactly the same. It seemed endless and huge, yet at times you forgot it was even there, and it would startle you when you noticed it again.

The boy felt small when he played on the shore, looking for stones and shells. He knew what the seagulls must feel like when he watched them picking at their pieces of fish, because the sea had a presence, and at times he felt that it was really the sea who visited him to see how he grew and changed every day.

Perhaps this was why the boy thought that the sea was ancient and wise and that it knew the answers to the questions he might ask. Maybe this was what drew him into talking with an old sea captain who he'd never seen before.

"How far is it to the other side of the sea?" the boy asked, his thoughts filled with images of the exotic lands that might exist there.

"The sea is the sea," said the captain. "It has no sides. Only land has sides."

"You mean it goes forever?"

"Yes," the captain answered, "with little bits of land along the way."

"But Mr. Danver said that ships have sailed over all the world and explored all the sea," the boy said, not quite sure. "Haven't they?"

The captain was rewinding a new coil of rope the way he liked it, so it would flow smoothly and not catch or kink. He looked at the boy.

"How can you tell if you have been to a certain place in the sea? The sea has no places, it only has water and waves and a rhythm. And it has a voice too, if you know how to listen.

"Yes, you could say, "I'm about halfway between Hawaii and Japan, for example, but those are land places, not sea places. You can spot the stars and watch the sun, but those are sky places.

"People forget that this world is mostly sea, but the sea is always moving. This is not the same sea here today as when I was last here, fifteen years ago. That was a stormy sea, too wild even for the whales. So how can anyone say they have seen all the sea? The sea is endless and always moving. Only the shores can be known."

The boy sat there, kicking his legs, wondering why he'd always thought this was the same sea each day that greeted him.

"But Earth doesn't go on forever," the boy said, still thinking and trying to understand. "So, how can the sea go forever?"

"You are still thinking landwise," the captain answered. "But when you are out upon the sea with no land in sight and only the stars in the sky—then the sea is forever. It has no places and has no time except night and day. These people who try to figure out the sea with their science and books, what do they know?

"They go to work every morning. They go to some place and come back to their home every night. They listen to the clocks telling them the time, they follow their roads to the cities and stores, and these places are always there. They never move. It is easy to be sure about things that never change.

"And so they make maps—millions of maps—but only land maps, with names that fool people, like the Indian Ocean, or the North China Sea. What do they know of the North China Sea? It is not one, but a thousand seas churning together, making new seas everyday. They know the land, so they think they know the sea. The sea laughs at their maps."

"Is that why people can't live out on the sea forever and have to always come back ashore, because they can't understand the sea and the sea thinks they are a bunch of pretty-pusses?"

The captain laughed. "Yes, I think you're right."

"But you have lived for a long time on the sea, haven't you?" the boy asked.

"Yes," said the captain, feeling very old.

"Where are you going next?"

"I don't know yet," the captain said. "My ship is for hire."

"How long will you be out on the sea?"

"That depends," said the captain, "on who I take, of course."

"Would you take me?" asked the boy.

257

The captain smiled. "Sure," he said.

"How long would it be then?"

The captain paused. He looked at the boy, and then at the sea. His thoughts rushed out far across time and across his memories. He thought of the years.

"It would be a long, long time," he said to the boy. "To answer the questions that you ask about the sea could never be a short journey."

The boy looked out at the horizon. Suddenly his legs stopped and hung motionless. He watched a seagull flying back to shore. He stood up slowly and looked at the captain. "When I am older, I think I will go out to sea." Then he ran up the wharf, toward town.

The captain understood the depth and wisdom of that decision, for he too had once been such a boy. And he knew that when it was time, the sea would send a teacher.

This represented a major shift in my realization of the spiritual teachings. Until this point, I had been judging the path by its landmarks and fixed reference points. I had mistakenly taken the land places as if they were describing the sea, as if they could tell me something about the ocean itself. But to know the ocean was something altogether different.

Captains of the sea are those who know the ocean without any need for stars or land to fix their reference. The ocean simply is what it is. It has a beingness that no landmarks can describe. It has a quality that can only be known through experience and intimate knowledge.

The world fights its wars over land, and all religious debates take place over fixed points. However, no one can own the sea. It cannot be bottled up. There is no place to fix a flag or a nameplate. After all, all names are really land names.

Then how does one describe the spiritual teachings? I now realized it was impossible. It is a reality that can only be known by becoming it. Now I could see that in a sense I was becoming the ocean and there was no way this could be given to anyone else. There are no land words that can explain this meaning. I could, when all was said and done, only let the sea speak through me. I could only let the sounds of the ocean, its depths and ever changing movement, shape my life.

This is what it meant to manifest the spiritual teachings.

A significant change came over me with this understanding. I began to see the silent questions in a whole new way. The questions were the call of the ocean. It was the sound of the surf pounding against the land, beckoning us out to sea. We worry about becoming lost at sea when we ask, "What is the meaning of life?" But, in fact, we have become lost at land.

We become so deeply trained in land languages that we don't realize the question, "Where should I go?" is but a land question, since in Soul the Isness of Being can be found in every place and is even where there is no place at all. Yes, of course we will become lost at sea. That is the reality of Self-Realization. It is not to become found, but to become lost. The silent questions come not to be answered, but to tug apart our answers so that we can Be.

Of course the world does not understand this language of the ocean, so when I said things that suggested leaving the land places behind, it sounded to some as if I was saying to destroy the land places. When I tried to describe how to step through the doorways to enter into the true teachings of Soul, some people took this to mean that I was preaching the elimination of doorways.

I could see this new truth I had discovered made some people extremely uncomfortable. They were not ready to become lost at sea. They weren't ready to give up THEIR answers. Nor did it seem right to them that I wasn't pointing to THE answers as if they were holy landmarks of the path.

If anyone thinks that Self-Realization is easy, they should think again. A part of me had no desire to upset anyone else. I could mimic land-speak as well as anyone else. But another part of me had become the sea. I didn't yet understand what this all meant yet. A series of dreams came to me around this time that foreshadowed what lay ahead. Here is one from my notebooks:

> An ECK Master came up to me and asked, "Well, what do you think you should do now?"
>
> I asked him, "What do YOU think I should do?"
>
> Then I realized he asked me first and I should answer first. So, I said, "I need to be true to myself and I should feel no hesitation in saying what I know is true."
>
> He said, "You should leave. When will you stop holding yourself back for others?"

I should leave? I should leave what? The Master's words shook me.

Suddenly I had this feeling that these Masters play for keeps. This was not just a game.

A series of dreams came just like this one, challenging me and suggesting that I was holding myself back. Another Master whom I had never seen before came and told me that I had accepted too many things. Even Paul Twitchell got some things wrong about the path, he told me. Then he asked me, "What do you think Mastership is?"

I could see the ocean wasn't going to let me go. It was out to indeed destroy all the land places I once held sacred. I felt as if I was being caught in a rip current and pulled out to sea. I wondered if I would ever see land again.

I then had the following experience that I recorded in my notebooks.

Woke up about 5:00 am and decided to do a Soul Travel exercise. Slowly I felt myself tipping backwards, but I didn't want to fall that way, so I tipped forward, all the way over and fell out of my body.

Immediately I was reversed, facing up, and I saw my luminous silver cord reaching up to my bed above me. I wasn't sure if I should go with the experience since it seemed more like Astral Travel (because of the silver cord) but I realized this was a foolish fear—so I went with it. I turned over and floated down into a room I had never seen before. There was no question that I was someplace physical.

Everything in the room was dull in colors and alien in feeling. Someone nearby held a paper with the date on it and I sensed I was not in 1985. I asked the man if I could see the paper. He handed it to me. I could hardly believe my eyes. "My God," I said, "it's 3911!" The man looked at me strangely, wondering why the date would surprise me like that.

It seemed that I was in something of a crude bookstore or a run down library that was rarely used. I couldn't see anyone in charge and there was a strange feeling of disorder and chaos, as if everything had fallen apart. The people there all seemed to accept it as normal, but it looked very depressing.

I looked through the bookshelves for something familiar and spotted what looked like *The Tiger's Fang* [one of Paul Twitchell's books]. It was red, which reminded me of how it looked when it was first printed. But when I took the book out to look at, I could barely see any resemblance. The title was changed, the shape was narrow and long, and a strange picture appeared on the front. The face was too large around the top, and too small at the base, but the resemblance to Paul was unmistakable. I could literally see how nearly two thousand years had distorted the image, as it was copied and recopied, and then touched up by hand. I flipped through the pages, and even though the words had changed, I still recognized them as Paul's.

I then spotted a volume of the *Shariyat-Ki-Sugmad* on another bookshelf. It was dark blue, and appeared to be Book Six. I exclaimed, at finding it, in disbelief [since Book Six has not yet been published]. Someone nearby said, "That's a favorite of mine, too." But when I opened the pages I found nothing even remotely what I expected. The pages were all light blue with colorful religious pictures on every page, illustrating the sacred verse. It was all heavy astral religious, filled with worship, and prayers. I couldn't see even a spark of revelation left in it. It had obviously become reduced to religious sermons held in worshipful adoration.

I looked around for someone to help me. A young lady and an older lady were nearby. That was when I looked outside through the sliding glass door for the first time. I had a flash of recognition and familiarity. "Why, it's Arizona," I said. The young lady looked strangely at me, as apparently I was using an odd name, but I sensed she had heard the name before.

I stepped outside to get a good look and was immediately seized with choking. The outside air was so smoggy it burnt my eyes and throat. I was forced to step back inside. I had seen enough to realize that this had indeed once been Arizona, but it was nothing like what I knew anymore. I also realized I would have to adjust the vibrations of my body to face the harsh air. Looking at the two women I could see that their bodies had learned to adapt, and somehow I seemed to know how to take on the same body pattern that they had. It all happened in an instant.

There was a deep booming sound, suddenly. I turned to the others and said, "Where did that come from?" There was some discussion between these two women because of my question. I was starting to worry them. Then I said, "That's where I must go," and I walked outside beckoning the women to follow me. They were both scared of my erratic behavior, as if I might be a lunatic. I could see that they followed me out of fear, figuring it would be safer to do what I said rather than upset me. I was surprised how quickly they fell into this feeling of fear.

Instead of following the road up to a parking lot, I climbed up a faster way, as it seemed that's where I needed to go. The younger lady followed easily, but the older lady could not. I could see that everything I was doing deeply disturbed her, as my actions were completely out of the ordinary. That was when I had a good look at her. Her skin was slightly darker than a white person, as if she had a slight mixture of black in her, with also a trace of Navajo to her face. I suddenly realized that the separate races had all disappeared through intermarriage long ago, but the traces were still there.

However, it was her consciousness that surprised me the most. She seemed to have the attitude and outlook of a slave on a plantation. Fear and a feeling of suppression filled her. I could only wonder where this had come from. To let her off the hook, and as a kindness to her, I said, "Those who cannot climb this will not be able to follow me where I must go." The old lady was visibly relieved. She had more than enough excitement for one day.

When the younger lady and I came to her car in the parking garage, other people were approaching. I didn't want her getting too upset either, so I asked if it was okay to be seen with me. She said it was okay, but I sensed she would rather not. So, I bent down to tie my shoes while the people were walking by. This was when I realized that no one had shoes with shoe laces, and so once again I was acting strangely.

The girl, as if trying to get her courage up and trying to calm me down, since she still wondered if I was a crazy man, said to me that she didn't let things bother her. It seemed pitifully weak, but I could see to her it was a statement of significant courage. An approaching man overheard her and said, "Well you're lucky. I have too much misery to escape."

I sensed that this man was a doctor and said quietly to the girl, "He has nothing to complain about. He flies wherever he wants to go," implying he had an easy life. However, by this time the overwhelming feeling of depression amongst the people was hitting me.

As I was getting into the car, which only somewhat resembled a car, I asked her a question about how it ran. She gave me an incredibly technical answer, as if it were common knowledge, but it went right over my head. I asked her where she learned such a thing and she said, "Oh I never learned it anywhere. I just knew it," as if it were nothing special. I said to her, "Then that is a talent you must have."

I was trying to make her feel more at ease, but in fact the whole world was filled with so many changes and different things that my own awareness was barely keeping up. I realized then that our consciousness can only deal with so much change at a time. More than our limit and we begin to blank out the rest. I knew there were things I was missing because of this.

We started driving in the car. I was in the driver's seat, which was on the left. There wasn't any steering wheel or tires on the car, but the girl showed me how to drive it. The roads were a complete shambles and all broken up. The buildings we passed were all falling apart. Junk and garbage was everywhere. It looked like a huge disaster had struck, and I had the sense that such a thing might strike again at any time. But there were people walking around as if this was just the way it was and had been for a long, long time.

There was a sudden sound of wind and then another boom, and for some reason I knew I must hurry.

I also noticed that amongst the people there was a strange lack of privacy, like people who come together in the face of a disaster. I didn't see anyone noticeably sick, but the air pollution was terrible, the sky was completely gray, with not even a sign of blue sky. The people looked beaten, apathetic and without any spirit at all.

As we drove I became confused over some people who would walk up to the road with what looked to be hand-held traffic signals. They had the green, yellow and red lights like a traffic light, but they were at the center of what looked like a Christian cross. Apparently they weren't traffic signals at all, but some kind of public notice to let everyone know when help was needed. However, the religious connotation was clear, and I sensed they were somehow connected with churches along the road. We passed many of these.

We came to one with a red light. I wanted to drive past, but the girl gave me a look as if I was being completely disrespectful. She had obviously been putting up with my erratic behavior, but this was going too far. I wasn't sure where I had to get to, but I had a strong feeling that I shouldn't get caught up in some kind of side trip, since my time was too short. However, I listened to the girl's pleas and finally decided to get out and see how I could help.

There was some sort of religious procession that seemed to be marking the opening of a new church, or the entering of a renovated old church by a new group. I couldn't understand all that was happening. The leader had long light hair, blonde-brown, with straight bangs. He wore a white flowing robe with gold-brown trim. He looked right out of Biblical times. He was even walking with a staff. One of his followers was a tall man with long brown hair, like a hippie from the 60's, with beads and a long dark robe. The leader, plus a few of his followers, showed the only smiles of anyone I had seen so far.

I held my hand out to greet the leader. He reached out, but not in the normal handshake. Instead, he laid his palm against mine and with his two middle fingers he touched the pulse on my wrist. I matched his greeting.

Suddenly I knew why I had come to this time and place. I knelt down on one knee with his hand still in mine, and I said out loud for him and his followers to hear, as a deep feeling welled up within me, "You are the one that was prophesied to come and lift the people."

Then I looked down for a moment at the ground, and quietly said to myself, "But oh, you have so much to learn yet."

263

Then looking back at him I said, "You think I look even younger than you, but I am over 1,000 years old. I have just returned to civilization after all these years and I am amazed at what I see. I was born in the time of Paul Twitchell."

The whole procession gathered around, struck by what I said. I had so much I wanted to tell this spiritual leader, but I started feeling myself returning to my body. I knew that I was disappearing right before the whole group and I could sense the impression this would leave.

When I came back it was about 6:30 am. I had been gone for an hour and a half, and it seemed as if it took exactly that long. I was completely conscious the whole experience and knew for a fact that I was in the year 3911.

It was a bizarre experience that affected my consciousness so strongly that for two weeks I felt as if I was half walking in some alien world. Everything seemed strange to me. There was nothing stable about the physical world I could count on. Time itself had fallen apart.

Long ago, I stopped wondering whether these experiences were exactly what they seemed to be. The question was not: Had I really been in 3911? All that mattered was the experience itself had been so real. I was completely conscious every minute, never once falling into a dream state, and it left me with a sense of reality so deep that I could see no element of imagination in it. Nothing I had experienced was even close to what I might have expected. I could not even recognize half of what I saw, since it was all so strange.

Some of the lessons from the experience were clear, however. I was there to help manifest the truth of the spiritual path for the sake of this new teacher. Yet, it was more as if some higher force was moving me, since the experience rolled out before me without any effort of my own. I only needed to recognize the meaning of the moment when it came.

While thinking about this, it occurred to me how little I knew about the ways in which the teachings reach this world. The message I gave to this teacher in the future struck home with me: How much I had to learn. My writing changed again, as well.

The Caged Bird

I have outgrown this old dusty ball of Earth. Its weak insipid desires strain at my heart. Its games of wealth and power tire me. I wander the lonely streets looking, searching, yet there is nothing to lift me but the love of God.

The dreams of others cannot move me. I see the endless hours upon hours they spend filling their wishes, but I have no wishes. I am the poorest of the poor, without even a desire, yet I am happy with nothing. I am happy with only a thought—to share the burning love of God. I have been scorched by love and nothing but love can soothe me.

Why is there no place for me upon this heap of a planet? There are holes for even the snakes and the weasels; am I lower than they? But I am a snake who will not slither upon his belly. I am a weasel who will not sneak away. How long can such a creature live in this ruthless world? I am weak and defenseless, knowing but one weapon; how to burn others with the love of God.

You who think you suffer; wait until you are burned by God's love! You, who can find happiness in your riches, wait until you see the treasures of heaven. You can go about your life, day by day, only because of what you don't know, like the animals of the forest who know not the comfort of a home. But what will you do when you have seen? Where will you go?

The world is but a prison from which only Soul can flee. The body is a chain—but it holds me no longer! Now I fly free and take wing into the very heart of God. There is no other way to heal these wounds from ITS great love.

Do the sting of these words disturb you? Then go seek your comfort in ignorance. I will not stop you. I will let you go, but do not ask me to follow. For I have drunk too deeply of God's love, and I know the caged bird cannot sing.

I wrote this piece from a state of consciousness like nothing I had experienced before. It was as if I was writing from a higher self and merely using my physical body to talk through. I could see with this writing that I was speaking with another voice. I was using a kind of inner matrix that could channel a deeper wisdom. It was a wisdom that even I was amazed to read and hear.

I had heard Paul Twitchell talk about this and heard him describe how he would sometimes shift to this higher self, what he called the

265

God-Self, and speak from it. He would say that he was not speaking as Paul the man, but from the higher self.

I had caught a glimpse of where the great spiritual teachers of this world have taught from. The wisdom that came through them was not their personal wisdom. It was not their personality talking. They had fashioned a voice through which the higher wisdom could flow. It was God's wisdom, in a sense, or the God-Wisdom if you want to call it that, but at the same time you become a part of it. It is not something separate when it flows through you, so it is also your higher Self at the same time.

There are many facets to Soul. We are in fact many selves with many voices, and it is important to know our many parts. This means it is important not to get carried away with delusions of grandeur simply because we have begun to speak with the voice of the God-Self. Everyone has such a Self, so this makes us in no way special or greater than anyone else.

Learning the lessons of responsibility that go along with this all took many years to understand. In the meantime, I felt uncomfortable speaking from the God-self. I had caught a glimpse, but still had much to learn about my Soul-Self, first.

As I looked at how completely my life had changed, I also realized I had left something very dear behind. I still cared about my old ideas of the path, like one might care for an old friend. We had been through so much together. I didn't even realize how deep these feelings went until I wrote the following.

The Old Path

It was a clear spring day in mid-17th century Scotland. A black-haired lad, looking travel worn, yet light of step, walked along a road trying to trace his memories. Blossoms of heather flanked him on both sides, like some strangely familiar hallway to the past.

"This was the Big Road," he mused. "Aye, the Grand Highway. It went forever to all the world!" He chuckled at his boyhood memories. Now it seemed so small.

His journeys through the exotic lands of the East had left their mark upon him. The battles he had fought for the Crown...the seas he had crossed in galleys, pulling oars beneath the hot sun...the strange cultures...the ancient Roman roads laid in stone, hundreds of miles long.

Now this old path seemed small. He had seen too much and walked too many paths, he thought. And yet...

He recognized an old elm on the hill, surrounded by a clump of white birch, like a circle of wise men left to themselves. Faint echoes of what he saw stirred long forgotten feelings. Like a stone clattering down an old well...he waited...listening...feeling...

Where the path should have been, he found brambles blocking his way, as if they were a locked gate claimed by the years, saying, "Go away. Let the dead lie in peace." For a moment he considered this omen, but then with a boyish grin he slipped his "Angel of Little Mercy" from her sheath and heaved to. "Take that and that, you cutthroats," he shouted while the metal blade flashed wildly.

Then he was silent. The cutthroats lay trampled behind him. An old thatched house waited ahead. It had been waiting for many years.

He drank in the sight, as if it held some secret of life for him. As if it could answer the meaning of himself. Armies might have fallen beside him, new kingdoms could have been born nearby, yet he would not have noticed. He was facing what had once been his whole world.

He wondered...dare he light the home fires again?

For an eternity he stood, caught between two worlds. He could not advance. No enemy had ever caused such hesitation. But this house, this old empty lump of weeds and clods...he had been born here. He had grown here. And a part of him was still here slaying dragons and ogres...sitting in his mother's arms, rocking before the home fires, while the rain dripped in puddles as they sang about the sea and far away lands—and his father.

Yes, his father. One day he would find his father and save him from...and then he heard once again that sweet, sad song of his mother crying for her love long gone, while she thought her son slept and could not hear her.

Was that why he left—to find his father? Was that why he had searched out and followed his father's dream? And now he had returned as his father, as his father once wished—to greet his devoted wife and wild son, to re-light the home fires...

To re-light the home fires...

"Nothing dies!" he shouted out to the house. Then silently he added, "I carry you all within me. You all live as I live. Nothing ever dies!"

This piece spoke to me at so many levels I don't think I can describe its many facets. I sat amazed at my computer after writing this. It was the story of some other man, yet it seemed to speak to me directly.

I had gone off to find my father and returned as my father. And the old path was too dear to forget. I could not leave it behind. I realized that I must bring it back to life, in a sense, through my recognition of it.

What I was doing, I can see now, was re-integrating my previous world back within myself. First I had to leave it, just as the ECK Master had told me, but now I could care for it like an adult. I was no longer the child. I no longer needed it, like a child, but in a sense I could see that it needed me.

I have seen many people outgrow their paths only to turn on their old teachings and attack them, as if such a thing could help them move forward and release the past. Of course we do need to withdraw from old states of consciousness to move on, but I found a sense of wholeness only after re-integrating my previous lessons into a greater perspective.

In the past I had looked to the path to help me at every turn, but now the path was something for me to manifest and to care for. However, I did not have to let my old world die and be forgotten. I could carry it with me as a part of myself.

I gave a talk at an Eckankar Seminar in California, where I tried to capture this lesson in a parable. The following is from my notes for that talk:

Leaving The Path

There was once a man who was so sure about the truth and validity of the Spiritual Path that he never wanted to leave it, no matter what might happen. In the beginning this belief was a blessing, as it strengthened his conviction and dedication to the Path. However, over time this feeling became so strong that it became an obstacle to him. So, God sent a huge boulder down to block the path, for his own sake.

When the man first found that the path was blocked, he turned back to search through his old tools to see what could help him remove this gigantic rock. Surely he must have been given the answer already, since God would never obstruct the path. He spent the rest of his life looking through what he had learned in the past, never finding a solution.

In his next lifetime, the man set out upon the path again finding it familiar and easy going, until once again he reached the wall of stone. He thought about turning back as he had before, but this time felt his desire to continue on the path was so great that he knew there must be a way. He began to climb over the obstacle. He must stay on the path. He knew that. So what other choice did he have? Half way up the side of the boulder, his grip slipped and he fell to his death.

Next lifetime, when he found himself before the "rock of ages" once more, he sensed that climbing it and turning back were not the answers, but he still had confidence that he could solve this problem. There had to be a way. Then it dawned on him. He could dig his way under. True, it might not be exactly "staying on the path", but it was pretty darn close. So, drawing on his own powers—and a shovel—he began the long difficult job of trying to dig under the boulder. Half way through, the weight of the earth fell through his tunnel and crushed him.

Next lifetime, the man finds himself facing the wall again, which he now calls the stone of God. He has given up all hope of using his own powers to find a way of staying on the path. So, he sits down in a lotus position on the path beside the barrier and begins meditation. He waits for an answer from God. God will send an answer or a miracle. He is sure of this. He spends the rest of his life like this, meditating and waiting by the stone of God.

Another lifetime comes and he finds the blockage upon the path again. He knows that waiting passively isn't the answer, nor is relying upon his own powers. Finally, his desire for God has become so great that it means more to him than staying on the path. So, he steps off the path and suddenly sees that he can walk around the rock to the other side!

The moment he steps off the path he finds the guidance of Spirit filling his vision and showing him the way. So, the man learned that the footworn path is not always the same as the spiritual path, and sometimes one must leave the path to find the Path.

It seems as if we are always leaving our old paths behind while struggling to find our new ones. I saw this over and over again amongst friends and family, and with ECKists and seekers that I spoke to.

They were holding onto the past, afraid to let go, yet knowing that they needed to take another step. I felt at times that half of what I was going through and what I was experiencing within my life was not just my own anymore. I felt these crossroads that others were facing. I saw with my heart the meanings of these tests that we meet up with.

Images often came to me, during this time, of people I did not know. It no longer seemed like Soul Travel, as if I was going anywhere. It was more as if they were all just here within my own world somehow. I wrote the following as an exercise to capture a few of these passing images.

269

They did not seem like my own, and yet it was clear that somehow I was a part of them.

By witnessing these glimpses, it seemed as if I was helping bring awareness to them, which is what they were calling out for. At the same time they came to teach me something as well.

Glimpses

The woman walked forward, slowly. She took each step with care, aware that she might never return again. She might never see Him, her master, teacher and spiritual father, again. Her purple silk robe hid her bare feet and her hands beneath its folds. Her dark hair hung straight down. She knelt before Him and bowed to the ground. Tears fell from her eyes and moistened the dirt. A mild breeze flickered the torch's flames and sent shadows dancing around her.

She did not want to rise. She wanted to just stay there at His feet. Time could freeze now and she would be happy, she thought. Why must this happen? Why must she go away?

His feet shuffled and she knew she was taking too long. She lifted her head. He was watching her. A worried look crossed his face and she knew he did not know what was going to happen.

"Oh, Master..." she said, and then bowed down again to His feet. She was crying out loud, now.

"What is it, my Mendina?" he said, still uncertain.

"Oh, Master," she said again, this time looking up into his eyes, "Will you release me? I feel I must go. I feel I am called elsewhere."

"What?!" he said so loudly it almost sounded like an explosion. "Called? Leave me? What do you mean?"

This was what she had feared; that he would not understand. That he could not gracefully let her go. That he would be hurt. She did not want to remember him that way—so human. She still hoped he could be her "Baba," that he could see into her heart better than she, herself. It once seemed this way, and she still wanted it to be true.

"Oh, Master," she said, "You have taught me well. From you I have learned the art of breath, to see without eyes and the thousand songs of Vishnu. But I have had dreams. Many dreams. And they have told me that I must go. I must leave you. I have fought these visions as if they were the enemy of vanity itself, but Krishna has come in his own form to deliver the message. As you have taught, I must obey. I ask for your blessings."

She could see clearly that he was upset. She knew of his hopes for her. Now it was all coming to an end. She would never be able to go back. She wished there could have been some other way.

"Where will you go?" he asked.

"To one called Quan-Tu. I have been given instructions to find him. I do not know anymore than this."

He gave an audible "Humpf!" half in disappointment, half in disgust. "You may leave," he said, then stood up and walked away.

The woman bowed her head to the ground and softly said to herself, "I am sorry Baba. I did not want to hurt you."

. . ● . .

Aaron the Tall was aptly named. A huge man, with black hair and black eyes, yet he did not look so fearsome now, lying upon a cot of birch and straw, alone in an old shepherd's hut. Fully cloaked in boots and mail, a quiver of arrows lay beside him on the floor. He held up a sword in his hands, as his eyes stared up into the dark.

He was silenced by an image he could not forget. He turned the sword over and over in his hands, while turning that image over in his mind.

He had scaled the walls of the abandoned Yonmir Castle, sure he had finally tracked down his enemy of 15 years—Garn of the Hills. For years he had been close, only to miss Garn by one or two days travel—and then to lose him completely. But he knew those tracks he followed there were Garn's.

He had never seen Garn, yet Aaron knew him just the same. Having followed Garn through towns and forests, across rivers and mountains, Aaron knew the man he was tracking. And knew that if he challenged this man to a fight, that he might not live. Yet the thought of retreat never even crossed his mind. His father's death must be avenged. There was no more to be said. He had always known this... until what he had seen this night.

He had climbed those walls to be sure it was Garn. The climbing was no great feat since vines and trees had broken the rock fortress, leaving foot and hand-holds everywhere. It was easy, even with only a bare moon lighting the shadows. And he knew he was close.

But he was not prepared for what he saw. It was Garn, all right, back in a small alcove, but it was not Garn the Resilient, or Garn the Bold. This was not the man he expected to find, for Garn was bowed forward on his knees in prayer before a pagan altar.

His voice echoed in the still night. He was praying and beseeching his gods for help. Aaron tried not to listen, knowing that each stands alone

271

with his God, and it is wrong to intrude upon another's sacred prayers. But he was transfixed by what he saw and a voice within told him that God wanted him to see this.

Garn's words came to him in bits, at times lost as Garn bowed forward, and then as clearly as if spoken just for him. Aaron pieced together what he heard. Garn's son lay dying from the fever. Garn's love for his son was strong and deep and he was asking his gods for help.

Then they came, the words that were for him. They pierced Aaron's heart.

"Oh gods," Garn spoke, looking upward, "is it I who have brought this death upon my son? Is it some act of my own, perhaps forgotten in my past? If so, do not punish wrongly. Take my life in place of my son's. If thou wouldst, show me how and I will lay down my spirit for his."

Aaron's eyes stared up into the dark, but that image would not go away. It was as if God, the Almighty, had spoken to Aaron and shown him. It was as if God had said, "See here, Aaron, Garn offers his life to you. He is ready to pay his debt. What more do you want from him? Will you give him what he desires? You, to whom I have revealed the healing powers of herbs. Have you not taken an oath before me, to heal any that are sick and commendable? Garn offers his own life to you in payment. Is not the son of such a man worthy?"

Aaron turned the sword over and over in his hands. How had it come to this? Such irony. For all these years he had hunted this killer of his father—now would Aaron become a killer of fathers? Or a healer of sons? If he should fight Garn and lose, then he would be unable to keep his oath of healing. Had he not made that oath on God's own book? If he should heal the boy first, then Garn would lay down his sword to him, and how could he fight a defenseless man? He felt both edges of the sword in his hands.

Aaron had always believed the difference between him and Garn lay in the different gods they worshipped: Garn's pagan gods of the earth; Aaron's Supreme God of the Holy Spirit. Aaron believed this to be a wall that separated them and made the avenging of his father all the more necessary. But now he was not so sure.

Garn's own prayer to his gods had reached Aaron and spoken to his own heart with the voice of the Holy Spirit. How could it be that through Garn's prayer to his gods, Aaron heard his own God? Were they one and the same? Was this God that led Aaron to take the oath of healing and led him to the wall of Yonmir Castle the same God that led Garn to kill his father? How could this be?

Aaron tilted the sword back and forth as if to see which way the whole problem would tip, but the sword stayed balanced between his hands.

"What am I to learn from this, my Lord?" Aaron asked.

"Let man worship me how he wilt," Aaron heard. "One man's love is not better than another's. All love comes to Me in the end. So treat all who love me as thy brother."

Dawn began to lighten the sky, as Aaron lay there. He felt a hardness missing within him. Something had died inside himself, a battle he had waged for years. Now it was gone. He wondered what life would be like without it...

These stories about people's lives in the midst of great change captured my attention. They might have come from another time or from places far away, but they seemed intimately close as I watched. I felt the intensity of their beings caught halfway between their need to move forward by the force of their own spiritual unfoldment and their heartsick sense of leaving their old ways behind.

I somehow connected to them and their stories through a sense of compassion and wonder. As I observed, I felt poised like Aaron's sword, balanced and unable to tilt one way or the other. After all, these were crossroads in their lives, not mine, but a sensation of awareness held me transfixed. Something in their experiences spoke to me. I too was changing, and I sensed that I would never be able to go back to my old consciousness. However, the shift taking place for me was different: The lives of others were no longer external, but were now a part of me, and I needed to care for them as if they were my own.

Soul's need for realization linked me with others going through their own awakening. This opened inner doors and linked me to people in a way I had never known before. I could see that all of life was moving in the same direction. Inscribed deep in our hearts is a desire to find the way back home to this greater realization of Self.

This now became my responsibility: To care for life and witness the arc of Soul as it created its unique life-story. Not to change anyone, but to become truly aware. A hush fell across my heart in the presence of these fellow seekers of Truth. The inner children of my own self felt a sensation of awe and became more harmonious. All of life made more sense, like puzzle pieces falling into place. It was the growing awareness of this deep connection to other lives that changed my experience. As I watched, something awakened within me.

I wrote the following in a writer's class I was leading at the time. We had taken a few moments for an exercise on being witnesses. Someone in the class suggested we all go back to the original moment of creation and describe what we saw. So, we did a short contemplation and then took paper and pencil in hand.

The Moment of Creation

It came into being in a moment that was eternity. It was everything and nothing. Soul watched in amazement, wondering what it was that was occurring. Never had this happened before.

Like a glimmering bauble that captures the eye of a child, so creation caught the eye of Soul. It drew Soul, as if calling to come fill this vast nothingness and give it reality.

Soul was charmed by a world that could only exist if Soul gave it attention. Before this everything had always been.

There was no beginning or ending to the realms of God, but this creation could not exist without Soul.

So, Soul was drawn to it and began to create, and these creations brought form to an empty nothing.

This was something I had never seen before – how Soul is drawn to the worlds of creation like a child fascinated by a colorful toy. Soul, pouring its attention upon the waters of emptiness brings about creation itself.

This void, this barrenness of the lower worlds is what draws out from within Soul the desire to fill it and make it into something. It becomes a way for Soul to display and project itself into the reflections of the world. Its own handiwork becomes visible to everyone, and there seems to be no game more fun than manifesting what it wants to see.

Only later, Soul gets caught up in the repercussions. The results of its own actions return as waves crashing on the shore, swamping it and carrying it far from where it wanted to be. It becomes confused and lost, surrounded by seemingly outer forces, until it can understand how all of this came from its own hand. It is not something separate. It is all a part of Soul, itself.

Thus, the worlds of creation become a school ground for Soul to learn.

Somehow I had stepped into this strange state of consciousness that showed the moment of creation from a new light. I found myself wandering

274

into perspectives like this during that time. I felt them drawing me closer to the heart of something. A growing presence was becoming palpable.

I began to wonder what it is I was experiencing. How large was this? Was it God I was touching?

Silence

If thoughts are universal,
    Then whose thought is Silence?

Dip even a finger in that stillness,
    And ripples shatter its mirror.

You cannot think of it
    And know it.

Few come to visit
    The deep pool
        And barren shore
            Of Silence.

I could not comprehend the largeness of this, yet the grandeur of it moved me. The surface of my heart suddenly seemed to be reflecting all of life, and it calmed me. Where did this stillness, this pregnant silence, come from? It took a while for me to understand that this was Soul's awareness I was sensing. This peace was the dawning of the higher Self. It was a mirror at the core of Soul revealing the whole of life.

I was trying to fully grasp this when I wrote that poem, which is why I asked: "whose thought is Silence?" I could not fully recognize this silence as my own, because it seemed much larger than anything I had known.

How could Soul reflect the secret thoughts of men and women, as if they were its own? Why was I now witnessing and tied into the imagination and dreams of the world as if these were my own children that needed my care?

I wrote the following article as I was exploring this and trying to understand what was changing within me.

The Call of the Inner Dream

If we could see the images secretly kept in the imaginations of man, we would see the dreams, desires and fears that propel mankind through life on this planet. We would witness here, first, on this inner screen, the wars and crimes that later enact themselves across our globe. We would see the controlling of the masses by those who know how to manipulate the imaginations of others, and see the inner battle of belief waging within all men.

Yet behind all this, beneath the desires of success and fears of failure, lay the unchanging sources of man's inner dreams. History and storybooks are filled with tales of those who have sacrificed everything for these longings of the heart. Leaving their families and traveling to foreign lands for the key to secret knowledge. Abandoning reputations and social position for love. Laying down their wealth at the foot of some holy man for the experience of God.

What can you say to such men and women? Life has no meaning for them but finding their inner desire. They might launch themselves upon their quest with such suddenness that it leaves their life in ruins. Or they may begin to withdraw from their friends and family, feeling the aloneness of the search that this inner force drives them to. Each day they wonder: Will this haunting dream come true?

Carl Jung, the psychologist, was one man touched by this inner call. In his autobiography he writes, "When religious teachings were pumped into me (as a child)... I would think to myself: 'Yes, but there is something else, something very secret that people don't know about'... I always hoped I might be able to find something—perhaps in nature—that would give me a clue and show me where or what the secret was... I was absorbed by it and had the feeling I ought to fathom it; and yet I did not know what I was trying to express... This possession of a secret had a very powerful influence on my character; I consider it the essential factor of my youth."

Jung had glimpsed the spiritual teachings—that great body of inner wisdom that has influenced this planet for untold ages. The Sufis call it the Wine of God. The early Christians knew it as the Gnosis, or the knowingness. These words only hint at what it is, but it is the impact upon our inner consciousness that awakens the inner dream within us. Then comes the longing to find it, the search that leads far from the protection of the masses. The Silent Questions call to us. It is a secret indeed, personal and powerful, that lifts us up and changes our world. But how far will we go for this inner dream?

Our family and friends may reject it. Then, should we force it upon the world like a religious zealot, a fanatic? Or do we forget the inner dream; ignore it as an unreality of the imagination? What if the dream is as strong as the powerful vision of Mohammed, who declared war in the name of God—a holy war that rages to this day? What if it is as deep-rooted as the dream of Israel, which inspired a whole race to call themselves the chosen people?

Hundreds of thousands of armies have marched across this planet conquering in the name of power, wealth and God, but all eventually stumble and fall beneath the weight of their own creations. Their dreams vanish like a mirage, so that only the desert wind and dry sands are there to bite their lips. Why do those age-old dreams of life escape them?

Life is strewn with the remains of those who have failed. It is an ever-present warning that he who dares follow the inner dream must pass the tests of his own sincerity. First, he must confront his reckless desires and harness their wild force, for this will be the power to carry him on his journey. Next, he must look beneath the surface of his mind and emotions, for only within the deep currents of his own heart will he find his guidance. And last, he must be willing to be changed by his dreams. Willing to give up all his limited conceptions, for this inner call is greater, always greater than we can imagine.

We think we are the hunters of a treasure that is our dream, but in the end we are changed. We are the ones struck down by the golden arrow. Thus we each face a choice: Either we must let our dream die, or our own self as we know it must die. When we believe more in the inner dream than our own puny powers, then the magic of the inner dream has worked its charm and our new consciousness becomes the treasure we sought.

Our inner dreams bubble up from within us, and they seize our lives, turning everything inside-out. When such realizations hit us, we can never go back again to see the world as we did before, and this was exactly what was happening in my life. My world was irrevocably altered.

I was brought face to face with a great decision: Would I give up my old dreams to live in the awareness of Soul? This meant giving up all of my preconceptions and pre-made plans to follow a living reality. I could see no other choice. But I felt myself stepping out across a bridge that was not yet complete. I was leaving everything I knew for something that was still beyond me.

This is when our dreams teach us more than we ever expected, when we let them take us to a place that is larger than ourselves.

The miracle of this, however, takes place within Soul, in a place I was still exploring and trying to understand.

The Altar of the Self

Hidden within the experiences of life is a lesson often learned by those who walk the far roads of the spiritual worlds: That the personal space of each being is the altar of God.

There is no greater altar than man's own Self. Yet this is hardly believable to the seeker who first discovers the spiritual teachings, for he has not yet found the mirror that can show him his true Self. He can only see an empty being in the mirror, lost, unsure, and seemingly the effect of the entire world around him.

This is why mankind is always giving up its personal space to causes that seem so worthy, or why most people try to lose themselves in the space of another. The first is the seeker of power, the second a seeker of love, but in both cases the altar of the personal individual Self has been abandoned. Weeds grow and claim the holy spot.

"Guard the doors of the Self!" the ancient teachers have told seekers of truth. "Guard the sacred gardens and pools of wisdom. Do not reveal those trees that bear fruit, nor the springs that nourish. You are the gatekeepers of God!"

This does not mean that the spiritual teachings cannot be revealed, or that this ancient knowledge is hidden, but that the forces of power and love shall tempt you to abandon yourself.

"Now I can see that no one can really know another person," a friend once told me. "It is painful because it seems so lonely."

This reminds me of the story of an oasis in the desert that once complained to a camel, "It is so lonely being cast out so far amongst the hills of sand. When travelers come, I give them my best water, but always they are gone the next day."

To which the camel replied, "I would give you all the cities of the world for a place of my own beneath the stars."

At this moment the camel owner approached, a man who was known to be a spiritual traveler of the highest sort. The oasis said to him, "You have seen the face of God and returned. Tell us, who is right, the camel or I?"

The man replied, "I have never found a place closer to God than where I am." Then he scooped up a bowl of water and walked away.

After the traveler was out of earshot, the camel chuckled to the water, "He is always saying such enigmatic things. But fortunately for me he doesn't eat much, and carries few belongings. He is light upon my back. In this way I see the wisdom of his ways."

"He was sparing with my water," said the oasis, "and in this way I see his wisdom."

The wind, who has heard many strange and curious conversations, carried these words to the spiritual traveler, who was sipping his water carefully, and thinking kindly of his camel. Hearing their words, he thanked the wind, and then the stars and all the wonderful celestial melody.

For in this way he saw the wisdom of God, and accepted it as a gift of love upon the altar of the Self.

This was the great miracle of Soul. Here, within the inner stillness, was the place where life was truly shaped. This was where the stirrings of awareness were first born into form. The moment I became aware of being in touch with all of Spirit, I awakened to the meaning of this sacred space. Listening to the silence and looking into the reality reflecting across the mirror surface of my awareness moved Soul into a dance with Life that united with the core of my being.

I suddenly realized that all the disillusionments of my life had come from placing my hopes on the altar of the outer world. There was no lasting satisfaction there, nor could there be. My inner dreams could not spring from an external reality. Their birthplace could only be found within me. Disappointment came to me over and over until I awakened to this higher Self that is a part of the whole. This was what I explored in the following article. I wrote this for others who might be going through similar realizations. At the same time I was writing to the children of my own self that were facing this same emptiness and aloneness, when old ideals die.

The Cracked Bowl

Have you ever watched children playing with stuffed toys? The love they give their blue elephants and floppy-eared puppies. The stories they tell them as they tuck the smiling animals into bed. The way the children fix their hurts and share with them their secrets. Their hearts rush out to their furry friends and fill them with life. This is the child's world, where their inner dream becomes real.

We call this dreamland or make-believe, but it is not as imaginary as we make it sound. For example, it does not end when the children reach the dinner table and the parent calls out, "Okay, enough with the games! Eat your food!" It merely changes. Now it becomes the dark world of rules, punishment...slavery. For the child it becomes a world of endless torture over a platter of vegetables. It becomes days...months...years watching their friends play outside while they sit there paralyzed, unable to move the green beans any closer.

"Man is lost in a world of his own projections," said an ECK Master to me once. "Man thinks he understands this world of solid reality, but he fails to see that he is the source of the creations that flood all life around him. He is like the painter who has forgotten his own paintings, and feels in awe of the great being who created such works of art."

We think we know this world. We think we know our family and our friends, but often they are just silhouettes we have colored in. We name them wife, boss, policeman, and expect them to fill the roles we've cast them in. And they struggle with these expectations from us, like the child struggles with his plate of beans. They too begin to ask: "Who am I?" and "What is real?"

We want the world to fill our dreams, but we struggle with the expectations of others—and this is the problem. Of all the dreams that fill our world, many are not our own. Many are not even dreams we like. There are dreams we run from or try to destroy, yet still they lurk in the dark shadows of our fears. Sometimes they rush out upon us in a sudden moment of anger. Sometimes they are dreams we feel trapped by, that we cannot control.

Childhood is filled with such myths and dreams because when we are young the world is beyond our understanding. Therefore, it becomes the screen upon which our imagination plays out before our eyes. Our inner feelings and desires are projected upon every event and object around us. The dark shadows in our closet become creatures, and the sticks we find become magic swords. This is the primitive world of the savage with his gods in every plant and element of nature. As we grow we begin to see these external forces for what they are, separate from our imagination of them, and our world becomes objective. But what happens to those who bury such myths?

What happens to those who reject their inner lives and accept only the outer reality? From that moment their life slowly erodes. Like a bowl that is cracked, their life spirit slowly begins to drain and no longer can the world reflect the rhythms of their heart. They have given up their birthright, they have denounced their keys to the God worlds, and now they can only ask: Why should I care about my work, my family, my future? There are no answers to these silent questions until their inner dream is restored.

Therefore, there is nothing wrong with men and women who bow before their savior, saint, master or God with absolute faith and total belief. For in that moment they are freed of the World Ego that clutches this planet in its hands and drives the lives of so many without mercy. No scientific proof or logical theories bring people to this point, because it is only true to them—it is their truth. And yet, without this release from "objective reality," how are they able to accept the gifts of their God-selves? Their bowl would be cracked, unable to hold the precious divinity that is their inheritance.

However, such total faith cannot be summoned like the genie from a bottle. It must spring from our experience and our understanding. To worship something outside us is like laying our hearts out on the city streets. We are never more vulnerable than in those moments of prayer, worship and love—when we set aside our cares for something greater. Just as the child must awaken from its childhood dream world one day, so too Soul must one day shake this cold outer adult reality and discover the great spiritual reality that binds all life together.

Therefore, our life needs to be whole—grasping a great dream that does not run from "the real world." A dream that out of strength trans-forms the world itself. A dream that flows from spiritual reality and is tied into the fiber of all life. It must illumine our day, reveal purpose to our existence and open our heart to love. We must not feel it shrinking our capacity, but expanding our breadth to a point without limits.

Thus, a true dream leads us to surrender our limitations out of love, not fear. It occurs within the most personal and private recesses of our inner self, never substituted by social rules or outer rituals. It must be an individual, personal experience that liberates us. It clears from our eyes the darkness so that we no longer see evil or weakness within ourselves, or within others, for such weakness is only the lack of a dream.

The key of the cracked bowl, then, is that we can never find our spiri-tual dream unless we first grant everyone else their dream first.

Unless we love and respect the beliefs of others as much as our own, the door to spiritual truth is closed. This is why Soul is required to blind-ly pass through the lower planes of reality before coming into the light of the self-realization state: To accept and pay homage to the gods, rulers and peoples of all worlds. We grow the most spiritually when we give of ourselves to life as it is and to people as they are.

Attaining the higher states of consciousness, alone, cannot solve the problems of this world. To see and care for all life as an expression of God is the door that leads to the God-State itself.

Almost all of my self-doubts have come from wondering: Is what I believed true? I finally saw that this was the wrong question. The question should have been: What do I want to create?

How else can our dreams become real except through our understanding and trust in them? The question is not whether they are true or not, but do we want them to become real?

If we only believe what is true, then we create nothing—we only reinforce what already exists. This is like throwing away our birthright.

Once I realized this, I saw that my beliefs were secondary. Consciously choosing what to believe was what mattered, and discovering what Soul desired.

This produced a new sense of respect for the dreams of others as well. Suddenly, I saw the millions of beliefs in this world as the creations of Soul. I became fascinated by what everyone believed, since it opened a window into the worlds they were choosing to create. Even the materialists who believed we should believe nothing except what could be proven scientifically, or the fundamentalists who believed their religion was the only true one. I could see that all these beliefs were simply their way of creating their world and the experiences of their lives.

Of Eagles and Dervishes

Around this time, I gave a talk at an ECK seminar in Spokane, Washington. I found myself preparing my talk not just for the ECKists and newcomers who were visiting, but for anyone. In other words, I chose to believe that my talk was for all of life, whether they were interested in the path I knew or not, including nature and the planet. Therefore, I wasn't surprised to see the strange weather that appeared out of nowhere when the seminar began.

I was not the only one choosing to believe that the seminar was for all of life. In fact, as an exercise, everyone involved in putting the seminar together had decided to focus on this intention as the purpose for the weekend event. So, after the forecasts called for clear weather, a number of us noticed when huge storm clouds suddenly appeared.

However, that isn't the reason I remember that day so clearly over twelve years later. It was not because this was the first time I had seen such strange weather around ECK events, on the contrary, but it was because of what followed.

A long time ECKist and friend wanted to introduce me to some American Indian shaman friends he knew, after the seminar. We drove out to see Bobby and Tela, both prominent teachers. Tela came from one of the oldest families of shamans, going back six or seven generations. Bobby had once been a university professor, until the day he found himself forced to leave on a search for truth that led him back to the teachings of his fathers and grandfathers. He had an illness that would not leave until he returned to his roots.

One of the first things Bobby said when I met them was, "Have you noticed the celebration of the Rain People this weekend?"

I nodded and laughed, because indeed I had noticed the storm clouds and intuitively knew what he meant by his name, the Rain People.

Then Bobby got very quiet for a moment and looked at me in a very strange way. He then said to me, "So the Rain People came for you? I wondered who they were honoring."

I felt strangely naked at that moment, as if my own beliefs and acts of creation, which had always seemed so invisible to the world before, now were being witnessed by this man. His wife, Tela, smiled when I blushed. This is why I remember the weather that weekend so clearly, even twelve years later.

Bobby and Tela went on to teach me some of their traditions and the meaning behind them. After Karen and I left, I sensed that Bobby and Tela had passed something on to me. It seemed as if I was carrying away a part of them with me. I felt a growing inner awareness of the inner teaching that they had been transmitting.

That night I knew a Soul Travel experience was awaiting me. So, I settled into a chair to see what it might be. It was nothing like I had ever experienced before. Out of thanks to Bobby and Tela, I wrote this letter back to them, describing what took place:

Dear Bobby and Tela,

Thank you for the many feelings of blessings Karen and I felt from our meeting in your home last week, and especially for your humor and openness...

I would like to share with you both an experience I had the night after we left your home. It had been a long, active day, and my body looked forward to sleep. However, my thoughts continued to return to you both, as I felt your presence strongly nearby...

Then, suddenly from within myself, I experienced this great opening and stretching of eagle's wings. I didn't know what this was at first. I then heard an eagle's screech, as if off in the distance it was calling my name. To answer this call, I let my body "die" and found myself with eagle's wings and an eagle's sight, flying through the air.

The sensation was incredible! I swooped down across a wooded mountain, clearing the treetops and found myself landing at the top of a pine. "This is amazing," I thought. "I can actually sit here at the very top of this tree." The man within me could not comprehend the experiences of the new body, or its instincts and vision.

However, this eagle shape was more than just a body. The best words I can find to describe it is that it was more like a power matrix—like some ancient vehicle that I had simply taken on like a cloak. It was an absolutely real physical experience. I then knew that all I had heard about the shaman's stories were true.

Through the eagle's form I also became acutely aware of the wind's meaning and speech. When I flew off again, the wind currents were filled with sound, patterns of energy and information that seemed as familiar as a native language. It is impossible to describe this or how real and clear this was. Through the eagle's eyes, I saw webs of light that crossed the land as if I was suddenly seeing an energy map of great precision. If I didn't know better I would have thought I was in another world.

You were both there, nearby. I was not used to the eagle's form, and Tela thought some of my antics quite funny. She was most graceful in her flight. Then she beckoned me and I followed her into the sky. "What is that golden triangle?" she asked. I looked up and saw it above us. I immediately recognized what it was. "It's a door, Tela. Fly through it," I said, and I flew through.

On the other side I was no longer an eagle, but became a man again. It was the next world beyond the physical, and before me was a council of Indian men, seated on the ground in a circle. It was a timeless setting, with discussions of the whole physical world and other worlds, their future and past. Once again I found a feeling of familiarity, and I instantly knew who these men were: Our Grandfathers. "How can this be?" I asked myself. "I don't have a drop of Indian blood in me, unless it was put there when I wasn't looking." And yet I knew these men were Our Grandfathers.

A question formed in my mind, as I knew it had been on Bobby's thoughts, "What is the future of the Native American Tradition," I asked our grandfathers. The answer came without any of them saying a word. "This world is beyond time and space, therefore it is eternal. Our ways shall always exist." It was a quiet answer, almost whispered, as if I were being shushed in a library for talking too loud. I wondered about this.

Then I thought I had better get back. I crossed through the golden door and became an eagle again. The feeling of flight was ecstatic. The wind and the heights were entrancing. Yet I began to realize I was being called. I knew it was a call I had to follow. It was the call of someone I must heed.

As I flew I began to see him. At first he was at such a distance that I could see him in my mind's eye only. But then I saw him standing there— arms crossed, legs spread in a stance of calling and waiting. He was the one who called me. He was the one I must heed. Who was he?

As I flew closer, I saw his great size. He seemed like an Indian giant, at least four times my own size. But then I remembered that it was my eagle's form that was small, and this Indian might be no giant at all. Yet, I was still awed by his size and my desire to obey him.

He held out his arm, and I flew as if to land, but instead found myself merging into his form. He and I became one, a man and eagle simultaneously. My senses reached out, as the senses of an eagle reach out, yet my power and strength were that of a man. What did this mean? I don't know. I only experienced and don't fully understand. Perhaps you can explain its meaning. I knew, however, that I was being blessed and could only reach out my thanks to you both who sent this experience my way.

After this encounter, I found a deeper understanding of nature and the value of religious belief. I then realized that I had within myself the ability to make anything sacred. Wherever I walked and whoever I met could be sacred—if I so decided.

How often do we throw away this power of our own to make things sacred? How often do we instead imagine that we can only consider things sacred if they first possess some special predetermined holiness?

Somehow I had forgotten how important it was to bring spirituality to the physical world around me. This had been essential to me when I had first stepped upon the path, but somewhere along the way I had lost touch with it.

At this time I found myself re-integrating within myself the whole physical world, in a sense. It was like awakening new senses that reached out into the world. I thought about this shift in my attention and how vitally important it is to have roots into the world.

It is true that Soul reaches to the highest heavens, but Soul also touches the deepest seas. It is not just upliftment that we need, but the expansion of consciousness—which means a broader reach of awareness, both higher and lower, until we touch all of life.

We can travel with great spiritual teachers inwardly, but we can also travel with the animals of the woods and fields. They all become sacred to our touch the moment we decide to believe they are. This becomes the moment we take back our birthright to create spiritual truth and realize that all of life is a sacred adventure.

Origins

Born of stones,
　　Grown from earth,
　　　　The birds sing my name.
River weeds and wild oaks
　　Call for me.
Have I been gone so long?

Cave paintings haunt me,
　　Like lost letters
　　　　Of some Word I once knew.
My starmap is no good here.

Draw the drumskin tightly,
　　Carve the flute.
My own hands know the way.

My own hands did seem to know the way. It seemed as if they were often my guides, rather than my mind. When I wrote, my hands found the words and seemed to bring forth a clarity in understanding beyond what I knew. My hands seemed to feel the way along the path as if I was reaching out in the dark and recognizing what was there and which way to turn.

I found myself more and more relying upon Soul to know the way. The starmap I had been given no longer showed the true picture of the way ahead. In other words, theories no longer worked, but Soul Itself knew the next step to take.

This led me to an interesting experiment. Here is how I recently described what happened next:

I was curious one day, as I worked on a new translation of Rumi's discourses. I was looking for feedback, so I decided to hold some open discussions on the first few discourses I had finished. I invited some ECKists I knew, along with some Sufi students and leaders I had met, who all had an interest in Rumi. I reserved a public meeting room and we met once a month for a period of 5 or 6 months.

The discussions and the interactions between the ECKists and Sufi students were fascinating. I could see that the Sufi students recognized and understood aspects of Rumi's traditional teaching that the ECKists missed, but the ECKists seemed to catch a deeper meaning of the inner teachings in Rumi's discourses.

However, there was one Sufi leader, Daniel, who seemed to immediately recognize the spiritual value in what I was trying to do. I learned later that he began telling other Sufi students that I was a leader in the Mevlevi Order, which is the Sufi teaching order established by Rumi.

A few months later, I got a call from Daniel inviting me to visit the annual meeting of the Mevlevis, known as the Urs of Rumi, which is a celebration in honor of Rumi's death day—or as they say: The day when Rumi re-united with the Divine. This is a sacred meeting where the famous Mevlevi Whirling Dervishes dance.

While standing in the outside circle with other visitors, surrounding the Whirling Dervishes, Daniel suddenly came over and invited me into their circle. He led me into a whirling dance where the two of us crossed our arms and grasped each other's hands. We then spun around each other in rhythm to the music. After a few minutes of this, we each split off and began the traditional whirling dance in the circle with the Whirling Dervishes...

I've met with many people from Sufi and Sant Mat groups, along with leaders in these groups. What has always struck me is that there are those who know. When you speak with these few, they recognize and understand no matter what words you might choose.

What does it matter if you lose all the other seekers, if you find those who really know and recognize the truth? Will those few not bring with them thousands? Are those few not the ones for whom the path really exists? Isn't everyone else learning recognition and understanding of the path from Them?

As Rumi once said, "What is all this talk of thousands and hundreds of thousands? The true ones are all One, and those thousands are nothing."

I had learned the form of the whirling dance from some Sufis earlier, but that day I learned the heart of it. My chest seemed to heat up with the spiritual currents that were transmitting the inner teaching of the Sufi Dervishes. It felt like the whole world was whirling around me, not the other way around. It was as if I stood stationary and unmoving at the center of the universe, while the universe was spinning around me. The whirling dance had gone on for more than thirty minutes, yet I never felt the slightest dizziness. My heart expanded out to touch everything. I then understood what could be transmitted through a sacred ritual if performed consciously with those who know. The teachings of ECK had always avoided rituals, but now I had a new appreciation for them as a means of transmitting a teaching.

The next day I wrote the following poem and sent a copy to Daniel with my deepest thanks. It is of course addressed to The Beloved, as the Sufis often name that One I have been calling the Inner Master, which some teachings call the Lord. Each name carries a slightly different meaning, but they all point to the spiritual matrix leading Soul back to Itself.

Whirling

The strings of this world
Have come untied.
Nothing holds me here
But Your handclasps and kisses.

But for Your hands
The winds would blow me away.
Even the eagles could not save me
For talons cannot grasp the air.

But for Your kisses
The blood would cease in my veins, and
My lungs could draw no breath.

Your touch spins universes about my feet
And lights a Sun in my heart.
I hold a handful of earth
And feel a million years of your life.

I will not give away these eyes and feet
   That You've given me
   Until the appointed hour.

I will not close this window
   Until the house is burned.
I can sleep no longer.
You set me whirling, and I cannot stop.

By this point I realized that I could no longer see any line that separated my path from any other path. I no longer saw an inside or outside to the path. I could see that there are only those who know. It does not matter what tradition or teaching that they come from. Those who recognize and understand each other shatter all the lines separating the religions of the world.

There really is no line separating those who are on the path of knowingness from those who are not—except perhaps the lines that people draw around their own lives by how they see themselves and the way they name their teachings. People draw these lines with their beliefs, but there really are no lines at all.

Not everyone I met appreciated this new truth of mine. Some felt threatened by it, as if I were trying to tear down their sacred walls. From their reactions, I learned the importance of these walls of belief.

When people declare their religion sacred, it is often a sacredness that only exists within the circle of their belief. They have a right to create this kind of sacredness, so I knew I must honor and respect their choices. But I had lost all sense of this within myself. For me, everything was sacred the moment Soul declared it to be. Therefore, there was no circle that alone could contain sacredness, since Soul encompasses all of life, every moment.

This newfound recognition spoke to a number of other people as well. I have found that many cannot feel comfortable placing a circle around their beliefs. They feel as if such things would be cutting themselves off from life, rather than revealing it, and so even the slightest sign of fences sends them far away.

The individuality of the spiritual path is something they recognize and understand. To follow a religious doctrine would be like going backwards for them. These are the outsiders who Paul Twitchell first wrote to when he started his teaching, so I knew them well. I was once such a seeker myself, until I realized that fences were as sacred as no fences, and both were gifts of God.

As Rumi once said, God is gracious with His gifts. But His gifts of covering are nothing like His gifts of uncovering, for in God's uncovering are the most beautiful realizations of life and love. In other words, I could now see that both covering and uncovering were part of the path, and therefore both were sacred.

I remember one such free spirit who attended a few of my classes. She had never been an ECKist, although she had read some of the ECK books. She had a particular ability that I will never forget. She was like the seers of past ages who spoke for the ancient Oracles, like the Oracle of Dionysus. She could speak with a higher wisdom that came through her. It would just open up for her and use her voice, yet she wondered what it all meant. She was both fascinated and bothered by her experiences.

One day while a few of us were talking after class, she suddenly said something that reverberated the depths of my consciousness. She said, as best as I can remember: "Your ideas of Mastership are too limited. There are many possible ways of Mastership, not just one. You need to explore the possibilities."

Indeed, her words came to me as if she were speaking thoughts so intimately a part of my self that even I had not yet realized I was thinking them. It was as if she was channeling my own higher wisdom just for me. The next moment she was back to talking from her normal self.

At the end of one of my classes, she came up as if she wanted to tell me something, then suddenly stopped, sat down and wrote a message to me that she was receiving from an inner source. She handed me the paper. It said:

Hello to you beloved companion.

Where is Sat Purusha? You are here. I am here.

I charge you with all humility to fulfill to your fullest expectations of your personal goals and ambitions to guide...all the brothers and sisters—in love—to new ways of finding individual paths through the light.

The energy fields that we are in at the present are quite intense, but are not contrary to the peace and love that is your goal to teach.

May the blessings be.

Always,

Reb-

She handed me the note saying that the message came through so strongly she had to write it down. She claimed the words were exactly as Rebazar Tarzs said them. I could feel his presence in the note even before I saw the signature of who it was from.

The Wind Changes Course

It was many experiences like this one that showed me this was indeed the universal Path I was working with. I was a brother to all who were seekers, and we were all attracted to each other and learning from each other. However, as this realization grew, so did a force that wanted to stop me. It was a strange thing. I never expected it would happen like it did.

It would have been easy for me to say that the criticisms and complaints that began growing against me were simply the talk of those who were envious or fearful of someone who felt enough freedom and self-confidence to openly talk about the spiritual path in their own words. This certainly seemed to be part of what was going on. On the other hand, I sensed that the growing attacks against me were also my own Fierce Children of the Light. They were somehow my own creations.

I felt as if I was beyond the drama that was unfolding around me, yet I could not shake the feeling that somehow I was also responsible for bringing these things to life.

What was behind this controversy? What would turn friends against me, or move people to denounce someone they once considered their brother? I turned inwardly for some advice on what was going on. I met with a Master who goes by the name Quan Tu. I wrote down the following after an inner experience with him. I found his guidance helpful.

Do not float across life's surface, but take root in its rich soil. To care too deeply about the battles and wars is to fill yourself with torrents of water that can wash your roots away. Surely it carries all new seeds far away from the earth where they must grow.

Do not be afraid to take root. Do not be afraid to reach into life and live upon its rich expanse. In its soil is growth. Even storms, earthquakes and the scorching sun cannot carry you away. Let life be your earth of stability, your sustenance, your bread.

In life's depth there is no conflict. Whoever dies in battle never knew life to begin with. This means that life fools the seeker whose roots do not

291

yet reach the earth. They live, instead, upon the storms of conflict. They respond only to war. They do not hear earth's wisdom saying, 'Let it pass. All things pass, but life endures.' They do not respond to life's voice, so how can they be said to live?

—Quan Tu

He was right. It was life that mattered, not the battle cries and the wars. I was after something beyond the sides that people take. I had lost all sense of the dividing lines, and yet I could still see how desperately people cling to their walls and fences.

I found it oddly amusing that on the one hand I was being criticized for not holding up the Master as if he were the head of some hierarchy of power that all should obey—and on the other hand I was being criticized for not denouncing the whole sham of religion and worship. But I had stepped beyond such useless fighting and found something that moved me across all these artificial lines that people draw in the sand.

People wanted me to support their battles, to raise their flags of war, but I had gone too far. I had changed too much. I was too much a part of Life Itself.

The Wind

How can they know whose side the Wind is on?

They rage, "You are against Him!"

Others cry, "Are you afraid to leave His side?"

Root-bound and boastful, they accuse the
    Sun of too much heat,
    Storms of too much noise.

Such pretty potted plants,
    Too delicate for the world outside.

They will never know the Wind.

"Take a stand!" they yell,
    But the Wind will not.

Foolish voices yelling at the Wind.

Their words are carried off by the Wind
Before they are spoken.

Something was reaching a crisis point, but I didn't understand what it was. People were drawing their sacred lines in the sand, and if I wouldn't take their sides then they considered me against them. But I couldn't take sides. I was the wind that blew across all the walls and fences and belonged to none, and yet belonged to all. So, suddenly I found people treating me as if I were their enemy.

For me, it was like being in the eye of a hurricane, as none of it touched or disturbed me. It seemed as if it were a thousand miles away, but I still wondered what I had done to create this. I couldn't just pass the whole thing off as someone else's creation. I began to realize that their problems were somehow my own, too.

Something similar began happening at work as well, when my boss started spreading false stories about me to damage my reputation. Some of the inventions I had developed for the company had become wildly successful, and managers were coming to me, rather than him, for future plans. Rather than working with me, he felt the need to undercut me.

I decided it was time to start withdrawing from what I had been doing. I realized that living my own law as Soul was creating problems for those around me. They could not believe that anyone had such a right. There seemed to be a common feeling amongst my critics that I had some kind of lesson to learn, and they wanted to take me down a notch to teach me that no one can live by their own law.

In fact, my boss used those very words, "You have a lot to learn," as he tried to teach me a lesson about the power that he had.

In my younger years, I might have stood up to challenge such foolishness, but I no longer felt so separate from their problems. The wind saw things from their side as well. Shortly after my boss said those words, he was demoted and removed from his position over me, but I decided to back away, to tone down my own inner authority. I thought it would be best to let things die down, out of sympathy for those who seemed so bothered by what I had been doing.

One day I was talking to a friend about what was going on. We ended up getting into a discussion about the problems of power. After our phone call was over, he asked if I could put down on paper what I had been trying to say. I wrote the following:

A Few Thoughts on Power

Power is like a poisonous substance that taken in small doses can actually heal, but once you begin to crave it—it becomes dangerous indeed. You should never forget about the ugliness of power—its ability to crush and drive over the space of others. By developing a great distaste for power and a deep distrust, you can begin to see it for what it is—a two-headed creature.

You cannot avoid power too long before it is thrust upon you. There are simply too many people who choose lives of limitation. They cling to the status quo. Therefore, simply exercising your innate abilities takes on the appearance of power to them. Others will rearrange their own lives to follow you—granting you a permission of power. But if you must accept it, because you see some good coming out of it, and you feel the need—never forget it belongs to the people who grant it. It is their power, not yours, and it is in your keeping only until they are ready to take it back.

The purpose of power is to serve. When it tries to raise itself above this lowly, servile place, then its acts of destruction have begun. Its only true value is to serve. All else is illusion.

Opinions and judgments are luxuries that those in power are not allowed. Their beliefs belong to their personal realms. But those in power must give up their personal lives—their lives now belong to those they serve. Many have destroyed themselves on this point—never realizing what power truly demands. They thought they were wiser than others and could outsmart the giant. They tried to grab the gold and run. But such gold turns to dust when spent on one's personal life, and curses the thief who wanted to rob instead of serve.

Think long and hard on this before the gleam of power fills your eyes, for a personal life is a very valuable thing. Do not give it away so quickly before you know its worth. Is the king's gold really worth it?

Even the Lords of the Lower Worlds, themselves, return to the personal life after ages of being gods over their domains—because only through the personal life can they grow further. The story of Atlas trying to trick Hercules into carrying the weight of the world is a story told over and over through a thousand ages.

Therefore, power is one of the lowest estates in life. Isn't this why so much gold is thrown at the feet of the powerful? They are given fancy titles and glitter to help them forget how much of their life is spent on serving the world.

Never see yourself as a figure of power or authority, for this is vanity and self-deceit. How can you become a figure of power to yourself? How can you look up to yourself as if you were greater than yourself? This is merely self-kissing-self in the mirror of vanity. This has nothing to do with God-Consciousness, which is carried out in secret, unrecognized, unseen and unheard by the world. The power of this world means nothing to the God-Realized.

Others may see you as a great channel for power, but remember—they are seeing their own reflections in you. It is themselves that they see, and their own power that they have granted you that they are unable to see in themselves. Be honest and truthful when you look at yourself. Are you thrilled by being in your own presence?

The greatest danger of power comes when it starts serving itself. When it convinces its captains and followers to serve and defend it. Never, ever fall victim to thinking there is any power worth defending for itself.

You, who have become scorched in the fire of power a million times, what are you seeking? To master yourself, or others? To scale the great mountain of God, or to run from the emptiness of yourself? To serve or to control?

Ask yourself these questions when passing before the great throne of power. Also, look and notice—there is only one seat upon that throne. And why is it empty?

Writing this out crystallized for me the difference between the Spiritual Hierarchy and the hierarchies of power in the lower worlds. Hierarchies of power are based on limitation. There is only one seat at the top. Whoever is sitting there prevents others from that place. Therefore, to have power means to have something that others don't have, as if it were a limited commodity.

The Spiritual Hierarchy, however, is based on the limitless. Anyone who attains a higher stage lifts the whole world spiritually. Therefore, everyone gains from it. No one in the Spiritual Hierarchy could ever limit our growth, since its whole function and purpose is the ever-expanding awareness of God. In fact, the Spiritual Hierarchy is nothing but the grace of God that allows Soul to attain the stations of the Path. No one stands as an authority over Soul, telling Soul what It can or can't do. It is Soul Itself, with the help of the Spiritual Hierarchy that knows the wisdom of advancing to God-Realization.

Some thought I wanted power, when I actually detested it. Some, whom I had considered my friends, began to turn on me. I had seen the fences that sometimes arise between friends and knew that there was nothing I could do to change that. Whether I was attacked, personally, or overly praised, I focused on giving others respect and acceptance for whatever they wanted to believe. After all, these were their creations, were they not? This was what they were deciding to make sacred.

In The Presence of the Lion

I thought that the conflicts would subside, but they did not. Around this time I began working on discourse twenty-six from Rumi's book, *It Is What It Is*. A section I read there jumped out at me, and I began to understand what was taking place within me. Rumi said:

> For someone to fly from here to the Kaaba in an instant is not so wonderful, even though there are such stories of saints having done so. But a true miracle is this: that God should bring you from a lowly estate to a high estate, that you should travel from ignorance to reason, from the inanimate to life. Just as at first you were earth and mineral, God brought you to the vegetable world. Then you journeyed from the vegetable world to the animal world, from the animal world to the world of humanity.
>
> These are true miracles. Through these stations and forms you journeyed, never once thinking or imagining where you would arrive, by which road you would be taken, or how you would be brought. Even so, you will be brought on to a hundred other worlds. Do not doubt it, and if you are told such stories, believe them.
>
> A bowl of poison was brought as a present to Umar. "Of what use is this?" he asked.
>
> They said, "When it is not publicly advisable to kill someone openly, you can give them a little of this. Then they will die secretly. If it is an enemy who cannot be slain with the sword, with a little of this they can be killed clandestinely."
>
> "You have brought me a very good thing," he said. "Give it to me to drink, for within me is a mighty enemy whom the sword cannot reach. I have no greater enemy in the world than he."
>
> "There is no need to drink it all up in one gulp," they told him. "Just one sip is enough. This bowl is sufficient for a hundred thousand people."

"My enemy, too, is not one person," said Umar. "He is a thousand strong, and has overthrown a hundred thousand."

He then seized the cup and drank it all in one draught. At once the assembled multitude all became believers, crying, "Your religion is true!"

"You have all become believers," said Umar, "and yet this infidel within me has not yet become a believer."

What Umar desired was not the faith of the common people. He had that faith and more—indeed, he had the faith of the veracious. He was seeking the faith of the Prophets in absolute certainty. That was what he hoped for.

The report of a lion spread abroad through all parts of the world. It was said this lion had a special quality: Anyone who approached him boldly, and rubbed their hands upon him lovingly, would be unharmed, but if they were afraid and timorous the lion would be enraged against them. Sometimes he even attacked, as if to say, "What is this bad opinion you have of me?"

A certain person, marveling at the rumor, traveled from far away to see the lion. For a year this person endured the rigors of the road and traveled from town to town. After finally arriving at the thicket and spying the lion from afar, this lion seeker stood still and could advance no closer.

The people said to this person, "You set forth on a long road out of love for this lion. For this creature you have struggled on for a year. Now that you have come so close, why do you stand still? Advance one more step!"

But none of them had the courage to take a further step. They all said, "The steps we took up to here were all easy. Yet this one step we cannot make."

What Umar desired was that step, to take one step in the presence of the lion towards the lion. That step is a great and rare matter, the concern of only the chosen and intimate of God. Yet this is the true step—the rest are mere footprints. Such faith comes only to prophets who have washed their hands of their own life.

When I read this I began to see that I too was looking to take one more step, yet all the previous steps had been easy compared to this one. It seemed as if I would have to leave everything else behind and set my own life aside if I would approach the lion.

My job had been threatened, but this didn't bother me. I wasn't concerned by the power of the outer world and all the outer authorities. I knew now that Soul is superior to all of them. Nothing they could do could move me from God. Not even the Irresistible Force could move the Immovable Object that is Soul. But this next step even Soul trembled at. Even Soul must be left behind. How could Soul, of Its own accord, gamble Itself away?

I was indeed unconsciously creating wars around myself, because like Umar I was fighting a thousand enemies to approach this lion. These enemies were my own and the only fears were of my creation, but this step was something beyond anything else I knew, and its very shadow faced me like approaching death.

An ECKist I did not know very well told me about a dream she had of me at this time. In the dream she followed me into a building that was both a store and a church. As I walked along the aisles, the statues and busts of Saints and Masters that hung on the walls began to vibrate. They shook more and more violently until they came tumbling down and smashed on the ground.

It no longer seems so strange that I might have had such an effect on others, since this was what was taking place within me. But there was no way to turn back now. I had no other choice but to take the step.

One day, shortly after this, Karen was preparing to do some deep-frying in the kitchen. She had placed a frying pan of oil on the stove and turned it on to cook while she went into another room to finish something else. I was wandering nearby when I saw the pan burst into flames. By the time I reached the kitchen, the flames were three to four feet high.

I reached for the stove to turn it off, but the flames were too hot to reach the switches. Karen came into the kitchen behind me and froze. I could see that the flames were so dangerously high that if it continued much longer, it was going to catch the walls and ceiling on fire. I grabbed for a heavy potholder and lifted the pan off the stove.

I thought at first that once I moved it away from the stove that I could reach the switch to turn it off, but the flames were too hot to move the pan anywhere. I also thought for a moment that I could carry the pan out the back door and toss it into the back yard, but as I turned around with the pan, I could see that there was no way to safely carry it through the house to the back door. It would have been far too dangerous.

I found myself with a roaring fire in my hands and no place to turn. I couldn't put it back because the stove was already too hot, and I couldn't go anywhere with it. It was starting to feel heavy and it felt like time was running out. Everything that happened up to this point took place in seconds, as I ran through my options. There had to be a way out, I thought.

I turned to the right and saw the kitchen sink. For a moment I thought I could pour it all down the drain, but realized immediately that would be impossible. I then turned on the faucet, wondering if cold water nearby could cool the heat coming from the pan. I then made a mistake that was over before I even realized what happened. I allowed some water from the faucet to get into the pan.

The pan of oil exploded into a fireball before my eyes. The whole kitchen was engulfed in flames. I felt a deep surge within me grow and heard myself saying a word, like an ancient yell, I had never heard before. It came out with a bellowing depth in my voice that shocked even me—and just as suddenly the flames all disappeared.

The frying pan was empty. The oil had completely vaporized. I ran and threw it out the back door onto the grass. I came back to see if Karen was all right. She had been standing behind me and was unharmed. But the same could not be said about the kitchen. The varnish on the cupboards was gone. The blinds on the window over the sink had melted. Even paper messages stuck on the refrigerator door, eight feet away were all singed and half burned.

You would think I should have been seriously burned all over, but in fact only my hand was hurt, since some oil had splattered onto it in a few places. Those burns were bad and required a visit to the emergency room, but except for some melted eyebrows and hair, the rest of me was untouched.

I felt a strange sense of calm after the explosion, even after I realized the mistake I had made with letting water get into the pan. I should have realized how dangerous that would be. I should also have known, as Karen pointed out to me, that throwing baking soda on the fire would have put it out and would have smothered the flames by robbing them of oxygen.

However, I found an immediate wave of sympathy pouring down on me from within, like a sense of grace, and I realized that something had changed for me.

Not everything can be described or explained. Not everything fits into words or stories. I knew one thing, however. I had much to learn. I now understood Paul Twitchell's story in his book, *The Tiger's Fang*, about how difficult it really is to pull the fang of the tiger. But there was one thing I could see: I had taken another step.

6

VOW OF SILENCE

PICK UP YOUR PEN," Life called, impatiently.
"Let it dance with your heart.
"Make your breath visible
With love's warmth
"Why do you keep me waiting?"

Forgive my silence, I replied.
But showing your jewels breeds envy.
Displaying your Truth sparks flames.
Since words only hide what they mean to reveal,
   Cannot love alone be my ink,
         And actions my stamp?
Buried gems are your secret beauty,
   But once in my hands the wars start.
Surely you have hidden yourself for a reason.
Before my eyes you have stripped off your many garments.
I stare at you, transfixed.
   I cannot move.
Dare I share such passion?
For your sake I keep you covered from the world.

"Then write me in secret, my love," Life answered,
"Yet write.

"For your words are music that stirs me,
"And my blush warms mankind."

. . ● . .

I COULD SEE that revealing spiritual truth was creating problems.
It was as if I had been sharing something too personal that did not
belong to the world. I did not completely understand this yet, but I
sensed that the ground rules had changed again.

Living by our own law and making our own spiritual path can be
upsetting to others who do not know such freedom. Yet their disturbed
feelings were not just their own. I felt them as if they were a part of my
world as well. Therefore, their response was a message for me and a
reflection of a deeper lesson.

Some things must be kept in silence. But why? What was I still missing?

Soul does not come into this world looking for hand-outs, but to gain
spiritual growth from its own individual efforts. Therefore, the treasures
we gain upon the path cannot be given to anyone else. In the end, we
must each earn them for ourselves. They must become our own.

If this were true, then what is the purpose of spiritual teachers? If
they cannot give to others what they have gained, and if living the life
of spiritual freedom creates problems around them, then what is their
role in this world? I found myself rethinking the meaning of the masters
and the spiritual travelers.

I wrote the following to explore what I knew and what I was learning:

The Travelers

There are those who claim that the spiritual travelers are perfected beings, but this is only true in the sense that they see and know a greater
truth. The perfume of perfection hangs on them. But that perfume de-
rives from the presence of God in their hearts. Through that scent we too
can experience God. But nothing perfect can be born, nor can it die—and
no jar can hold the whole ocean, only a few drops.

Therefore, the travelers never see themselves as perfected unless they
are in the grips of vanity. To someone inside a house, the window seems
to frame the whole view of the outside world. But to the window, itself, it
merely holds but a few panes of glass.

304

A sea shell to our ear reminds us of the sea and brings the sea closer. But to the shell that has lived in that ocean and intimately knows its depths, such a sound is nothing like the true ocean. It only reminds the shell of how far from home it is.

So, to us who are seekers, the spiritual travelers are the windows of God. They become the matrix through which pours the light and music of the higher spheres. But to the spiritual travelers, this image of themselves is an illusion. In reality they have completely forgotten themselves in the presence of that great ocean which draws them on. They know they cannot take one iota of credit for what belongs to God.

The Sufi Master, Hakim Sanai of Afghanistan, once said, "Do not prattle before the People of the Path. Instead consume yourself. Your knowledge and religion are inverted if your face is toward this world instead of toward God."

It is often a surprise that spiritual vanity could be such a danger to those who approach the state of God-Realization. Some believe that the spiritual travelers move into and live only in a state that is beyond egotism and illusion. But whoever thinks they are free of illusion is more deeply embedded in it than anyone else.

Mohammed said, "Allah, show me things as they truly are. You show a thing as beautiful and in reality it is ugly. You show a thing as ugly, and in truth it is beautiful." That is the experience of this world. Everything bad has some good and everything bright casts some shadow. This is why we are always humbled here; because only within God Itself can we find perfection.

One day a seeker was walking by the house of a saint. A wall surrounded the garden, and the seeker heard the saint praying on the other side.

"God," the saint said, "people do not hear you, nor see you anywhere. They see only themselves. They are so filled with themselves that they cannot hear your call. O God, what can I do?"

The seeker heard God's answer to the saint: "Now you see things as they truly are."

The saint said, "There can be no curse greater than this!"

God answered, "Nor any greater blessing."

The saint pleaded, "O Lord, share with me your great wisdom. Show me the purpose of this and what I can say to these people who are lost and so far from your presence."

Silence was the answer.

The saint could not accept this silence. He thought there should be an answer. So he stumbled upon his trust in God. The illusion of separation from God was too real for him. He could not see the wisdom in a world that did not know how to live in God's presence. He could not see God's hand behind it all. His foot slipped upon the path and his name was forgotten.

But that eavesdropper who thought of himself as the seeker became illuminated in that moment, for he realized that perfection exists only within God Itself—nowhere else. He went on to become a great teacher of the Way.

Yet, his name has also been forgotten. What? You thought he should be remembered and famous? Not so. God has hidden Himself from this world, and so does the spiritual traveler. He may hide himself in secrecy or in fame, yet still he is hidden.

This is the meaning of the story the Greeks told of Daedalus and his son Icarus. Daedalus, in a vision granted by the gods, was shown how to fly by making wings of wax and feathers. This was a rare secret to be revealed to a man, but with this vision came a warning: You must never give this secret to another mortal, and do not fly too high. Do not think you are a god.

One day, returning from a flight, Daedalus was spotted by his son, Icarus. Icarus wanted to fly, but no matter how he begged and pleaded Daedalus would not give in. Icarus was not one to give up easily, however. So, one night he climbed up the outside of the rock wall and hid himself in the private room where his father prepared to fly.

The next day, Daedalus, still grieving that he could not share this wonderful secret with his son or anyone else, since the gods demanded a vow of silence, began to make his wings of wax and feathers. Icarus watched and saw everything. After his father flew out the room's window that hung out over the edge of a cliff, Icarus immediately began making wings for himself.

Icarus was soon flying. "This is easy," he thought. He flew after his father and found him out over the Aegean Sea.

"Look, Father," he called out. "I can fly, too. It's easy."

Daedalus was shocked. "Go back, Icarus. Go back before the gods see you. Go back before it's too late!"

But Icarus was emboldened by his own small success. He suffered that common problem of the spiritually vain: He could not hear the warnings and messages that God was sending to him through others. In trying to fly too high, in trying to join the gods, he was scorched by the sun, his wings melted and he was drowned in the sea.

Daedalus was struck with sorrow. He wondered: How could such a blessing bring such destruction to those he loved? But this is the danger of taking up God's work: It also attracts those who would dare to assume the role of Teacher out of desire for personal gain.

To see ourselves as spiritual travelers creates two things:

First, the opportunity opens up for us to journey through the spiritual worlds as co-workers with God.

Second, some will react to us as if this were vanity. Whether it is truth or not does not matter. When some people sense or perceive that we see ourselves as spiritual travelers, they will react to this as vanity.

There is no way to escape this Catch-22 except through God's hands. Therefore the spiritual travelers don't expect any respect to be gained from spiritual success, for it appears as only vanity to this world. This is why they listen to the criticisms of others, knowing that there are often secret warnings hidden beneath the surface. They know that learning is more important than teaching, and that truth will always be invisible to this world. Thus, they discover the benefits of being taken down a peg and bowing before the God in others.

Rumi, the Persian Sufi said, "All who criticize the seeker's ego are not enemies of the seeker, but his friend—for the seeker's ego is his own enemy, too."

In the end, we are all spiritual travelers. We are the Path. We listen only to our own selves, because no matter what someone else might say, we can only hear and understand what is a part of us.

Therefore, on this journey of Soul we must speak in that language of Self—that language where we are not two souls, not hundreds of souls, but only Soul of Itself. This is the language of the travelers. Do you recognize it? It is a conscious language that is not just spoken but must be known.

Our language and wisdom, as the travelers, is not only composed of an inner spirit, but has an outward form as well. Our body needs its outer skin as much as its inward heart. The seed must have its shell or it rots in the earth. Rituals and religious traditions are outward forms, but few remember that the true purpose of such traditions is to carry a teaching that words cannot describe.

Modern society on planet Earth has been driven toward destroying its traditions as if it could find freedom this way. We think we know so much more than our primitive ancestors. This is the illusion drawn over the eyes of mankind so that he will continue on the path that is his fate.

For this reason, when modern man hears about the spiritual travelers, he imagines it means complete detachment from all traditions, families, the world, and a total escape from the limitations of form. He does not see that the spiritual traveler's love for God is so great that he takes on the forms, the families, the traditions, for the sake of a teaching the world does not understand.

What use is total freedom to the spiritual traveler except to spend it on God? What could he want for himself? Having been given all by God, he wants nothing more than to give all back to God.

The false self is the greatest discovery to the spiritual traveler. This is the ego the world sees. This does not disappear for the traveler, but rather for the first time becomes truly visible.

There is no place to go. There is nothing to become. Any image the world has about the traveler is false, for to become the traveler is to become something the world can not see.

This is like the story about a cave that went deep into a mountain range. There was a legend about this cave; that anyone who traveled far enough into the cave without falling into the pitfalls would come out into a wonderful world of bright sunshine, blossoming fields and comfortable living. Having arrived, no one ever wanted to return.

This is the same with those who approach God. According to legend, if you go far enough, you never come back. This doesn't mean you cease living in this world, but having arrived there you can never return. There is nothing left of you that is separate from God. This self that others see and call by your name is merely the false-self.

But who wants to take such risks? The people who look into the cave say, "How do we know that those who never returned haven't perished?"

Of course they have perished! How else could they cross into that land where Soul has never trod, and the Soul body Itself must be dropped before entering? Yes, they have perished. Even THAT I AM has perished and only "God IS" is left.

Before the travelers start hinting at perfection to others, they remember "There is only room for one in God." Even a hint of otherness puts us outside. If a beautiful lover showed you perfect love, would you share this with the world? Even one boast would send that loved one away. For, by this boast we show our desire is not for love itself, but to show it off for worldly rewards.

Therefore, the travelers hide the perfection of God from the world as you would hide a lover. The compulsion we feel to share the love of God is like an unripe fruit. Wait until it ripens.

That compulsion is the same urge that the salmon feels when it swims upstream, or the swallow feels when it seeks out Capistrano. Where is that compulsion leading? It can lead us to the leash-holder and free us from the leash. If it brings destruction and devastation then it has worked its miracle.

The travelers are those who have been destroyed. They did not run from their annihilation, but walked right into it. They have never returned. None have been heard from since. Those that you see are but empty leashes. Like empty window frames. They are empty shells cast upon the shore.

It is an emptiness that holds oceans.

I can see my own conceptions of mastership were changing even as I wrote this. At the point where it says, "In the end, we are all spiritual travelers. We are the Path..." something shifted for me. My perspective changed and the idea of being a spiritual traveler no longer seemed so far away. It seemed within reach.

At the same time I realized how little I really knew about what it meant. I had been following a dream of God-Consciousness that was almost the opposite of what it really was. It is not something great in the eyes of this world. In fact, it has no value in this world. It means nothing here.

How could this be?

I was working on rewriting a translation of Rumi's *Discourses* at this time, mainly as an exercise for my own learning, when I ran across this quote from discourse ten. It struck me, and for the first time I began to understand what Rumi was saying:

There are certain lovers of God who, because of their great majesty and jealousy for God, do not show themselves openly, but they cause disciples to attain important goals and bestow gifts upon them. Such mighty spiritual saints are rare and precious.

Someone said: "Do the great ones come before you?"

Rumi answered: There is no "before" left to me. It has been a long time since I have had any "before." If they come, they come before an image they believe to be me. Some people said to Jesus, "We will come to your house." Jesus replied, "Where is my house in this world and how could I have a house?"

It is related that Jesus was wandering in the desert when a great rainstorm broke. He went to take shelter in the den of a jackal in the corner of its cave, until the rain ceased. A revelation came to him, saying "Get out of the jackal's den, for the jackal's little ones cannot rest on account of you." He cried aloud, "Lord, the jackal's pups have a shelter, but the son of Mary has no place to call home."

Although the Jackal's whelp has a cave to live in, still it has no Beloved to drive it out of its home. But you do have such a One driving you out. If you have no home, what does that matter? The loving-kindness of such a Driver, and the grace from such a robe of honor that singles you out to be driven forth, is worth far more, exceeding a hundred thousand heavens and worlds here and beyond.

It is a robe of honor to become nothing in the eyes of the world. It is a loving-kindness to have Someone driving us away from the false self and drawing us on. This was a truth that spoke to me at this time, but it also seemed to be telling me that everything I had learned up until now meant nothing. I had attained nothing, spiritually, and was nothing. Yet, strangely, this was more valuable than anything I had understood before.

Was this the meaning of the Vow of Silence? Had I been revealing truths as if they were significant, when in reality they were nothing? Was this what had created problems? I began to sense a new law emerging from within myself, but still wondered where it was taking me.

I wrote the following:

I get the feeling that I'm slowly turning around and looking in a new direction. It is as if I had been focused upon the outer worlds and the many ways that Spirit flows out, creating wonders and bringing love. But now, turning around, I see something very different—something much truer. I've only been looking at the mirror of the world all this time and seeing reflections of myself. But now I am slowly turning around to look upon the Face of God.

Now, the outer worlds no longer look like something separate from Soul. Suddenly, it's as if Soul encompasses all of Life, and my role now is to wander through this world of Self to be a Witness to its workings. To see it as it is.

I feel a loss of the creative drive with this new state of consciousness, since creativity and giving form to Spirit has been the means of spiritual growth to me for so long. On the other hand I now find the subtlest inflections of my thought become mirrored out upon the world, and the subtlest feelings of the world become reflected upon the mirror of my heart.

It seems that something much deeper is taking place than creation. It is neither great nor small, so it goes undetected. Yet the whole of Spirit moves like tides across the world.

To see life as it is. Is this the meaning of God-Consciousness? I felt like I was catching the glimpse of something far beyond what I had ever thought. This was not just observing the world. It was a way of seeing that made everything conscious. It was like a way of awakening Life, Itself, by consciously recognizing Life as it was.

I was also beginning to see the huge difference between the outward flows of Spirit and the currents that return back to God. I had been creating the path for myself, but didn't realize that all my efforts had been focused on manifesting the outward flows. This is what creativity and creation are all about in the lower worlds—the outward flow of Spirit. I had mistakenly thought that this was what mastership meant: First, to create one's own world, and then, to work with the spiritual forces of the world.

Now it was beginning to dawn on me that I had been looking the wrong way all along. I had been facing the world and creating for the sake of the world. I had only been working with the outward currents, but it is the returning waves that the spiritual travelers are most interested in.

I wrote the following:

I've changed in how I see things. I now see the value that comes from the downward cycles as well as the upward changes. In fact, I've almost reversed my thinking, since I now see that the down cycles are often where our greatest spiritual growth takes place.

I'm reminded of something Rumi once said that captures this for me. He wrote that there are those who love the blossoming of the rose, and there are others who love when the petals fall and are blown away by the wind. Rumi was saying that there are those who see the signs of death as an indication that Soul is returning to Its source, and there is a hidden beauty in such moments. There is a poignancy and meaningfulness in death.

This world praises anything that praises this world. Therefore, spring, which brings birth and youth, is good, while autumn, which brings death and the withering of old age, is bad. But in fact youth is the time when Soul becomes lost in this world, and old age is when Soul withdraws from this world to return home.

This is what the creative cycle is about. The creative outward phase builds and gives birth to new things, spreading ourselves across this world. The inward phase withdraws us back to our center. The outward flows of Spirit move us out into the world, creating, and the inward flows bring detachment from the forms of the world, to return us back to the ocean of unmanifested reality.

Rumi gave another example to illustrate his point. He said that when people give a party, everyone sees the spending that goes into it, but few see all the saving that went on beforehand. People see when the tree sends forth its new green buds, but no one sees what is happening in the winter when the tree withdraws its sap and collects itself back from the world.

Spirit leads us down, just as It leads us up. In following It down, there is even more growth and spiritual transformation, but it takes place invisibly to this world.

The more willingly I follow the ECK through Its down cycles along with Its upward cycles, the more I find the two merging into one. Going along with the falling apart and decay of life, as well as the birth and growth, has shown me the secret that Soul lives and grows spiritually beneath this outward show.

I no longer felt so deeply moved by the forces of creation that pull mankind along in its cycles. I was connected to something outside of creation. Something else was drawing me along.

I felt as if I was unlearning habits and patterns of behavior that were as unconscious as breathing. One of the strangest discoveries during this time was the realization that most of my motivations were tied back to the world. Even many of my deepest searches for spiritual truths were, sooner or later, used as a way to help myself in this world. It was as if I would make sincere efforts to lift myself out of the mess I had created, like someone gasping for air, only to use my new found gains to turn around and create something new and better for the sake of the world. This "dance of Lila," which is the dance of Soul losing and finding itself, went much deeper than I realized.

What did it really mean to work as a co-worker with God? What motivations are left within us once we have turned toward the face of God?

It is like fleeing from all directions and from all motivations. This is not a natural condition to have no desires. How is it even possible to attain such a state, without desire?

I came to realize that only God causes this change within Soul.

I wrote the following in a letter to a friend:

You mentioned that you find yourself moving farther and farther away from an anthropocentric approach to the spiritual teachings. I must say that I have journeyed so far away that I've lost all sense of centricities of any kind.

The vast majority of people living in the planetary worlds are much like the planets they live on—caught in the gravitational field of some spiritual sun around which they revolve. But I feel more like one of the comets coming from someplace too far out to know, that passes by for perhaps a brief period and then is gone again. There must be One beyond all centricities that guides my path.

We have been trained to be centric—to revolve around some greater body. We build our belief systems to reinforce our worldviews, but sooner or later we get knocked out of our normal orbit. Then we quickly struggle to find some other sun to revolve around. This is our nature. We rarely leave our orbit unless pushed by some force beyond ourselves, and then we seek some new pattern of life, some new sense of what is home.

It seems that Someone has pushed me too far away from any orbit to ever find home here in these planetary worlds. I've been knocked from my orbits too many times and now belong to none of them. Yet, strangely, I now see them more clearly than I have ever seen them before.

Turning around a center is the way of creation. It is the result of the creational forces flowing out into the world. A sun sends its rays out to the planets around it, breathing life into those worlds. Parents give birth to children who fall into the orbit of their parents, who protect them and give them shelter and sustenance. Nations grow from a central capital around a government, because they need a hub around which to spin.

However, this world is not the home of Soul. The origins of our conscious being come from far beyond, and sooner or later we begin to remember that we are more. We then look for the returning waves that can raise us above and release us from the centricities of the worlds. We begin to drop our needs and dependencies. That is when we discover the real source of Life. That is when, for the first time, Soul truly begins to grow in spiritual capacity.

Realizing how wrong I had been about so many things and how much I now had to learn, I went back to see Quan Tu, the master whom I had visited from time to time via Soul Travel. He wouldn't answer my questions directly, but I felt something coming from him that was leading me to a deeper understanding.

I could feel my old preconceptions falling apart, as they no longer seemed to fit. It was as if this great edifice I had constructed was now a fraud. I had been trying to climb higher and higher towards God, like Icarus, as if that was truly the direction where God resides. But of course,

God has no directions, no place and no time. I had only been climbing the edifice of this world, and now realized that it meant nothing.

I wrote the following after my visit with Quan Tu:

"Be Silent"

"Be silent!" you say
But words rush to my mouth.

"Be silent!" you repeat
Yet I cannot keep from speaking.

Is there no bottom to this well of useless talk?
Will my donkey never shut up?

"Silence and poverty are my doormat," you whisper
Yet you have no doormat but the earth,
   And you do not care for words.

"Eagles never say 'fly' to fly," you say,
"And babies who haven't learned 'cry' still cry.
   "What is the use of such talk?"

"They fill the silence," I think with my donkey thoughts.
You don't even crack a smile.

I think you hear a song I have only dreamed of.
"Will you take me there?" I ask.
"Be silent!" you say. "You are there now."

           . . ● . .

I walk in your footsteps
But my feet do not have the roots that yours do.

I listen to the breeze
But the music that surrounds you seems far away to me.

In the dark, your face is aglow.

314

I search your eyes like a child
    Looking for a Christmas present.

You sit me down sternly.
"Stop these games," you say.
"Are you seeking God or Santa Claus?
    "Life is what it is!"

I feel like a junkie hooked on dreams
Caught stealing from his lover.

I step into your footsteps again
But the earth is hard and cold.
So cold my feet are frozen,
With a cold that reaches up into my legs,
    Like roots.

You smile.
"A cold that sprouts roots," you say,
"A dark that lights flames.
    "You will never be the same."

"Where are you leading me?" I ask.
"Down," you say.
"Down?" I ask.

"Even lower than down," you say,
    "Until you've lost everything you do not know.
    "Until you've felt that true hunger like the emptiness of the desert,
        "How can you know?"

"But must I go all the way down?" I ask.
"Even lower than all the way," you reply.
"Have I angered the gods?" I ask.
"You have charmed them," you say.

"I'd hate to think of those whom the gods dislike," I say.
"Yes," you answer. "They are left to sleep
    "In their soft beds of illusion."

I had been so busy making my own path that I had not seen the importance of the Silence. This is why Life was now asking me to keep a vow: To return back to the silent questions. This was, in fact, the call of God, the call to return.

To feel that primitive spiritual hunger, the original desire—this is what I needed. It was like starting all over. Not just starting over with the path I found in this lifetime, but going back thousands of lifetimes to the very first moment of existence. I had to unlearn thousands of lifetimes of creating and becoming lost in my creations. This was why I came back to learn about people.

It is a strange passage, when Soul suddenly finds Itself without desires. How do we live? What do we center our life upon? It seems as if something we have been hooked on for lifetimes has vanished. We are left only with God. The desire of the ego to create simply dries up.

But over time, and it seemed like years, gradually something new began to fill the void. Not my old desires, but an eternal desire that belonged to Life. A desire beyond my little self was now becoming a part of me somehow. It seemed ancient in some way, and for the first time I began to glimpse the real meaning of the spiritual teaching that pours out of the heart of reality.

Little by little, I began to understand the meaning of this vow of silence. What can be said when none of the God Truths mean anything to this world? The returning currents have nothing to do with the created worlds. They are about Soul's capacity to grasp something this world will never understand.

Perhaps this explains why so little is written about the path beyond this point. I wrote:

That reality is speaking to us all the time, but we do not hear it because our ears are not attuned to its form.

The Masters bring into speech what is formless. We hear the words but miss the silences between the words.

How can that Great Reality stop speaking out to the world continuously? What could hold ITS voice back?

We have learned to speak to describe our meanings, but the Silence of God pulls all meaning from words.

God has hidden this great secret by placing it everywhere.

We can say nothing about IT, and those who see this reality willingly give up their voice to take the vow. What else could they do?

Yet, how can we not speak of IT? Everything we do and feel springs from IT.

Suddenly, I could see the whole meaning of the spiritual growth of Soul. It was as if I had never really seen it before.

I could now see this great current that pours out upon the world like a wave of light. We call it the Voice of God. It is beyond all paths and all religions, yet all spiritual teachings spring from IT. No teacher can give it out or explain it, still, everything we do after bathing in this light becomes a part of the teachings and a part of the path. It is not an organization or a tradition, but something beyond all forms. It is this stream that calls us back to God through the silent questions.

I now understood the purpose of the Master, the stages of spiritual growth and the importance of the individual path. It was not what I had expected. I had to break free of all the dreams of centricities to find this current leading to a source that was everywhere.

I wrote to a friend a series of e-mail messages that reflects some of my thinking at this time.

DOUG: Phil, a lot of people know that after Shams of Tabriz (Rumi's Master) died, Rumi came to realize that Shams was within himself. He wrote the following in his *Diwan-i-Shams Tabriz* (from Reynold Nicholson's translation):

Cross and Christians, end to end, I searched.
    HE was not on the Cross.
To the Hindu temple, to the ancient pagoda,
    In neither was there any sign.
To lofty Herat and down to Kandahar I looked.
    HE was not in height nor lowland.
Determined, I climbed to the top of the Mountain of Kaf.
    There was only the place of the 'Anqa Bird.
I made homage to the Kaaba.
    There was no answer.
I asked for a hint from Ibn Sina,
    But HE was beyond the limits of the philosopher...
I looked into my own heart.
    In this, HIS place, I saw HIM.
HE was in no other place.

317

But not many realize that Rumi also took one of his own students and treated him as the Master, after Shams died.

PHIL: Are you saying that he looked to the student as his Master? In other words, he gave the student the power to be an Oracle for himself (Rumi)? Or are you saying that Rumi took on the role of Master for one of his students?

DOUG: Rumi looked to the student as his Master and treated him as the Master. The student was humbled by it and objected, but Rumi continued. Finally the student, out of love for Rumi, allowed Rumi to treat him this way. In fact, Rumi wrote his famous six volume poem, The Song of the Reed, known as the *Masnavi*, as a dedication to his student, calling him the light of the world.

From this, I believe Rumi was saying that even though he had become a part of the Master, inwardly, he still needed a North Star in his life outwardly. Even if he could create and manifest the North Star within himself—it still needed an outward form.

Rumi wrote in discourse thirty-one of his book *It Is What It Is*:

When someone follows a star and finds their way by it, the star does not speak. Merely by looking at the star, they discover that invisible road and reach their goal. In the same way, it is possible by merely gazing at God's saints to find the spiritual path. Without words, without questioning, without speech, the purpose is achieved.

PHIL: How would you describe the process of creating and manifesting this North Star?

DOUG: When one knows how to become the North Star for one's self, then one can manifest their own North Star in another.

We can always say that we have love within ourselves, but how can we know that love without another?

PHIL: Doesn't the concept of an authentic Master satisfy that need? Or are you referring to an additional spiritual/physical relationship that is more intimate in nature?

DOUG: The question I am getting at is: Who is the Master for the Master? Rumi showed that even the Master needs Someone to serve and look to as his North Star.

PHIL: Fascinating. In other worlds, the Master needs the student as much as the student needs the Master. A device that keeps one humble and focused on the spiritual need of another, and in so doing amplifies one's spiritual growth.

What you're suggesting here, unless I've totally missed your point, is the value of selecting a special student for this relationship. Yes?

318

DOUG: Or at least selecting someone. Or maybe we should say, letting our heart select someone.

Yes, it is fascinating.

PHIL: What do you make of the idea of reaching a point in spiritual development where you see the Master in all of life and are in a constant state of humility by virtue of ITS presence?

Doesn't the assignment of a North Star somehow limit the spiritual exercise?

DOUG: I think this sounds great as a theory, but without the North Star it all becomes impersonal. Yes, we can see the Master everywhere, but that will not evoke the personal love for God.

If we only find the Master everywhere, then where can that highly intense personal experience of God center itself on?

Many prefer that sort of path, not because the results are better, but because it fits their ideology better and seems less messy from a personal standpoint.

That of course is the problem with Love. It is personal and comes with pain and struggles, like thorns come with the rose. Yet, this is what brings significance and purpose.

On the other hand, voyagers only need the North Star when they are out at sea. At home, who needs a guide?

If all the stars in the heaven are "equal," then there is no reference and the world loses its meaning. This, I found, is the secret of living as a person in this world.

Therefore, our relationships are what grant purpose to life and give a reference frame to everything we experience. The value of what we say and do springs from our connections. It is not within them or in us alone, but can only be found in between the two, where we are joined as one.

Although I had left all the orbits of the world for a while, I now found the realization that it was relationships that make this world, and life is not possible here without that. But this was still a different place than I had ever been before. The spiritual teachings and the silent questions come to this world with focal points of their own, but they release us from the gravitational forces of the world and cause us to move towards something far beyond.

The secrets of God are indeed hidden everywhere.

319

Whispers of the In-Between

Between a blade of grass and the sky
  Is too much for words to express.
Between one root and the earth
    Is something too sacred to be exposed.
      Do not pull apart the fabric
        To learn.
    Like fine rain,
      Seep into thinner and thinner spaces.

From the surgeon's hand to man's heart
  Are miles of separation.
From the scalpel's edge to a single truth
  Are a thousand doors
    No knife
      Can unlock.
    True friends have a way of opening hearts
    That leaves no scars.

Even this thread of a poem is too thick for the fine curtain
  That heaven draws between moments.
Even the pause between breaths
  Is not thin enough
    To know without looking.
  Have you never noticed—
    You become lost
      At the instant of discovery?

The fabric of hearts is infinitely fine and delicate.
Tear even one thread and it frays
  Into a million fragments
    That no tailor can restore.
  If you must know the secrets hidden
    From prying eyes,
      Then follow the whispers of the in-between.

We can write about cities or people, about stars or nature. These are the stories of this world. We can write about specifics. Our histories are created from these stories. Our language is made for this.

But how do you speak of everything? How can we talk about the all-in-all we call God? Our tongues and throat become speechless. Our fingers can not find the letters for such words. As Rumi said:

The pen broke and could write no more.

We can talk forever about the smallest of things, but we must fall into silence about what is most significant.

This is why our lives are made of speech and silence.

So, after the long journey of the silent questions I find myself at the end of the path of words. All I have written were stories hinting at the silence drawing me onward. But now I realize that I can say no more. Not that the path stops, but it is no longer my story. It is God's story from here on. This is the real meaning of the vow.

It is not a rebuke to stay silent, but an act of love. It springs not from a desire or need, but from a Will that is God's that has become our own.

The Will of God

What is this Will of God that waits patiently, forever if needed, for Soul to realize the gift it has been given?

What is this Will that cares nothing for right or wrong, but only that Soul chooses, acts, and learns from those choices and actions until Soul comes to know what It is?

What Love is this that causes God to withdraw ITS Face into the invisible, until such time as our eyes can search for and find IT even where it cannot be seen?

It seems that this Love and Will barely even resemble the "love" and "will" we know as human beings, yet Soul knows and recognizes these words etched on paper. Soul senses the greater meaning, like one who is lost in the wilderness understands the comfort of a single voice.

I believe there is a Language that only Soul can hear. It hides behind the words we use, as well as the events of our lives. We shouldn't confuse it with the language of mere mortals.

Strangely, when we try to reveal that Reality, we hide it, and when we hide it, it becomes revealed. This too is a sign of God's Will and Love.

And so I come to a place where silence says more than anything. Having crossed the deserts and deep forests of the world, having explored the many heavens of the many religions, as well as the sciences and philosophies of doubt and disbelief, having seen wars and birth, youth and death, having found treasure and given it away, having left all orbits and returned—I can only say that all of this is the path.

This, and everything that came before, is the path. It is all the path.

The Tremblers

Some let their dreams die because they become disillusioned. I let my dreams die because the reality of Life and Truth is more captivating and stunning than any dream.

I feel as if I am trembling before God, like one who is caught without breath before the awe of ITS beauty and love.

This is God's gift and I know how valuable it is.

Rumi once said:

> Trembling and passionate love are necessary in the quest for God. Whoever does not tremble must wait upon the tremblers. No fruit ever grows on the trunk of a tree, for trunks do not tremble. The tips of the branches tremble, and the trunk supports the tips of the branches and the fruit securely, even against the blow of an axe. Since the trembling of the tree trunk would end in ruin, it is better for the trunk not to tremble. It suits the trunk to be quiet to better serve the tremblers.

Thus a spiritual teaching is made up of those who build pillars to provide strength and support for the sake of those who tremble. Some need a doctrine and a form as something firm to hold onto, but the words they protect come from those who quiver in awe before God. The path seems ageless...beginning with a form and shape from ancient times...continuing into the timeless future. But in fact I can now see that it is reborn each moment.

Today it seems to me that the spiritual travelers are not the trunk but rather the leaves that tremble at the ends of the branches. While the trunk remains fixed and solid, the leaves are barely connected to this world. They know nothing solid, but only the wind and the rays of light from the sun. Yet that thin thread, which holds them to the tree, connects them to something ancient, with roots as old as time itself.

All of this is the Path. One day I will let the winds of God carry me off and I will leave the tree completely. I will go where the winds take me, becoming more wind than earth and settling far from this place.

But for now I feel fortunate to be connected, if only by the slenderest of threads, to a tree whose roots are in God and whose shadow is cast upon this world.

How many travelers have I met who stopped along the way to plant the flag of their belief, satisfied with what they had found? But for some reason the silent questions would not let me go. They mocked all my great convictions and accomplishments. They showed me something more. They showed me that there is always something more.

The path has pulled apart all the strings of my life until my own unfoldment means nothing and only the unfoldment of Life itself now moves me.

Candles

Love came...
  I brought her into my bed,
    And she gave me keys to all the bedrooms of the world.

Wherever I sleep
  I find her waiting.
She says,
  "How can you sleep?
    "Hold me, and don't let me go."

When some lovers come
  We turn the lights out,
But when Love comes
  All the candles are lit,
  And you can't put them out.
You say,
  "I had no idea there were so many candles."

In every heart I have found candles
   That only Love can light.
All the forms of this world
   Are dark and invisible without the light from those candles.
Have you ever seen what happens
   When candles get too close?
They all melt into one
   And can no longer be parted.
Then they burn brighter
   And melt more candles,
     Until all the candles become many wicks
      In one piece of wax.

Love is plotting this.
   I warn you,
     But it is too late for me.
   Love has lit a desire for God
     That can never be stopped.

EPILOGUE

Leaving Terra Firma

I'M LEAVING TERRA FIRMA and stepping out onto the waters. I wonder who will follow?

This ocean and these seas are all of Life, tossing and churning with the unseen and unknown. Our conscious minds float like corks on the waves, with our heads above water, but we know nothing of the depths. We bob in little circles, never seeing the far reaches. We must leave behind everything we know and hold onto, if we want to know the ocean.

These seas continually move. They never rest. Their energy is inexhaustible. Composed of billions upon billions of vortexes, they move, ever shifting with the currents that swirl around us and beneath us. Follow those streams, the rivers within the ocean. Let them carry you far away from terra firma.

Look deeply. Listen carefully. This is the edge of awakening.

I lost everything about myself, but found something greater. I found YOU. There is no other name for You but "YOU."

Even as I call "YOU," You begin stirring everywhere. But I am the one who fell asleep. It was I who forgot Your wisdom, Your beauty and Your voice.

"YOU" is the name that awakens Life. I call it aloud. "HUUUUU…" is how it is spoken. I cannot even utter it without waking from my sleep. I can not speak it without seeing YOU everywhere.

325

Even as I awaken You, You awaken me. You are the awakening of Soul. Every "you" spoken is but a reflection of YOU. How can there be love without "you"?

You lift and carry me across the ocean, beyond the horizons of all horizons. Down into the depths beyond knowing. There is no measure of Your seas. The mind cannot follow You as You move back upon Yourself, as You turn without space and without turning. You shift too quickly and change too fast. Nothing can cease Your moving, always moving.

What is "stopping," but a terra firma word? How can death touch You, when You die and are reborn every moment? Your knowledge and teaching seep into the unconscious, unseen. Your wisdom is not a language that can be fathomed. It is inscrutable.

Your speech is not made of ordinary words. It is reality. It pulses with a heartbeat that slips behind the spaces of all things and all beings. Like invisible shreds and bits filtering into consciousness. They are too small to see, like infinitesimally small threads, they weave together the visible tapestry of all that is. How do You do this?

I am asking and I listen.

Even the cells of my body are attuned to You. I never knew this before. How could evolution be a surprise to anyone, when all things are carried along by Your song? Our greatest discoveries are but what little of You we have let filter into our lives. How much have I missed? How much have I forgotten?

"Your awakening is My awakening," You say to me. "We are not separate."

"Are You God?" I ask.

"No. I am but the Voice of God reverberating throughout all that is. I have been singing to you my song down through the ages, through the subconscious of your dreams.

"Give up this clay self," You say. "Lose the little self and dive into My ocean. Let the Whole seep into your being. Give up trying to understand Life with your thoughts. Put aside such insignificant goals. Those are but bits of terra firma clinging to you. Let me carry you far away. Let me pull you apart until nothing can hold you together again.

"Then you will be as I am. Then you and I will move and grow together. I long for your awakening within Me. It is My own awakening.

"Reach out with your being to touch Me. I will give you a Throat that can speak My Voice. Then utter Truths for Me. Become a Spiritual Traveler and accept the birth right of Soul. A million have come before you. A million more will follow. These are the waves of My ocean lapping against the shore of terra firma.

"My waves can carry you away, but you will never return. Your clay feet may walk upon the firmness of land, but how can you ever forget? How can you ever sleep again? Listen to my Voice with the whole of your being."

I can no longer resist Your call. I have left terra firma and stepped out upon the waters, where everything I see shows Your love for Soul. I now know that all of Life is searching for nothing but You through the yous of the world.

Words pour through me onto paper, but this is not me speaking, it is You. Who can understand this kind of talk? I wonder, now, who will follow these trails You leave in the heart?

. . . . .

MY PERSONAL GROWTH no longer matters. What needs could I have when the currents of the whole Ocean have become my own? My heart and life are now rooted in something beyond all names. Love has led me to the God-Reality everywhere. That is where I find growth today.

How could this miracle come about? I don't know. It is not something within the power of mankind.

What else is there to say? Beyond this point the words are no longer mine, they belong to God.

It has been quite a journey, so far.

I wonder what comes next. . . .

ABOUT
THE AUTHOR

Doug Marman has been writing, lecturing and leading classes on spirituality and the exploration of consciousness for over thirty years.

His varied work has led him through successful careers in a wide range of professions, including: reporter, photographer, editor, inventor (with more than 20 patents), engineer, marketing manager, and corporate executive at one of the largest companies in the world. He is now co-founder of a technology start-up.

He is also the author of: *The Whole Truth—The Spiritual Legacy of Paul Twitchell*, and a new book coming soon: *It Is What It Is—The Discourses of Rumi*.

He lives in the United States Pacific Northwest, with his wife and son.